SIMON AND SCHUSTER *New York London Toronto Sydney Tokyo*

THE EARTH IS ENOUGH

Growing Up in a World of Trout & Old Men

HARRY MIDDLETON

Simon and Schuster
Simon & Schuster Building
Rockefeller Center
1230 Avenue of the Americas
New York, New York 10020

Designed by Liney Li
Manufactured in the United States of America

10 9 8 7 6 5 4 3 2 1

Library of Congress Cataloging in Publication Data

Middleton, Harry.
  The earth is enough.

  1. Middleton, Harry—Childhood and youth.
2. Ozark Mountains Region—Social life and customs.
3. Children of military personnel—United States—
Biography.   4. Fishing—Ozark Mountains Region.
5. Hunting—Ozark Mountains Region.   I. Title.
CT275.M5136A3   1989   976.7'1053'092 [B]   89-11261

ISBN 0-671-67459-5

To
Kelso Sutton and Nick Lyons,
two who love the good Earth
and the good word.

And, at long last, for
Norwell, who pulled the pin
for God, country, and the
men he admired most—those who
marched to the Garry Owen:
7th Cavalry Reg't, 1st Cavalry Division
(Airmobile)

Once in a lifetime, perhaps,
one escapes the actual confines
of the flesh. Once in a lifetime, if
one is lucky, one so merges with
sunlight and air and running water
that whole eons, the eons that mountains
and deserts know, might pass in a single
afternoon without discomfort.

—Loren Eiseley, The Immense Journey

What is life? It is the flash of a firefly
in the night. It is the breath of a buffalo
in the wintertime. It is the little shadow
which runs across the grass and loses itself
in the sunset.

—Last words of Crowfoot, a Blackfoot warrior

Creek runs to river,
River runs to sea,
Ain't never caught a trout
That ain't caught me.

Oh, listen what I tell you,
Tell you true,
You fool with trout,
And they hook you.

—Albert "Salmo" McClain, improvising on
Muddy Waters singing "Lonesome Road Blues"

THE EARTH IS ENOUGH

Growing Up in a World of Trout & Old Men

PREFACE

I am along the banks of Snowbird Creek, not far from Sassafras Falls and Burntrock Ridge. Snowbird Creek is on the
eastern flank of the Great Smoky Mountains and is full of wild
trout, not people, which is why I am here. I enjoy trout. They
are never disappointing company. They like the things I like—
clean mountain streams, swift-moving water, wildness. There's
not much of it left.

Just a few minutes ago I let a fine brook trout go. The gorgeous and tenacious little brookies are the only native trout of
these mountains. Spooky as a blind horse. Suspicious, intolerant, elusive, malingering. Fine, noble qualities.

I am sitting on a massive slab of gray stone lodged near the
creek's edge and enjoying the morning's rich silence. Another
benefit of seeking out mountain streams and trout. The brook
trout I released has disappeared into the creek's deeper waters. It
slipped from my hand like a shadow moving across flat stones.
Sunlight refracts off the water in layers as distinct as the strata
deposited in stone. Yet the light is fluid, moving easily over the
creek's surface, changing endlessly as it falls upon the side of the
ridge, in the deep woods, on the galleries of stone.

Layers of light and wild trout and these mountains. Enough
to fill a man's mornings, you'd think, and yet here I sit on this

warm chunk of ancient rock thinking of that last little knot of umbilicus that is my navel. I worry about it from time to time, worry that the knot won't hold. I feel as if I'm leaking. I wouldn't be surprised. A dyspeptic German doctor tied the knot. A nurse handed me to him with giant forceps. He was still upset that Germany hadn't fared better during the war and there I was, another American. Who's to say he didn't tie a quick slipknot? My mother was fast asleep, heavily and happily sedated, after I popped out in the back of a U.S. Army ambulance. In those days there was nothing either natural or chic or glamorous about childbirth.

Many years later I had to go before an American judge. This is what he asked me: "Do you want to be an American citizen?" He had to ask, I had to answer. After all, I had come into the world on foreign soil. My country had to be certain of my loyalty.

Just another rite of passage, another of childhood's puzzling and uncertain moments. American writers are mesmerized by childhood, the quizzical journey from innocence to adulthood. What a journey it is, too: precarious and wonderful; frightening and alluring; delightful and tragic. Not one journey, but many, and every one of them different. I am told that money and privilege sometimes make for a smoother passage. I would not know. I only know about being a soldier's son: the military life and the unexpected fortunes such a life brings. Luck has a lot to do with it, and I was lucky in that my luck went sour early and put me on another road altogether, a road that took me deep into the mountains, a road that led to a trout stream and into the curious and captivating lives of three old men who, by having so little, laid claim to having everything that mattered, was worthwhile, and would last. When my friend Norwell, who was just thirteen, found a grenade in a clear, cool stream deep in an Okinawan jungle valley, and pulled the pin, my journey began. The long trip home. It continues still.

Have I told the whole story of my time with Emerson and

Albert and the lunatic Elias Wonder? Hardly. This is but one slice of it, a single beginning. There were others. As for endings, there are none, no final ones anyway.

This is a boy's story. Just that. It harbors no messages, no great quest. There are more questions to it than answers. Just one boy's story of growing up: my story, my memories. All mine and remembered as I want to remember them. Because this is my story and because the living, like the dead, have a right to peace and privacy, I have changed names, places, dates. I have played with memory and time, shuffling them about at will. I know the counties of Arkansas well, and there is no Oglala County among them. Likewise, there is no town called Mount Hebron. Yet, years ago, in the high country of the Ozarks, there was a county very much like Oglala County and a town almost identical to Mount Hebron. And through the narrow valley ran a swift mountain trout stream in every way identical to Starlight Creek. If I have changed the names, I have not changed the emotions, the experiences, the details of it all, those years with the old men in the mountains when I felt my life changing, felt it as clearly as the warm sun on my face and knew from that time on that life for me would be somehow different. I followed the old men into the woods, to the stream, into the high country, not because I had to, not because they asked me along, or because they put it on me as a test of character, but because I wanted to, because I wanted to know the source of whatever it was about the natural world that gave these old men such solace, such contentment. The land gave them their greatest joys and, too, some of their greatest sorrows. And yet they held to it tightly, refused to let go. Its course was theirs, and after a time, mine as well. Never did they push their beliefs or way of life on me. Indeed, they spent many days and nights cautioning me against such a life, a life steeped in an unshakable attachment to the good earth. "Wildness ruins a man, sooner or later," Albert told me. "It's like a voice calling you home. A voice you try to deny and can't, like that of a beautiful and seductive woman." I listened, but in the end I simply could not resist.

As I said, this story is mine. Its perceptions, its coloring, its interpretations are likewise mine alone, in all just a story of how I had the mixed luck of slipping so willingly into the embrace of the natural world, how I knew a time, a time with three old men in the high country, when the earth was more than enough; it was everything.

Some last words, then, from my stone next to Snowbird Creek. Words of thanks. Honest words and necessary. A writer may write alone, live alone, but sooner or later he must get up from his desk, leave his garret. When he does he is more than likely out of his element, an awkward sort. So it is with me. Such a writer needs all the help he can get. I've had more than my share. More good fortune. Thanks, then, to my family: of course—my father, a soldier's soldier; my mother; my kind sister and brother-in-law, a soldier, friend, scholar, writer; and my wife and two sons—and especially three friends who see in me more than I see in myself—Bob Bender, Philip Osborne, and Julian Bach. Many thanks. Many thanks, indeed.

Harry Middleton
Hazel Creek, North Carolina,
1988

1. FAMILY TREE

Vietnam? Sure, it's that Asian aphrodisiac.

— Pfc. Bernie "Wild Man" Wascomb, 1965

Winter gave way to spring and spring to summer and I had not yet been in the mountains a year when Cody, my grandfather's hunting dog, died.

On the morning that we buried him, Uncle Albert ran excitedly back and forth across the lush, damp grass that grew ankle high in front of the house. He held out a long length of fishing line that trailed behind him and onto the end of which he had tied a brand-new trout fly, one he had just christened "Cody's Wish." Snapping behind him as he galloped about the yard, the thing looked like a diminutive kite fluttering in a small wind. Large and burly, the trout fly imitated no particular insect, stream or terrestrial. Albert had spent most of the night fabricating it out it of clumps of rabbit fur, bits of chicken feathers, loops of colored thread. It was meant to somehow celebrate Cody's deep and unending fascination with everything. Nothing had escaped Cody's attention, especially if it smelled of trouble or adventure. That had been true all his life, twelve years. The old man had found him dead the day before up near the head of Starlight Creek by Karen's Pool. Albert figured he'd been fishing. Cody was an angler of consequence, unable to tame his obsession for trout. His body lay on the creek bank, the cold water lapping at his enormous paws. And Albert had tied his commemorative trout fly and named it after the old dog and now we were going to bury Cody out behind the barn alongside the white stone that marked Zeke's grave. Zeke was a mule. Big as a pickup truck, said the old man. The color of wet granite and an animal of deep character, unshakable loyalties, and strict beliefs. Zeke never pulled stumps on Saturdays. Just Saturdays. "It was a religious thing with him," said Albert.

I had dug the hole for Cody. It was wide and deep and dark, and the old man split two burlap potato bags, mended them together so they made a shroud, and sewed Cody's handsome black-and-gold body inside. It took all three of us to put Cody down into the hole. On my hands and knees, I packed in the damp reddish-brown soil with a flat-faced shovel, kept pushing till the hole was full, swollen with its new burden. Albert marked the grave with a large chunk of leached limestone that he had taken from the cold pale-green waters of Karen's Pool.

We stood there beside the grave for a long moment, hats in our hands. The old man spoke. "He was a good dog, as dogs go, and a fine angler, a true friend." A pause. "What's done is done, what's past is past, but that don't mean we won't miss him. We will." The only sound was the low rustle of leaves in the soft wind. The old man put his hat on, told me to go and get the fly rods. "Amen," said Albert.

Hesitating, I lingered there for a time and a sudden warmth crept up my legs, spread along my spine, into my arms and shoulders, settling finally in my belly, chasing out the insistent fear, the mistrust and uncertainty, the doubts that haunted and paralyzed me. Such a strange warmth. Conversion at the grave. Baptism of earth and tears. "Get the fly rods," the old man said again. I had come home. Whatever came to pass, these mountains were my place and these old men were my family, my blood.

Out of an old dog's death a homecoming, an arrival, a complex and difficult merger of a gypsy past and what turned out to be a remarkable present. As for the future, the old men rarely speculated, but it seemed dangerous, a volatile mix of unstable chemistry. And all this burning in my gut as I stood looking down at Cody's grave. Albert stood near me, a tight-lipped, almost envious grin on his wrinkled face. Death had joined Cody to the land he loved. I could see on Albert's face that when death came he coveted a similar ending.

Uncle Albert and my grandfather had lived in these low-slung, hogback mountains for nearly a century. My great-grandfather, a disgruntled ex-Confederate soldier, came here in the late 1870s after serving as a scout with the U.S. Army in Indian country, the Great Plains, the wild expanses of Montana, Wyoming, Colorado, Utah. As a boy he left his father's hardscrabble farm in the North Carolina piedmont and at fifteen joined Lee's Army of Northern Virginia. I saw an old cracked and wrinkled photograph of him once—a sad-eyed, sunken-cheeked boy. The eyes dark, staring, peering from under a rumpled wide-brimmed hat: a look that reached out beyond the geography of time. Small hands. One clutching a crude, homemade knife, the other holding an antique shotgun. Two pistols tucked in a wide black belt. No childish smile, no patriotic glow, no heroic gleam. He survived the war only to risk his life fighting the desperate Sioux and Cheyenne. Of a sudden he quit, moved on, moved south again.

According to my grandfather, he had fallen in love with a young Oglala Sioux woman named Evening Star. On a warm spring morning in 1877, the prairie meadows vibrating with birdsong and the wind sweet with the smell of the season, a cavalry detachment had boldly attacked an unsuspecting Sioux camp. They were greeted by old men, children, women, including the woman Evening Star. The camp had had no fresh meat for weeks and the young men were hunting. It took only moments. Guns were emptied, fires set. No birds sang. The wind had the sharp stinging smell of sulfur. The dead cluttered the meadow in grotesque poses. The former boy Confederate had tracked these Sioux, led the cavalry to the rise overlooking the camp.

A year later he laid down his savings for more than a thousand acres of hilly, rocky, rolling land in the upper reaches of the Ozark Mountains that every sane man for miles around knew was worthless. He married a hardworking, soft-spoken, respectable mountain woman named Allyson Moultrie. She had blue eyes and thick red hair. Over the next four years she gave birth to two sons and died in the winter of 1885 after cutting her shin with an ax while chopping stove wood. The leg went bad, turned black as oxblood. She was dead in two weeks.

My grandfather was the younger boy. His name was Emerson, a shy, quiet child who grew into an even shyer, quieter man. He had his mother's stormy blue eyes, her fair skin, and his father's coarse auburn hair, which he always kept short and parted down the middle. He attended school for a time, but education disappointed him. He missed spending his days afield, hunting the high country, fishing the cold mountain streams, working the unforgiving land, so at the age of fourteen he resigned from public education. There were no good-byes and no regrets. His school years did, however, deepen his passion for reading. Books obsessed him, thrilled him, comforted him all his life. Indeed, it was books alone that competed for the precious hours he set aside for the outdoors, those long days walking the mountains, camping in the mottled shade of the thick, cool woods, searching out the elusive, alluring trout of Starlight Creek.

At eighteen, Emerson married. Her name was Sally Ann McClain, a small-boned, energetic girl of sixteen from up the valley, the fourth of eleven children, nine of them girls. Sally

Ann had shining hopeful eyes, thin, sincere lips, weathered skin, strong hands, and a touchy disposition. She was the only living creature Emerson shrank in fear of. "She had a voice that could take rust off metal," he recalled fondly, more than forty years after her death. Before her death from bone cancer, Sally Ann bore three daughters. Faye Eileen, the youngest, had fine red hair, big, doleful hazel eyes that always seemed on the verge of filling with tears, a bobbed nose laced with freckles. Faye was short, trim, and tireless. She was my mother. Just as she completed high school, World War II broke out. A stroke of marvelous good fortune for her and her sisters. Opportunity knocked and it made no difference to them that the fist was that of a desperate world. War meant change, and change meant a chance to escape the mountains, the unyielding oppression of a merciless land. The war eased the Great Depression, and impending prosperity lured my mother down into the delta, down into the cities, left her giddy and lighthearted, as hopeful as a child. She packed her small leather suitcase, walked to town, took the first bus to Memphis, a bus to another world, a bigger, more complex, angrier, confusing world, a world at war.

She ended up in Washington, D.C., a secretary at the War Department, a patriotic position of high responsibility that exposed her to an endless tide of handsome young officers from every branch of the armed services. A young woman's notion of paradise, at least in 1944. In less than six months' time, two sailors, a Marine, and three Army officers had proposed to this quiet, hardworking young secretary with the tireless smile and bright eyes. Like just about every other young woman in Washington in those years, she was irresistible. It was wartime and my mother felt strongly that it was every woman's duty to get behind the war effort one hundred percent. Everyone was expected to do his part and it was her part to innocently flirt with every young officer that passed her desk. She bid them farewell, told them honestly that she would miss them tragically. Sadly, it was their duty to fight, even die.

Meanwhile, in 1940, Albert moved in with Emerson. Not a big move, really. Albert had the farm across the creek. His fifth wife had died the year before. Tuberculosis. For weeks Albert couldn't eat or sleep. "A man shouldn't have to lose five of anything," he said. Emerson agreed. "There, there," he said tenderly, while cooking Albert a plate of eggs and grits.

This, then, was my mother's family, or as my father called them, "those people." They were generous, hardworking, content, forgiving, unambitious, intelligent, and dirt poor. My father couldn't stand them.

"Socialists," my father said. "It's people like them, people who have no desire to get ahead, people with a work ethic rather than a profit margin, that give people like us, people who are working their asses off to get it over on the other guy before he gets it over on us, a bad name."

My father's people were for God, America, and progress at any price, just as long as it didn't cost them anything. They believed that America was the greatest nation on the face of the earth and they were willing to take on any other nation that didn't feel the same way. They were honorable, courageous, decent folk who believed passionately that there ought to be a law giving them and their kind more happiness, more prestige, and more power than those who weren't their kind.

"Republicans," said my mother, the word vibrating deep in her throat like a death rattle.

My father's mother was a Jones. She grew up in the tiny northern Alabama town of Eva, not far from her grandfather Jones's old plantation that had gone to hell after the Civil War. The old Confederate officer spent his last days on the porch of the big house gulping cool well water and talking to ghosts or working the fields. On a muggy afternoon in July 1900, he fell in the bean field, collapsed to the hard, dried ground like a tree split by summer lightning. My grandmother found him there, soaked in pools of sweat, staring up at the summer sun. A neighbor rode a mule to Eva to get the doctor. After being carried to bed, the old man threw off the wet compress on his sunburned head, shot straight up in bed, and told the gaping family members gathered about his huge oak bed that a dark cloud had hung directly over him as he bent down to pick beans and engulfed him like a vapor. He looked up and found himself staring into Willy's pitiful eyes.

Willy was Robert William Jones, his older brother who had been killed at Gettysburg, thus marking the farthest point north that any member of the Jones family had ever traveled, armed or unarmed. Now Willie had come back: death's messenger dressed in moldy butternut, bloodstained and hollow-eyed. He had found his brother, touched him with a bent, icy, spectral finger. Seeking to comfort the dying old man, his oldest daughter, Kate, clutched his bony hands and whispered, "It's me. It's Willy. It's all right. Everything's all right." Family legend— which is always better than truth—has it that the old Confederate lurched forward, his dim eyes full of fresh horror as he screamed, "Egads, Willy! Are we bound for hell, then? You're as stone ugly as your niece Kate!" Exhausted, he flopped back onto his pillow, closed his eyes, and died.

Sometimes late at night when I am on the road, sleepless in some nondescript motel room in some unfamiliar town, I will take out the local telephone book and look under Jones. They are always there, often by the dozens. It is comforting to know you come from such a large, sprawling family. And if there are no Joneses, I try the Middletons, another common American name. I am rarely alone.

My branch of the Middleton family were restless folk, drifting from the Carolinas into Tennessee and then into northern Alabama, where they might have stayed had the Great Depression not come along, crushed their hopes, and put them back on the road again. After their marriage, my grandfather and grandmother moved from Eva to Sheffield, Alabama. Work proved scarce and soon enough there were three sons. My father was the third, the last to be born in Alabama. A machinist by trade and a man who believed in luck, my grandfather Middleton found work with the railroad, the Cotton Belt in Shreveport, Louisiana. The family moved and if it didn't prosper, it survived, hung on, even expanded with the birth of the last two sons.

Late at night, at the end of his shift, my grandfather would stuff old sacks with as much company coal as he could smuggle out to his neighbors who had no jobs and couldn't afford coal. He was the Robin Hood of Shreveport, and I never knew him. He fell dead of a heart attack in the early 1950s. My grandmother lived on alone in the small red-brick house for more than thirty years, a television with bad reception keeping her company. She talked to it, and it answered. The point of their conversations was of no importance, only the sound and the passed time. For me, my grandfather existed only in photographs, mementos of incalculable loss, a big man with thick dark eyebrows and brooding eyes, enormous hands and a puffy face turned jaundiced by the aging photos pasted in the big black albums my grandmother Middleton kept in a trunk at the foot of her bed.

My father enjoyed a hearty, all-American childhood, spending equal amounts of time fighting his brothers, being an average student, charming girls, and working for the railroad with his father. He loved the train yard, the smell of heavy oil, the sound of hissing steam, the endless metal clank of motors running. He liked hanging around with the other workers, rolling cigarettes, knocking back cheap liquor, and listening to the bawdy stories told by his father and the other older men. Then the war broke out. War tends to upset things. It brought my mother down from the high country and yanked my father out of the train yard. The way my father told it, the Army plucked him from the backseat of a 1936 Ford and the arms of love. Actually, he had tried to enlist in the Navy. Too small. The Navy had standards, requirements. "Besides," said the recruiter, a bald-headed sailor with a pimply face, "I just signed up three guys named Middleton. You some kind of gang? You ain't on the lam, are ya?"

The Army had fewer restrictions. By then the war was chewing up young men faster than the Army could shave them, feed them, arm them, and hurl them into the front lines. Being six months short of his eighteenth birthday, my father had to get his father's consent before enlisting, which my grandfather did gladly, proud that he had fathered so many sons fit and healthy enough to lay down their lives for their country.

Eyeing the signature carefully, the Army recruiter broke into a broad grin. "Well, well," he said, "a bona-fide flag-waving American youth eager to go off and put it to Hitler, eh? Proud of you, boy. Damn proud. Not every boy these days is so willing to die for what's right."

"*What?*" yelled my father in disbelief. "What in the hell are you talking about?" The thought of actually dying had never entered his mind. When boys go to war, it seldom does. My father thrust his face into the recruiter's and bellowed, "Look, Mac, all I want to do is beat the shit out of sailors."

Before he knew it, my father was a proud and dapper private first class, ready, even eager, for the pfc next to him to get it and get it good for the good old red, white, and blue.

My parents met in Washington, D.C., after the war. Peace proved to be a powerful aphrodisiac and they were soon married. The ceremony took place on a sultry August day in Shreveport, waves of humid Louisiana heat settling like clouds in the high ceiling of the Methodist church.

Black-and-white photographs of the event show my father handsome and dashing in his uniform, an officer's uniform. My mother's eyes were wide and tender, her smile shy, flirtatious. Behind them, my grandmother Middleton dabbed tears from her eyes with a white lace handkerchief. Uncle Albert and Emerson were not in attendance. Couldn't make it. Went fishing.

My father had his orders tucked inside his coat pocket. Back to Germany. Having destroyed that nation in order to purge the evil from its heart, he was now asked to reconstruct it, heal it, nurture peace and friendship between the German and American people. Peace, like war, can be a terrible thing, especially for an Army officer hungry for advancement. Peace was often tedious and uninspiring, marked by endless days of banal paperwork. War held no charms for my father. Indeed, he hated it in that special, deep, and palpably fearful way that all soldiers hate it. But peace brought into force the full weight of the Army's vapid, mundane bureaucracy, and he hated that and his life as a low-level functionary in it more than anything.

Still, there was the Cold War and war was hell, hot or cold. It was also his business, and business was good. In fact it was prospering, since the Cold War kept everyone tight as an overwound watch and in a constant state of high-strung anxiety and anticipation because everyone knew it was inevitable that sooner or later somewhere, somehow, some whacko would screw up and peace would come apart as easily as Humpty-Dumpty.

The fighting man had to be ready. So my father kept a clear and disciplined mind in a tight, hard-muscled body because as a career officer it was his job to see to it that when things got tough everybody suffered—everybody, that is, except the career officers, who were pugnacious, stern, God-fearing men who held the firm belief that it was the right of every American soldier to believe passionately in whatever he wanted to believe just as long as it jibed with what the Army believed.

Being in charge of young men who could be stone dead in a breath-sucking instant turned out to be a full-time job, and as far I as can recall, my father never dreamed of cool, deep woods or of rising trout. He never thought about fast cars, a decent Italian meal, Rolex watches, a place in the country, seabirds on the wing. Whatever emotions or secret desires he harbored he kept cold and buried deep, so deep they were unreachable, untouchable. He never boasted, never ruminated about honor or courage. Among career officers, courage didn't count; it was a deadly luxury, one that could get a man waxed, greased, boxed-up dead, and there was nothing like death to bring a halt to a rising young officer's career. Zap and no promotion, just a Glad bag, an aluminum box as some smug-faced general handed your widow a folded flag and a limp salute. No, the idea was to live, whatever the cost. For lifers, death wasn't an option; it was a dead end. My father used to tell me in a voice as serious as hell that I shouldn't worry about him because he was official U.S. government property and as such he wasn't allowed to die.

My father never talked of war, never emptied out a soldier's usual bagful of stories. Except once. On the night in France after he bought his first reel-to-reel tape recorder, he sat in the kitchen, the big machine on the table, as he drank bourbon-and-Coke and bellowed into the microphone he was holding only inches from his mouth. He was telling a story about a landing. No places mentioned. No dates, no names. Just before the men were to board the landing craft, a tall, smooth-skinned chaplain with a cherub face and smiling eyes gathered them together, then climbed on an ammunition box so he stood above them. He asked them to kneel, fold their hands, pray as he prayed. "Thou Lord, our God," he chanted in an upbeat rhythm. "Lord of hosts, grant our glorious forces victory on this great day of liberation, total victory over the hideous forces of evil spread over the land before us. Steady our hands, O God. And shield us. And watch over us through these long and dark hours, for in Christ's name we pray. Amen."

"Yeah, all that," piped a corporal from Sheridan, Wyoming, who stood helmet in hand. "But begging your pardon, Pastor, don't you think we could skip all the divine generalizations and get to the meat of it?" And the boy from Wyoming began to pray. "God, help all these greasy low-life swabbies to aim their big guns straight and true so they can obliterate every evil-eyed son of a bitch waiting to kill us on the beach. Sober up the fly boys, your Greatness, so their bombs will fall with fearful deadly accuracy, annihilating entire cities, towns, and villages in the blink of an eye. Let the gunners melt down their artillery, disemboweling our enemies before they disembowel us. If you love us, rain death upon our foes. What did we ever do to them, anyway? Spare them no mercy. And, sweet Lord, we, as your children, ask that you might do all this quickly because we are scared shitless. Amen."

When the landing craft dumped them near the beach, the kid from Wyoming was the first one to get it.

Playing back the tape, my father sat there at the kitchen table all night, drinking and listening, and listening again.

My father exuded confidence and demanded obedience, swift and unwavering. For the most part he tolerated life by making it well ordered, well greased, a simple problem of tactics and strategies, all possible outcomes pondered in advance. So our life went, as neat, as tidy, as disciplined as a parade march, snappy as a cadence call.

My childhood? A childhood. Some of it good, some of it lousy. I'm not going tell the whole story. Some secrets need to be kept, neither spoken nor written down.

Some people I know claim to remember things from when they were warm and innocent in the womb. Life for them was instantaneous. Others detail experiences from when they were two or three years old. I must have been otherwise occupied. Life held back with me. I didn't understand that I was alive and alone and adrift in the world until I was five, a very old five.

It was midday, the hot sun high in a cloudless summer sky. A band played loudly, a military band. The musicians wore starched blue uniforms with gold braid; their freshly polished instruments flashed in the sunlight. Notes hung languidly in the humid air over the parade field like a mist. A timid wind barely stirred the air and the flags drooped limply against wooden staffs.

The tune, I would later learn, was a favorite Sousa military march, a steady beat of brass and drums, richly mixed. Music to speed up the blood, I suppose, renew old loyalties, stir up wan-

ing patriotism. I only recall that it hurt my ears. I wanted it to
end, be over. My mother stood beside me, trim, tanned, eyes
that broke down the sunlight into flecks of absinthe green and
soft hyacinth blues. Her hair was cut short, the bangs combed
just so across her small forehead. She wore a blue dress, the
hemline falling discreetly below the knee. A black handbag in
one hand; my hand in the other. She had on white gloves that
buttoned primly at the wrists.

Troops passed in front of the reviewing stand, eyes right,
young faces that to me looked identical, like dolls. Uniforms
pressed, buttons polished and shoes shined, medals and ribbons
proudly displayed. My mother's grasp loosened only when the
troops came to a halt and the music ended. A single line of
officers approached the stand, stopped, stood ramrod straight in
the sun. Attended by a curt and precise major with a runny
nose, a general moved quickly down the line handing out
medals. Salutes and handshakes were exchanged. My mother
ushered me down onto the field. A photographer from *Stars and
Stripes* moved gingerly among the officers, snapping pictures.
Everyone seemed jovial, even festive, except for the short, wiry,
balding captain at the end of the line. My father. He gave the
photographer an icy glare. He detested cameras as much as he
loathed mirrors. Both, he thought, had it in for him. They were
shameless liars that had an annoying habit of making him look
small and slight. One of the things he was best at was nimbly
avoiding cameras and mirrors. Just as the *Stars and Stripes* photographer focused, my father pushed him abruptly aside.
"Prick," he mumbled.

It's true about the mirrors. Even the wobbly reflection from
a store window could throw him into a nervous rage. According
to military records, he stood five foot seven and weighed 119
pounds, but the years were good to my father and by the time I
was five he had grown considerably, so that he stood five foot
nine and weighed close to 150 pounds. Like the fish that haunts
the angler's dreams, he was forever gaining size. To appease him

and somehow keep the family in balance, my mother spent a lifetime making sure that my father never encountered a full-length mirror. In our homes the mirrors were always the first things to go. Early on, my father got the reputation of being a mean little bastard, an opinion that made him blush with boyish pride.

Another sound permeated my childhood, one that came every morning, as regular and dependable as daylight. My father rose at 4:00, made coffee, and promptly at 5:00 he appeared at my bedroom door. "Hit the deck," he would snap, the sound like a bark, more noise than anger. Just as he said the words, somewhere on post some sleepy-eyed, hungover enlisted man flipped a switch that sent the first chords of reveille blaring out of enormous loudspeakers, shattering a thousand unfinished dreams. My father was hard; we would be hard; he had proven himself; we would prove ourselves. "Never let any prick tell you you're small," he ordered. "I won't," I said, uncertain of the strength of my commitment. I loved the man, even though I only rarely saw him and never knew him at all. While I still sweat at the memory of his sharp voice and pitiless eyes, I do not recall if he had a favorite song, understand why he poured ketchup on his scrambled eggs, what he dreamed of, if anything, or how he looked in civilian clothes. Were his eyes brown? It's hard to remember, for it seems in every memory of him his face is turned away.

In Germany my parents took a small apartment outside Frankfurt. It was my father's job to see to it that communism stayed where it belonged—behind the Berlin Wall.

"Middleton, they're everywhere," said the sandy-haired colonel with the ruddy complexion as he chewed on the stump of a wet, sticky cigar.

"They are?" said my father incredulously, wondering who they were and how they got the drop on him so easily.

"Everywhere," the colonel assured him. "Communists, fellow travelers, socialists, Marxists, Bolsheviks, Leninists, Reds,

Maoists, populists, movie actors, atheists, iconoclasts, hordes of nonbelievers."

"I see," said my father, who didn't see anything but another colonel who had lost his mind.

"Hell, Middleton, even my cook's a goddamn pinko," said the colonel, who had worked himself up into a fine patriotic rage as he spit bits of tobacco into the air. "You got a cook, Captain?" the colonel asked apprehensively.

"Yessir. A damn fine one too, sir. Got her fresh from Mount Hebron."

"Mount Hebron?" whispered the colonel, rubbing his wide, square chin thoughtfully, running the name through his mental file of suspicious geography. "Keep an eye on her, Captain, especially if she's feeding you anything that tastes remotely like beet soup." The colonel saluted smartly, jumped into his jeep, and sped away.

"Prick," muttered my father.

Soon enough my mother became bored with the lackluster life of an Army officer's wife. She hated getting together with the girls for bridge even more than she hated the inevitable weekly teas. Everyone cheated at bridge, a fact that upset her only because the ladies cheated so poorly. At the teas the gossip was insipid, as cold and watery as the tea itself. She stopped going altogether when Colonel Townsend's wife, whom my mother didn't know, told her honestly and in the greatest confidence that Captain Middleton's cook, some anarchist from Mount Hebron, a well-known communist client state, was poisoning him slowly with beet soup. My mother put her face down close to Mrs. Townsend's good ear and whispered, "No, dear. It's a pinch of arsenic in his grits twice a week."

My mother turned to spending her free time at the base infirmary, where she visited the wards filled with enlisted men, boys who were more lonely than sick or just recovering from a handsome case of syphilis. As a volunteer, she took their temperatures, wrote comforting letters home to their families, sweethearts, parole boards, and read them uplifting, inspirational literature, pages and pages from Joyce, Thomas Wolfe, Descartes, Nietzsche, Freud, and Robert Benchley. She drove them crazy. In fact, she drove them so crazy that they recovered in no time at all and all the wards emptied, leaving my poor mother to discuss the ramifications of Cervantes and the modern novel with the moody floor nurse, who didn't care as soon as she found out Cervantes was dead and didn't date. The nurse took my mother's temperature, gave her a bottle of aspirin. Even the private with the shattered spirit who slept all day in the mental ward bolted the day after my mother began reading him the German edition of Heinrich Böll's latest work.

Amazed and pleased as punch at the soldiers' remarkable recoveries, the Army doctors gathered together in happy little groups to congratulate themselves on a job well done and to marvel at the wonders of modern medical technology.

My mother was happy too, because no matter how many enlisted men she nursed back to health from Germany to Okinawa, there were always more, waiting in long lines at the infirmary doors eager to check in and get some sack time.

Fourteen months after my parents arrived in Germany, I was born. It happened in late December, a cold and snowy Wednesday morning. Sitting by the small gas heater in their apartment, my father bitterly went through the latest promotion lists printed in *Stars and Stripes*. Again and again, he examined the M's: Mickles, Micklow, Micporil, Middlebrooke, Middlesworth.

"Pricks," he muttered.

"It's time," announced my mother. Actually, it was a little ahead of time, but she wanted to make certain that the Army doctors kept their promise about knocking her out. She had nothing against motherhood as long as she was asleep when it happened.

My father called for an ambulance, which showed up twenty minutes later under the dubious command of Pfc. Leonard Epes. A boy of medium size and limited aspirations from Santa Fe,

New Mexico, Epes had wheedled his way into the motor pool by refusing to decorate his barracks locker with splashy, full-color photographs of naked women with huge breasts and small minds. Instead, he dedicated his locker to a photographic gallery of flashy cars, all of them red convertibles.

Slinging snow and slush, the pea-green Army ambulance with the red cross painted on both sides pulled up in front of the small apartment building. My mother got in the back and my father covered her compassionately with a wool blanket. He banged on the cab. "Step on it, prick!" he said. And Epes stepped on it, the broken-down ambulance lurching uncontrollably, spinning and swerving like an amateur downhill skier. A mile down the narrow road and what had been a low, bothersome grinding noise became a loud, worrisome grinding noise.

"Hold on, dear," my father yelled over my mother's screams, gently consoling her as she beat her fists against his chest and covered him with a rain of invective.

"Faster, pinhead," my father bellowed to Pfc. Epes.

Epes stomped his foot on the accelerator and the ambulance let out one last high-pitched whine and then quit. Pulling to the side of the road, Epes bounced from the cab, quickly popped the hood. He stood there in the light snow looking knowingly at the engine.

"Well?" my father urged in an irritated voice.

"Well?" retorted Pfc. Epes.

"Look, prick, what's the problem?" said my father.

"Well, sir," said Epes confidently, "looks to me like something's wrong with the engine."

"Eh?" yelled my father, who couldn't hear Epes over my mother's clangorous shrieking. "You little twerp, did you say we've been hit by a pigeon?"

"No, sir," said Epes, pointing animatedly at the motor. "There's something wrong with the engine."

Just as he was going for Pfc. Epes's throat, my father noticed a haggard-looking man across the road bemusedly watching the confrontation. The man had the look of an ill-conceived scare-crow. He wore a moth-eaten Russian Army overcoat, German hightop military boots, and a rabbit-fur cap. He crossed the road and stood next to Epes, peering down at the motor.

"Trouble?" he asked in a heavy Bavarian accent.

"Naw, bub, we enjoy standing out in the cold and snow discussing engines while a pregnant woman lies in back yelling her lungs out," said Epes in his best sarcastic New Mexican slur.

"You Americans?" grunted the German. Without waiting for an answer he went on, "The greatest nation of all, and still you can't make a practical and efficient internal combustion en-gine."

Pulling off the distributor cap, the tattered refugee wiped it off carefully on his coat sleeve, snapped it back on.

"Try it," he said.

Epes leaped back into the cab, hit the key, and the engine sputtered to life. The old German smiled, as if he had at last experienced the taste of victory, and walked on down the road, his shape finally dissolving in the falling snow.

Suddenly the morning had turned quiet. No sound save that of the ambulance's engine cooing. My mother had stopped screaming and with good reason—I had showed up. I was bruised, lopsided, wrinkled, and purple, but content under the warmth of the wool blanket. In the cab my father searched for a pencil and paper.

"How's things, sir?" asked Pfc. Epes with genuine concern.

"Well, Private, just between us, I'm worried. That's the odd-est-looking human being I've ever seen. I'm no doctor, mind you, but I don't think it cooked long enough. Looks raw, like something's maybe missing or out of place or something. Who knows, Epes, what with your driving you might have jostled something loose. The sad, ugly thing has a lump for every bump you hit."

At last he found a pencil and a scrap of paper and asked Epes for his address back in the States. Smiling broadly, proudly, as if expecting to get cheerful Christmas cards from his former commanding officer, Epes gladly obliged. With a foxlike grin, my father folded the slip of paper and slipped it inside his pocket.

"You believe in God, Epes?" asked my father.

"Certainly, sir. America's God."

"Good. Then you better pray earnestly to him from now till the day you die that I never get within twenty miles of Santa Fe. Now let's go, Private, slowly and gently."

My birth certificate is in German. Translated, it says I came into the world in Frankfurt at 10:07 A.M., though actually I had already fallen into a blissful sleep by the time Pfc. Epes stopped the ambulance at the hospital's emergency room entrance. Weight: 7 pounds, 14 ounces. Length: 21 inches. Head size: 14 inches, if the lumps weren't counted; 17 inches if they were. A German nurse handled me with forceps, while a disgruntled German doctor cut the cord. My father added "Jr." to my name, which is curious only because my name is not exactly my father's name. The "F" in my name is for Frederick, Frederick Koppel, formerly Sergeant Frederick Koppel, a tank commander in Rommel's Afrika Korps, the old ragged drifter who managed to get the ambulance started.

As a boy, I used to stand for hours in front of the bathroom mirror (the only mirror in the house) working my jaws, hoping they would one day be as taut and muscular as my father's. Not knowing my father well, never spending time with him, did not dampen my natural boyhood urge to imitate him, to idolize him right down to his traplike jaws. Sometimes I worked my jaws all day long by chewing great wads of bubblegum as I sat in my room reading Sun Tzu's *The Art of War*, Clausewitz's *On War*, and "The Instructions of Frederick the Great for His Generals." I worked overtime to be the perfect doting military son. Plans were made for West Point. Every morning at dawn, PT, physical training, no matter the weather or my health, as I ran the route the troops ran wherever we were. Often I ran behind a particularly snappy-looking platoon so I could feel their rhythm, repeat their cadence. Military rap. Pick 'em up and lay 'em down.

> *I like workin' for my Uncle Sam*
> *Let's me know just who I am*
> *Up in the morning at the break of day*
> *Goin' run, goin' run, goin' run all day*
> *PT, PT*
> *Good for you*
> *Good for me*

The drill instructor would trot to the front of the line screeching, "Again, hogs. Sing it till you drop."

As the 50's became the 60's, the calls took on a gloomier, more desperate tone. Vietnam soured the Army's cadence songs the way too much wormy tequila or yesterday's cold pizza can fracture the digestion and embitter the spirit.

When morning broke in Okinawa, as the F-4 Phantoms screamed overhead, the young pilots jovially practicing low-level bombing runs, this is the song I ran to as the soldiers sweated in the damp, sultry air.

> *I wanna go to Viet Nam*
> *I wanna kill the Viet Cong*
> *With a knife or with a gun*
> *Either way will be good fun*
> *Stomp 'em, beat 'em, kick 'em in the ass*
> *Hide their bodies in the grass*
> *And if I die in a combat zone*
> *Box me up and ship me home*
> *Pin my medals upon my chest*
> *Tell my mom I done my best.*

Even today, when the past seeps into the present, when something startles me into thoughts of childhood, I hear the cadence calls, the sound of young men's voices on a morning wind, lyrics of death and violence drifting placidly over manicured parade grounds where no one ever got hurt. To me, as a boy, military life, for a time anyway, seemed a grand adventure. We belonged to no one place, and no place claimed us. We were perpetual wanderers. Such a life could hold advantages for a child because so little was lasting, permanent. Every two or three years, things changed. New place, new school, new people, new world. If things fell apart in Texas, there was always Virginia and Fort Meyers to look forward to. If someone let you down at Fort Lewis, there might be a true friend waiting in France or Germany or Fort Huachuca, Arizona, even though your mother swore to murder your father in his sleep if he ever requested that "moonscape." So much left to chance. All in the dice. If you got snake eyes, you just bit your lip and waited, for the dice would be rolled again.

If nothing else, military life taught a child world geography. There was always that touching moment at the base school near year's end when the fathers got their orders. Invariably, the teacher would pull down the big wall map of the world and all the kids had to file past it and point out their new destinations. Erin to Ismir, Turkey, where they didn't even have Armed Forces Radio, for chrissakes; "Cross-eyed Pete" to Virginia (his father got the Joint Chiefs of Staff); Maria, with the twelve cats, to Schweinfurt, Germany; lovely, dark-eyed Belinda, the cheerleader who wore the black underpants and who was half Spanish and half German, off to Guam. And so on. Chances were you'd never cross paths again. Some you never missed; others you longed for desperately for the rest of your life.

It was late in May at Fort Leavenworth, Kansas. The school, like the post, sat on the bluffs overlooking the swift waters of the Missouri River. By midmorning everyone knew it was map-pulling day in Miss Hillman's class, and down it came, nearly covering the entire blackboard with brightly colored continents. We marched up by rows. She handed each of us the long wooden pointer so we could happily locate our new homes. A quick, professional, unsentimental exchange of good-byes. Frank to upstate New York; his father had gotten the "honey hole," West Point. Wendy to Fort Knox, Kentucky, even though she pointed to Canada. Peggy to France ("Watch them frogs, baby," said Frank, "they'll give you warts!"). Mike to someplace called Fort Benjamin Harrison in Indiana. Bill to Taiwan, which greatly upset him because he did not recognize Taiwan as the official China. As an act of personal belief and defiance he boldly took the pointer and placed it on China, saying, "If I'm going to China, I want the real thing, not some cheap imitation." I had been through this ritual dozens of times, yet I was nervous and kept wiping my palms on the back of Henry Mitchell's shirt. Henry didn't care; he was bound for Fort Bragg, North Carolina. "This time next year," said Henry, "I'll be up to my ass in dim-witted southern belles and you'll be up to yours in fried rice, he-he-he."

My turn at last and I took the pointer from gloating Henry Mitchell and stared in hypnotic terror at the sprawling map. Sweat trickled down my forehead and into my eyes, throwing the flat world before me out of focus. On my first attempt, the tip of the pointer jabbed Burma. I moaned, "Sorry." Another quick parry found me bound for Nepal. My stomach tightened and my knees threatened to buckle. I stepped closer to the now swaying map, steadied it, studied it. Whatever prompts the chemical reaction that transforms fear to panic kicked in. I couldn't find the place. It wasn't off Malaysia or New Guinea. It didn't lurk near Australia or New Zealand. I found no trace of it in the Sea of Okhotsk, the Bering Sea, the Sea of Japan, or the Coral Sea. Nothing. It had finally happened, I thought, my mind reeling. The colonel had thrown craps at last. We were being shipped off to oblivion, a place so obscure, so insignificant that even modern-day mapmakers ignored it. Sensing my malaise, Miss Hillman jumped to my rescue. "Just exactly what are you searching for?" she asked, a touch of pity in her voice.

I said glumly, "It's an island."

"Which one?"

"It's called Okinawa, Miss Hillman, and I know it's gotta be here somewhere. The last great battle of World War Two was fought there."

Facing the map, Miss Hillman found Japan and began moving her right index finger down its coastline toward the China Sea. Her finger moved slowly, carefully, as though it were a ship marking its course. "Here," she said, proud of her geographic prowess, her finger stopping suddenly. "The Ryukyu Islands. Okinawa is the big one, not too far off the coast of Vietnam." Everyone knew about Vietnam because more fathers were going there than almost anyplace else, and they were going alone. No families. Vietnam was a war zone, though no one wanted to admit it yet.

I learned that the Ryukyu Islands are beautiful. The famous war correspondent Ernie Pyle got it on one of them. Okinawa was the only island in the chain I spent time on, but I got to know it well, very well indeed, in 1964–65. A lousy year by most judgments. Kennedy already assassinated. General Douglas MacArthur died. My father said on hearing the news, "Poor bastard. Wanted to be king more than he wanted to be a first-rate soldier. Guy went nuts. Too bad. Yeah, too bad." Dr. Martin Luther King, Jr., won the Nobel Peace Prize. Former President Hoover died, too, and hardly anyone noticed. Ian Fleming, author of the James Bond thrillers, died, and everyone noticed. It was that kind of year. The Beatles were everywhere. "I Wanna Hold Your Hand" blasting on the radio every ten minutes, a song the GIs particularly loathed because the last thing they wanted to hold was a girl's hand. If the Beatles left you cold, there was My Fair Lady or Mary Poppins or Dr. Zhivago. Picasso painted his "Self-Portrait." Everybody I knew thought it looked like a fresh road kill. Rachel Carson died. Some guy named Cassius Clay beat Sonny Liston for the heavyweight title. We listened to the fight over Armed Forces Radio.

Clay's victory cost me forty two mint baseball cards. Clay later pupated into Muhammad Ali. Imagine that. Riots in New York. Riots in Washington, D.C. My mother moped about the house saying, "Bad karma . . . bad karma." Altogether, a touchy year.

GIs gathered at the base snack bar to ogle the officers' daughters while they worried about their fate. At last, they had something to worry about. Just across the China Sea. Vietnam. Their jive talk had a frenzied pattern. "It's for real, man. For real. The shit's coming down and on our heads. Like I told my platoon sergeant, brother, I can't be going off to no war. I'm just coming into the full flower of my fun years. Hey, we're going. The Marines. Christ, they're the bait, the warm-up squad. We're the clean-up crew, the bad boys. You think the women there are any cheaper, man? A pilot told me stuff there's really cheap. Got him a Rolex for next to nothing, he said. This war stuff won't be so bad as long as they keep me where I belong— in the rear with the gear, my man."

But mostly it was just talk, exciting talk, and they went ahead and spent the bulk of their time and all of their money at the strip joints and whorehouses that clogged the island from Sukurian to Naha to Kadenia. The young girls were always waiting just outside the gates, awkwardly dressed in miniskirts and too much makeup and smiling, talking, pitching their universal spiel. "Lay you money down, honey. GI No. 1. Funky Chicken with me, GI. I love you long time so you take me States, yes? No Funky Chicken. I teach you Okinawa Watusi. I Monkey you to death. Ten doll-a plenty cheap for good love. American GI tops. No. 1."

My father paced the floor every night, more nervous than I'd ever seen him. He told my mother in whispers, "It's this Vietnam thing. I don't like it. The whole thing stinks. We can't defend a country from communism that doesn't particularly want to be defended. I tell you we get too deep into this shit and we'll be on a one-way roller coaster ride to hell."

You heard them even at night sometimes—the drumming of

the 105s and the pounding 155s, a constant shattering peal of artillery practice—and you got used to it and fell asleep to the echoes of the man-made rolling thunder. On the other side of the island the Marines trained deep in the thick, hot jungles. Rumor circulated until it became fact. They were going. Vietnam. Officially just to protect the big air bases. But nobody believed the Corps would be content to sit around, protect the fly boys, play jacks in miserable, stinking bunkers. "It's not in their nature," theorized one GI. "Marines ain't that smart. They'll move out beyond the airfields sooner or later and when they do, the shit will start. The bad shit—the dying."

Heady stuff for schoolboys. Each day after school we'd go to the air base to watch the endless stream of big cargo planes coming in and leaving and the jet fighters screaming overhead —a sight that sent the adrenaline shooting into our young, ignorant blood. Or we would scrape together seventeen cents for a cab ride out to the Marine base and hurl insults across the heavy wire fence at the young Marines. After all, we were soldiers' sons and envious, so envious that we were willing, even eager, to sacrifice our fathers for the hollow glory of having the Army get the jump on the jarheads and get to Vietnam first. "Send the Army, not the Girl Scouts!" yodeled Norwell in his brassy voice. He was almost fourteen. He kept on taunting, yelling. "Yeah, eat the apple and fuck the Corps." And the young Marines beyond the fence just grinned and went on looking at us in wide-eyed befuddlement.

And every day my father got gloomier. "The whole thing stinks," he told a young captain at the officers' club who couldn't wait to get into combat and whose only fear was that the whole thing would end before he had a chance to bloody himself, kill his country's enemies with cool dispassion, win medals and honors, and, most important, get his promotion to major years before he would without a good little war to fight.

The captain seemed confused and slightly miffed at my father's pessimistic attitude. "They can't win, sir," he said.

"They can't lose," my father said emphatically, and explained to the baby-faced captain how the Vietnamese had waited out the Japanese and embarrassed the French. "Technology ain't worth crap against a people who thrive on adversity and ease their hunger with determination." My father had never sounded more eloquent. Bourbon tended to bring out the poet in him. He went on. "You wait. If we go at them piecemeal, they'll nibble away at us, reduce our overconfidence to dust."

His face red with indignation, the captain replied stiffly, "Sir, the South Vietnamese are a good and noble people who deserve the right to decide their own future."

My father just smiled as if he'd heard it all before. "Look, son," he said, patting the captain knowingly on the shoulder, "I don't mind fighting for a guy and his country just as long as that guy is willing to fight and die along with me. You're right, the South Vietnamese want to win, and they're willing to sacrifice every eighteen-year-old American boy to do it. All I'm saying is, why should I or you or anyone die for a country that its own people won't even fight and die for."

"Because your Commander-in-Chief tells you to," tweeted the captain. Sensing he had gotten the upper hand, he added: "And because every other soldier is gladly marching off to help the South Vietnamese."

"Not Private Bernie 'Wild Man' Wascomb," said my father, taking one last drink and wishing the good captain a pleasant evening.

In those days there seemed little doubt about our course of action. Everyone from the President to the Joint Chiefs of Staff agreed that defeating, even destroying North Vietnam, if it came to that, was the American, the democratic, the right and Christian thing to do.

This is what my father, the colonel, said: "Politicians. Bureaucrats. Functionaries. Pricks."

That summer I got a job at the motor pool. Once again, I found myself among Army ambulances. What goes around comes around. Only this time, I washed them, cleaned them, kept them a fitting and wholesome environment for the wounded and the dead. My immediate superior was Private Bernie "Wild Man" Wascomb.

"Call me Wild Man," he chimed.

"Sure, Bernie. Whatever you say."

Bernie combed his black hair straight back and examined his acne in a jeep's side-view mirror. As mentors go, Wascomb turned out to be unusual and entertaining. He came from Ohio and was determined to get back to Ohio intact, all bodily parts accounted for. While officially he backed the Army's policy in Vietnam, he didn't see what it had to do with him personally. As far as he could figure out, he hadn't done anything to the Vietnamese people that would cause them to want to murder him and he wanted to keep it that way. His plan was brilliantly simple. Rumor on the island was that there was a particular strain of VD going around, called the Asian Revenge, that resisted all known treatment. It could be controlled, but never cured. Consequently, Wild Man Wascomb spent his every waking moment with every tart he could buy, rent, cajole, sweet-talk, harangue, threaten, or lie to in hopes of contracting a whopping case of the Asian Revenge, a case so extreme and medically frustrating that the doctors would be forced to send him back to Ohio.

"Better a pervert than dead," Bernie crooned every morning as he stole the general's jeep to cruise the local bars in search of a stricken young girl and his ticket home.

As it turned out, the Army didn't care how much gonorrhea Private Wascomb had in his blood, so Wild Man decided to stop getting the clap and to start going crazy.

Like clockwork, every Monday morning he would shuffle over to the hospital, report to the psychiatric ward, and confess to being a lunatic.

The bored nurse always gave the same reply: "So you're nuts. Who isn't?"

"No, really," pleaded Wascomb. "I'm sick. Batty. Flipped-out. Dingy. Loony-Tunes."

"No shame in that, honey," answered the nurse as she gave him a cherry-flavored placebo and sent him back to the motor pool.

By summer's end, Wascomb really was crazy, but the doctors didn't notice and kept giving him cherry-flavored placebos.

In the fall, when the air felt almost cool, when the temperature actually dropped a few degrees and the rains came, heavy and constant, four of us made plans to launch a patrol into the deep jungle valley across the highway. The site of hard fighting during World War II, it was laced with old Japanese Army caves, grottoes that hadn't been entered in twenty years. It offered another campaign, one of many. I had already lived and fought around the world, serving with imagined distinction on many battlefields. I had been with the forlorn British at Dunkirk, the damned at Verdun, the hopeless at the Sommes, the doomed Confederates at Gettysburg, the triumphant Allies at Normandy. Oddly, despite these daring exploits, I never once dreamed of glory, valor, heroism. At home, the day's battle finished, wherever it was, I rarely dreamed at all, and when I did, I always dreamed of death. Dying, it seemed, was what grunts did better than anyone else.

We pulled out on a damp morning, humid and warm. Full packs, two canteens filled with grape Kool-Aid, sharpened machetes and K-bar knives. By midday we had shucked the packs and stowed them in a hidden cave entrance that faced the sea. We sucked at the canteens in a vain effort to ease our thirst. Norwell handed out salt tablets. Hordes of insects enveloped us, biting our arms and faces mercilessly. We moved on deeper into the valley, our boots caked with sucking mud. Norwell picked a leech off his cheek, crushed it between his fingers. It made a soft popping noise. We discovered another cave. More souvenirs to bundle up—rotten boots, rusted uniform buttons and canteens, a bent rifle barrel, spent cartridges, a twisted pair of wire-rimmed spectacles in a leather case, bits and pieces of human bone. Down, down into the valley, Norwell on the point. You could hear the rhythmic slicing of his machete and, below, the sound of a stream that ran cool beneath the jungle's thick canopy.

At just before two o'clock Norwell saw it, lying along the stream bank. A grenade miraculously preserved. Breathing heavily, wiping the sweat from our eyes, we all gathered around it like pilgrims at a holy shrine. Here it had sat, I thought, for twenty years: death in a metal jacket waiting patiently like a seed waits in the ground for just the right combination of rain and sunlight before it takes root, blooms. So this grenade, dispassionate death, had waited, and we had come. Secretly, perhaps each of us had hoped for such a moment, an authentic test, a true measure of our mettle. The honor went to Norwell, who was the oldest. Overweight, jolly, good-natured, a permanent smile on his flabby face, Norwell bent over and picked up the grenade. Wearing a pair of his father's fatigues, Norwell had rolled the baggy trousers up above his knees and his soapy white flesh was covered with mud and red welts. He started singing, mimicking the Beatles' "I Wanna Hold Your Hand," changing it to "I Wanna Pull Your Pin." Great stuff. We laughed. Norwell laughed, biting down on his lower lip. He said, "Okay, I'll heave it there, down in that ravine. You shits spread out, get down." The clatter of web gear as we instinctively followed orders. I jumped down behind a fallen log but could not resist looking up. I saw Norwell's plump index finger snug against the rusted pin. Nothing stirred: silence so absolute that it sat on the valley like iron. My heart pounded fiercely, roared in my ears, beat so wildly that I imagined it exploding. For an instant, Norwell studied the grenade, his prize. Then a flash, spontaneous combustion. No explosion registered, just that flash and the pain of hot metal slicing into my hands and arms. For an instant, I couldn't see. The world was a milky orange mist. Everywhere it rained Norwell, a cherry-colored vapor that coated every surface. All of us were covered with bits and pieces of Norwell. The hazy light shone pink, a rising sticky cloud that had once been human, vital, alive, now evaporated in the sun. Norwell surrounded us: burnt skin high up in the trees, viscera in the stream, along with shards of bone and chunks of brain. No message, no postscript for the ages. Norwell had just vaporized, an instantaneous exit.

We picked up what there was, wrapped it in a poncho.

"Holy shit!" sobbed Frank hysterically.

Yes, holy shit.

"For chrissakes, did he pop like a balloon or what?" cried Bob.

Yes, like a balloon.

"Oh, my God! Oh, Jesus Christ!" I screamed frantically.

Yes, oh, my God. Oh, Jesus Christ.

My father had faith in luck, believed in it. His first time in Vietnam, he bought a tiny 18-karat gold Buddha encased in plastic on a gold-link chain and never took it off. He said, "A soldier knows he's getting old when he has to start buying his luck." After Norwell vaporized in that jungle valley, my father figured my luck, too, had run thin. He came to the conclusion that I had seen quite enough of exotic, alluring Southeast Asia. "Time to get up, get clean, get packed, and get the hell out," he told me two weeks after Norwell's transmutation into that gazpacho mist that drifted up out of the valley and out over the Pacific Ocean.

My father decided that what I needed was a drastic change of scenery, so I was bound for my grandfather's place in the mountains. I said angrily, "I thought you said they were bums, socialist bums." I didn't want to go. "They are," said my father. "But they are live bums."

With his face turned from mine, my father busily stuffed clothes into my duffel bag.

He said, "Did you understand what Norwell said?" The

words were spoken with what, for him, was alien tenderness.

"He didn't say anything, Dad. He smiled and exploded."

"He said everything," he said emphatically.

As he leaned over the swelling duffel bag, the little gold Buddha swung hynotically from around his neck.

I didn't understand what he was trying to say.

"You shouldn't forget Norwell's good-bye. You owe him that."

"Christ, Dad," I shouted, "he didn't say anything! Just that big, stupid grin." I was angry now and sad, and I could feel the tears starting to come. I fought hard to hold them back.

He talked on about terrible truths, about how man was such a pitifully vulnerable and fragile creature. So temporary. A silly sack of skin and poorly protected organs. No immortal soul, just life, frail and flimsy. He said, "James Bond, Sergeant Rock, the Green Hornet, Rocky the Flying Squirrel, Zorro, Dick Tracy, Spiderman, the Lone Ranger, Mighty Mouse, Superman. Bullshit. It's bullshit, all of it." Man is unsuspecting flesh, entirely vincible. Entrails, brains, blood, and bone. A perilous environment for something as fissile as life to reside in, much less survive. Put a bullet in a man and his plumbing goes to hell and he dies. Cut him with a knife and the blood pours out of him like water over a shattered dam. Expose him to a virus and he succumbs. Throw a hand grenade at him and he explodes. Soak the air with bacteria and he comes down with a rattling cough and expires. Drop a bomb on him and he vanishes so completely it's hard to imagine he ever was. Throw him off a bridge and he drowns. And once the life has been knocked out of him, what's left? Compost, not some wondrous, mysterious otherness. Just organic chemistry. Death is permanent, the great forever. Blood makes the grass grow. You've got to keep the spirit vital, he said, warm and vibrant as long as you can. Grab life with both hands. Hold on to it desperately.

At the airport, my father shook my hand firmly, a man's grip rather than a father's, told me to take care of myself. "Think law school," he said. "Think medical school. Christ, be an engineer or an accountant. That's an order."

Kissing my cheek with a light brush of her lips, my mother pressed a paperback edition of *Don Quixote* into my hands. Her way, I suppose, of saying that while one journey was ending, another was beginning. My mother was a kind woman who had a fondness for touching, meaningful, symbolic farewells.

2. HOMECOMING

Life ain't what it's cracked up to be, no matter how many times you live it.

— Miss Emma Hamm, time traveler, aboard the eastbound Greyhound bus somewhere near Nevada's Smoke Creek Desert

Four in the morning at 33,000 feet and it was cold. A disenchanted stewardess with deep green eyes meticulously spread a TWA blanket over me as though I was a doll packed in straw. The captain's voice crackled over the microphone. We were nearing the International Date Line, that invisible, arbitrary, imaginary line extending from North Pole to South Pole that lets man keep his calendars neat, tidy, up to date, his watches and clocks accurate, on the money. I stared out the window. Somewhere down there on the dark waters of the Pacific was the 180th meridian. Another of man's imaginary lines. The earth is bound in a mathematical corset of man's devising, an attempt to make the natural world more orderly, presentable, understandable. The Date Line and the 180th meridian keep company, run roughly the same course. Deviations are made here and there so that places like the Aleutian Islands and Alaska can enjoy the same day at the same time. Thanks to the

Date Line, the traveler journeying east loses a day once he crosses the line. The traveler headed west across the line gets the day back. All time accounts balanced. No overdrafts and no surpluses.

"Yesterday's today, again," chuckled the captain as we crossed the line. "Remember TWA, the airline that let you re-live the past." Passengers immediately began fooling with their watches, grateful for the gift of time, an unblemished twenty-four hours.

The jet entered an immense swirl of clouds, was instantly enveloped by fingers of lacy, visible moisture. Pools of eerie light, light the color of ancient copper or decaying hyacinths, drifted freely within the clouds' soft, permeable tissue. Norwell's cloud had had the same strange, startling color about it. It, too, had drifted to the east, and I wondered if it had ever reached the 180th meridian, and if so, if the journey had made a differ-ence. Surely, there would be no urgent need for Norwell to reset his watch.

Behind was the island of Guam, where we spent an hour refueling, stretching. I sat in the snack bar drinking cool orange juice and listening to the mastodonic B-52 bombers taking off, a thundering sound, deep and growling, the vibrations rattling the ice in my glass. A resonating, mindless grinding, like the sides of mountains collapsing. Then gradual silence as the dino-saurian planes rose heavily over the Pacific heading west where Vietnam was going on, a wonderfully alluring and exotic land where each day human beings died in staggering numbers. Guam was just close enough to the Date Line that time was forever threatening to come unglued. Any moment today could become yesterday. "I feel like I've fallen down Alice's rabbit hole and time is out of whack, has no meaning," said the young airman wearing two flag jackets. "Like being buried in quick-sand, sort of. Something you can move in, but can't get out of. Bad vibes, my young man. Bad vibes. Soon I'll cross that line headed home, open my eyes and it'll all have been a dream. I'll discover I was never here at all."

Hours later and the ragged coastline of California. Long before Guam I had lost track of the days and hours. I only knew the sun was up, and inside the jetliner the air was still thick and tundra cold. In the distance, the ocean finally gave way to land, blurry and indistinct, a haze of moss greens and browns. Again the static of the microphone and the talkative co-pilot's chipper voice. "Welcome back," he said. "Welcome home."

A top sergeant named Clemens met the plane. I offered my hand; he saluted. He had a face as round and smooth as an Edam cheese and eyes hidden behind dark flight glasses. Sergeant Clemens drove me directly to the Greyhound bus station in town. He handed me a sealed white envelope containing my tickets and saluted crisply again. I studied his face. Nothing. Expressionless. I found my bus, turned, and Sergeant Clemens had gone, disappeared. First Norwell had vanished. Now Clemens. I wasn't lonely, just alone.

A tiny black man with a tremendous dome of hair on top of which sat a silly-looking gray hat opened the bus door. Wrinkles cut across his white shirt like canyons. The shirt nearly swallowed his elfin body. He looked like a child that had been haphazardly folded in a quilt and acted like a man who had seen too much sameness. He leaned dejectedly against the steering wheel.

"Time, folks," he said in a dreary monotone. "Time to roll."

Hours later, ominous clouds moving like a tide from the north and west. Enormous columns of mud-colored air billowing up from behind the craggy pinnacles of distant mountains with the worn look of abraded primal incisors. A fulvous runny meld of sticky road grime and splattered rainwater leaving viscous yellow tracks across the windows. The landscape seemed cold and desolate. Cold crept through the bus's metal frame like a vapor, and yet I was so hot I peeled away my heavy coat and sweater, rolled up my shirt sleeves. Even so, sweat dripped down my chest and arms, beaded on my forehead. What now? Malaria. Hyperpyrexia. Traumatic fever. Sorrow. Anger. Boundless fear. Calenture. Delightful, simple delirium. The bus headed on into the building storm, into a geography of perfect darkness.

The bus seat felt like solid concrete. As the miles clicked off, I squirmed for comfort, any soft spot. There is something soporific about humming wheels. Fitfully, I slipped in and out of sleep. Nevada, I heard someone say, was just beyond the next range of mountains. Nevada, I whisper, as if it were a soothing mantra, and close my drooping eyes, and I am seven years old and in Orléans, in France. It is cool and sunny, a bright, clear, day. Bands play, crowds cheer. A fete. Joan of Arc Day, and I am in front of a legion of swaggering Cub Scouts, carrying the American flag, holding it high into the wind. The wooden staff is heavy and my arms ache as the shabby blue-clad column of young boys marches down the narrow streets toward the plaza dominated by the imposing statue of Joan of Arc. The streets are clogged with people—French, Americans, British, even tourists from Japan happily snapping photographs of everything. In the sidewalk bars and old hotels along the parade route, every seat and every room are taken. Revelers hang precariously out of hotel windows, drinking cheap champagne, singing patriotic French songs, laughing loudly, and filling the cool spring air with a constant rain of confetti, crumpled paper cups, wet cocktail napkins, champagne corks, caps, even a couple of bras, which in the tinted shadows of the narrow street look like dwarf parachutes, one red, one white. Up there somewhere, hanging out of one of those windows, are my parents, both of them smoking Salems and drinking white wine from dark green bottles because they detest the pretentiousness of French champagne, even the cheap brands. And the noise, I remember, seemed to have weight and substance and was animate, moving along with the snaking line of marchers until it suddenly transformed into uncharitable screams and a volley of sharp stones.

The rocks and other missiles were coming from behind a cemetery wall not far down the street from the sculpted figure of the martyred Joan, timeless in her armor, incorruptible, godlike. Unfortunately, though, not only was she granite or bronze or whatever, she was also stone dead and did not lift a divine finger to halt the heavy bombardment zeroing in on us from the cemetery.

Cub Scouts and Brownies were everywhere breaking ranks, fleeing as the little band from the city's fire department played a snappy minuet. Some of the older Boy Scouts began returning the fire, throwing whatever was at hand into the cemetery. Our attackers turned out to be our French schoolmates, who thought Americans marching in their Joan of Arc parade demonstrated a certain lack of taste and correct manners. Never breaking rhythm of their assault, the drumming fusillade of rocks, vegetables, and eggs, the French boys began chanting obviously insulting slogans in a slurred, broken English that I never did understand, though I believe it had something to do with what they perceived to be a special relationship between Americans and pigs.

Undaunted, the flag waved on mostly because I couldn't find a spot of cover that wasn't already occupied. Like a warm virus, the brawl eventually began to spread, overtaking the adults, who each gave their loyalty and whatever was handy enough to throw to their respective countries.

Then I heard it, clear as a bell tolling, even over the boiling mixture of trumpeting band music and hysterical Japanese tourists—my father's unmistakable voice, like boulders grinding.

"Move it. Move it. Shove off, Pierre. Where were you at Normandy, you prick!"

He was wearing green trousers, a harsh green turtleneck sweater, and a red beret cocked defiantly to one side of his head. Suddenly he leaped on top of one of the stalled taxicabs, their horns blasting. Up one cab, down the next; up another and down again, and the tumbler of wine he held aloft never lost a drop. He charged ahead sporting the manic grin of what the French call a *fou*, a screwball. Reaching me, he placed the red beret atop his wine glass and waved it high over his head in an attempt to rally the dispirited Scouts.

"*En Dieu est tout!*"

"*Enfants perdus!*"

"*Vivre ce n'est pas respirer, c'est agir!*"

"*Bon jour, bonne œuvre!*"

"*Jamais bon coureur ne fut pris!*"

"*J'y suis, j'y reste!*"

And finally, in a burst of fevered emotion, "*Vive la bagatelle!*" which I took to mean either "Long live truffles" or "Let's hear it for frivolity." Then the balding little man donned his wine-soaked beret, grabbed the flag from my hands, and exhorted the disoriented members of Troop 321, screaming "Forward, you little bastards!" And before we knew it, he had taken the statue and sat tenderly in Joan of Arc's sacred lap removing banana peel from her cheek. Even the French boys in the cemetery were moved to spontaneous expressions of reverent awe.

The Greyhound moved on, crossing from Nevada into Utah. Another of man's geographic lines had been crossed. Rain turned to snow and I woke up shivering, my cramped muscles aching, my skin cold and pasty white. Putting my coat back on, I rubbed a small peephole in the slick fog building up on the window. An almost unfathomable darkness over the landscape, as dense as greasepaint. No stars. No moonglow. No creeping shadows. The fog quickly reclaimed my window and I curled up tight in the seat, tight as an insect under a stone. Safe, secure, invulnerable? Hardly. Just a comfortable way to wait out the inevitable rush of miles.

The wheels hummed, and the black driver was humming too, Motown tunes. Soon I was drifting into dream, a warm haze enveloping me. I found myself on my hands and knees in our house in Fort Sam Houston, Texas. My mother and I had been sitting on the cool floor under the kitchen's ceiling fan.

She held a photograph album in her lap, pictures of seemingly endless family members and friends whom I'd never met. Suddenly she stopped, pointing at a small black-and-white picture of a baby lying on its plump stomach naked on a cheap imitation Hopi Indian rug.

Tapping the picture excitedly with her finger she said, "That's you, dear. Daddy took one look at you in the back of that goddamned ambulance when you arrived so unceremoniously into the world and said you looked like ten pounds of ossified, pre-chewed bubblegum."

I winced.

"Not so," she cooed. "You were the most beautiful thing in the world."

And the dream evaporated and it was almost dawn as the bus pulled into a rest stop in Green River, Utah. As I moved down the aisle, my tennis shoes stuck to the tile floor, as slimy as the floor of a slaughterhouse. Ordered two hot dogs and a Coke. A young woman and two children slept on the station floor, shoved up against a rack of gray metal lockers. The children were tucked beneath a thin yellow sheet. At the door, two soldiers chain-smoking Camels waited for the next bus west. I recognized them instantly; one bore a morbid resemblance to Norwell, the other was the spitting image of Wild Man Wascomb. Both seemed doomed. I turned away, walked into the seedy restroom, splashed handfuls of wonderfully cold Utah water on my tired face. Reflected in the broken mirror, water running down my cheeks and chin, my face in that flickering fluorescent light seemed to have the consistency of day-old oatmeal.

Back on the bus, a new driver had boarded, as well as a new passenger, who plopped down in the vacant seat next to mine. She was small and old, with shaggy, smoky-gray hair and wrinkled skin. Liver spots covered her hands like islands of mold on white bread. She stank. Perspicacious, slightly meddlesome eyes peered out from behind thick glasses. She carried a small brown suitcase secured with two lengths of cattle rope. On her lap she clutched a plastic bag packed with scraps of colored yarn, one blue tennis shoe, a yellow rain hat, a dirty red bandana, a half jar of salted peanuts, a pocketknife, and a broken compass.

She introduced herself in a quavering voice. "Miss Emma Hamm," she said, extending a tremulous hand. "Time traveler."

"Eh?" I gasped, and scrunched into the corner of my seat, trying to put as much distance between us as possible on a bus speeding across Utah at seventy miles an hour.

Digging through her bag, she pulled out a yellowed calendar. Year 1857. She flipped through it, asking me for the current year, month, and place. I fingered the outline of my pocketknife in my pants pocket.

"Nineteen sixty-five," I said. "Winter. Utah."

She threw up her hands, the loose folds of skin on her upper arms shaking like Jell-O. "Well, there goes another lifetime." She tossed the calendar aside angrily. "Two hours ago it was June 14, 1857, in the gold fields along the American River in California."

She reached deeper into her bundle, came up with a tuna fish sandwich, offered me half.

I visualized the whopping case of food poisoning possible from a tuna fish sandwich slapped together more than a century ago in some pestilential California mining camp.

I said, "No thanks. Just finished two hot dogs."

Miss Emma tore into the tuna fish, telling me between bites that she had led fifteen previous lives. At least, that was how many she remembered.

She looked dreamily out the bus window as the blood-red Utah sun moved higher over the horizon. "This time traveling wears a body out, son. That's for sure. Oh, yeah, you think it's romantic and all. Not so, not so at all. Heartbreaking is more like it, truth be told. I been far back as Greek times and still ain't never got a break. None at all. No matter where I pull up, it's the same slice of woe. You'd think just once I could move among the Du Ponts or Vanderbilts. Maybe do some time as a minor Greek god or an Egyptian princess. Maybe some trifling duchess. Naw. I can't even get into the body of a middle-class housewife. I starved to death in Russia in the nineteenth century, was trampled to death in a food riot in Ireland, thrown in paupers' prison in London and eventually died of dysentery. Dropped dead on a barren farm in Turkey in 1653; died elsewhere of the plague, cholera, TB, childbirth. As a Crow squaw I died a drunk on some reservation in the Dakotas singing ancient chants to extinct buffalo. And so on."

Little chunks of tuna and mayonnaise were stuck to the corners of her mouth. She didn't have any teeth.

"God knows how many times I've died, and every time I weep for joy thinking this is it, the last time, peace at last, and then I wake up as a bag lady digging through garbage in summertime Chicago or a young girl with a bloated belly and disappearing breasts digging roots in Ethiopia, and it starts all over again. Just like now." She looked about cautiously as if suspecting to be done in by Time again any moment, then fumbled in her coat pocket and pulled out a bus ticket to Kansas. "Found it rolled up tight in my hand this morning back there, back wherever it was I came from. Last night, I was in the mining camp up along the American River, a young girl working a claim with her father. A dark night. Rattling noises and my father suddenly screaming. Dark-faced men tearing at his clothes, looking for gold. Then tearing at my clothes. I woke up cold, lying next to a dead man in a cardboard Kenmore box in an alley. I had my hand in his coat pocket. This ticket was in my hand."

While Miss Emma Hamm talked, she closed her eyes and her head bobbed gently against her chest. I took a napkin from my coat, one I had left over from the hot dogs, and wiped the dried tuna from her chin. As the bus zipped from Utah to the Uncompahgre plateau of Colorado, Miss Emma Hamm opened one eye and told me in a whisper that soon she would again be just a speck of undifferentiated energy, a speeding flash of mindless atoms traveling through time and space. "You know where I'm going next?" she asked, smiling hopelessly, apathetically.

I shook my head.

"Germany, 1944. The Holocaust. My name will be Vonya Moshe. I am so beautiful it would break your heart. I will be gassed at Auschwitz while I stand naked crammed in a shower room with my mother and sisters and cousins and a hundred other naked women and girls. Surely, this time I will really die, be given peace. Don't you think?"

"Yes, without a doubt," I said as softly and kindly as I knew how.

And Miss Emma Hamm went back to sleep, making tiny, wet sucking noises with her pinched lips.

The bus drove on to Salina, Kansas, where she took up her bundle, shook my hand, and departed, saying softly in German, "*Um so besser.*" As the bus pulled away, I watched her through the window, watched her cross the highway and disappear into a landscape of dark, fallow fields and low, gray winter clouds.

Another hot dog and a quart of chocolate milk somewhere out in the plains of Kansas. After Salina, the weather turned worse. Someone said the temperature was 15 degrees. There was talk of more snow. To the north the sky was sooty gray again, threatening, clotted with swollen clouds that seemed to hang just inches above the flat terrain. The bus kept its eastward course, headed for St. Louis. In Topeka I bought a map of Missouri and Arkansas and spread it across my lap. I found St. Louis, then Interstate 55, a thin red line, smaller than a capillary, seeping south past places that meant nothing to me, were not even images. Just names. Crystal City. Perryville. Cape Girardeau. East Prairie. New Madrid. Portageville, Oscela, and finally into West Memphis, where I changed buses.

A drastic change in landscape. An older bus, one that smelled of sweat and cheap wine and sour beer, headed north and west into gently swelling blue-green hills, then climbed to rocky, brittle-backed ridges, worn and ancient. Groaning up and down the steep, narrow mountain roads, the bus seemed to travel along the backbone of time itself. It was a disarming geography of low clouds and thick forests, occasionally relieved by a broad meadow of brown grasses and fallen leaves. Here and there brilliant shafts of sunlight penetrated the forest, pellucid and shimmering like gaslight. Wisps of clouds edged down the hillsides, mingling with the rich veins of light so that each finger of cloud transected the hill like a mountain stream. Where it fell unobstructed, the sunlight highlighted diaphanous reds and yellows, somber browns and muted greens, charcoal blues—the colors of the season. Below enormous bluffs with protruding limestone brows, in the hollows, caliginous shadows flickered against the sides of stones, obscure shadings like black-and-white prints slowly coming to life in a chemical bath. In the more precipitous crevasses there seemed no light at all and the faces of the canyons looked darker than a moonless night, blacker than a crow's wing. Everywhere there was water, moving water: pale green, blue-green, endless tintinnabulations, as creeks and streams and cold springs edged perpetually over layers of stone, around exposed gravel bars white as bone. And the bus rumbled on, farther into the hills, deeper into the maze of narrow, interlaced valleys.

After West Memphis, there were no cities of size. Just Jonesboro. It and the isolated hardluck mountain towns that got smaller and smaller and farther and farther apart, their presence announced by small green signs along the side of some hill and the sudden appearance of a lopsided clapboard house, brick chimney puffing gray smoke. Scrawny chickens pecking at the roadside; a disemboweled washing machine or icebox on the porch next to a threadbare sofa half buried under a quilt of autumn leaves. Set up on blocks in the front yard, a ward of automotive paraplegics—a Plymouth, a Dodge, always a Chevy or two, all the color of wormwood, hoods popped, engines ripped out with wires and hoses jutting this way and that, just so much iron and rubber digestive plumbing. Grass and weeds up to the decaying doors, winter violets blooming from pitted grilles. Skinny, raw-boned dogs of uncertain breed curled up on the wooden porches, their eyes dull, drained of all curiosity.

Little towns with curious names like hard, sharp-edged poetry. Augusta. Bald Knob. Hoxie Strawberry. Black Rock. Ash Flat. Evening Shade. Zion. Walnut Ridge. Just to the north of the bus route, the Missouri Ozarks, and to the south, the great White River valley falling off into the flatlands along the Arkansas River toward Little Rock and the great river, the Mississippi. West of the descending White, the sudden eruption of the jagged Ouachita Mountains, and westward from the rim of the Boston Mountains lay the eroded heart of the Arkansas Ozarks and the hazy vastness of Oklahoma, Indian country. My grandfather liked Oklahoma. "Where's there's desolation and heartbreak," he said, "there's beauty and magic." He credited what he called the Great Mystery with keeping several year-round residences. One up in the high country of the Wind River Mountains. One amid the stony-eyed reptiles, hardy cacti, warm stones, and alkali water of Arizona. Certainly, one in New Zealand. Others in Alaska, the Ozarks, the Smokies, Montana. The Great Mystery was a trout angler and got around. And surely, too, a home in Oklahoma, somewhere up on the old black prairie along some little-known stream where, unknown to any man, wild trout still spawned, lived and died undisturbed.

At the rim of the Boston Mountains, where the bus limped along, it was as if the earth had suddenly cracked open, stranding me among these ancient hills, another time traveler. Unlike Miss Emma Hamm, though, time had been kinder to me. There was a comfort, never fully explicable, a soothing immediacy to these hardscrabble hills, an intimacy missing from the bleak, wide-open immensity of the great West I had just traveled through. Here beauty lay not on the surface; its grandeur was more subtle and lacked the heady pretense of the obviously glorious. The mysteries of this desiccate primeval sea floor were as plentiful as ghosts, pleasantly haunting one's days and nights, forever provocative, evocative.

Miles before reaching Mount Hebron I felt an easing in the great cavern of sour, bitter emptiness that had inhabited my belly. In the soft sunlight filtering down through the hills, I could feel the knots of fear untangle, the pools of anger and confusion evaporate. At Bower's Corners, I opened the window wide and the wind was cool and fresh and sweet, and there was in it no hint of cordite. Nowhere the smell of uncertainty or death. I found myself gulping air, filling my lungs with it over and over, as though I were drowning, then suddenly, incomprehensibly washed up on some beach, a man too frightened to question his fate, too thankful to reject it, too hopeful to deny it. Gasping, huffing, the bus slouched up yet another steep grade, past one more luminescent green sign, this one heralding Mount Hebron. I sat back, took another lungful of cold mountain air as the soft convalescent, analeptic sunlight warmed my face and arms.

Mount Hebron: a dozen ramshackle buildings strewn haphazardly along the lip of a curve, on both sides of the mountain highway. Coming in from the east, the bus first passed a handsome white house that sat well off the highway behind a fence of split-rail logs. Behind the house stretched a wide meadow where a small herd of cattle methodically grazed on lush winter grasses. Off to the right, a boarded-up store, a rusted sign over the doorway reading "Webster's Appliances & Beauty Shop." More houses, small, some almost secretive, retiring, hidden behind tangles of trees and shrubs. Suspicious looks from behind screen doors. Cultivated seclusion. Other houses simply expressionless, anonymous, not even a potted geranium on their wooden porches, a name or even initials on the battered mailboxes poised recklessly along the highway.

At the apex of the curve, Wulff's "Dry Goods & Law Firm & Notary Public," just across from John William Pete's Esso station, garage, and Ford dealership, the most modern building in town, complete with air conditioning, central heat, soda machine. Two gas pumps out front and two newly washed and waxed and proudly displayed 1965 Ford pickup trucks, both burgundy red.

Where the highway straightened out, just before dipping into the next valley, stood K. M. Bates's "Hardware & Grocery," a two-story brick building, a dull red, with thick hobnailed glass windows and tall oak double doors with white enamel doorknobs. Two wooden benches sat on the porch in the shade and ran the length of the building. Two wooden steps led up to the porch and the imposing double doors, which opened wide to a vast array of necessities and tempting frills, fillips, the new, the superfluous, the alluring, and the simply curious and fascinating, all enough to bewitch any man, prosperous, lousy rich, or decently poor. The café occupied the small building next to Bates's. Although the place belonged to Miss Donna Bly, no one called it Donna's or Bly's. It was just "the café," five wooden tables with red-and-white plastic tablecloths, cheap metal chairs, and an atmosphere that always smelled of hot coffee, fresh apple, cherry, and chocolate pies, great potfuls of spicy chili, hot grease, cheeseburgers, and Pine Sol. Directly across from Bates's store was Mount Hebron's second gas station, Reilly Larson's Billups. One chalky white pump, regular gas only. Flats fixed. Oil checked. Minor repairs extra. On warm afternoons Larson sat in a wooden chair propped up against a bold red Coca-Cola machine that spit out warm bottles of Coke for a dime. Larson sat against the big machine wiping down his artificial left leg with a clean rag and Windex. A veteran of World War II, Larson had lost his leg in Germany. The well-kept prosthesis was one of the town's great prides and Larson spent a good deal of his time showing and explaining it to admirers.

Every town in these mountains, no matter its size or importance, had its heart, its center, its secular anima where the mail arrived and departed, news was passed, troubles reported, sorrows voiced, deaths mourned, births announced, a place where fortune and catastrophe struggled for dominance, where joy and gloom descended in equal measure, where dreams were fulfilled or hopes shattered. A kind of public wailing wall, emotions laid out like a restaurant's daily bill of fare. K. M. Bates's Hardware & Grocery was Mount Hebron's groaning board. There the town's soul was laid bare promptly every morning at seven thirty, except Sundays, when Mr. Bates swung open the heavy twin doors and you could hear it all so clearly, the murmurs, the cackling and nervous whispers, the whining and troubled sighs, the hosannas and the tears, the unabashed weeping and grieving, the jubilation and yowls of petulance. There at Bates's store, people got their blood to pumping, railed at life. Bates's was also the bus stop. Right beneath the metal sign hanging from Bates's porch roof, boasting two-foot-tall rooster-red letters, so many journeys began and ended.

Here my bus, too, eventually pulled up, stopped, and idled. I felt dizzy, as lightheaded as a diver with too much nitrogen in his blood. Like a paralysis, terror seized every muscle and bone. I needed time to decompress, steady myself. Unable to move, I looked out the window, watched particles of dust in the red shafts of evening light. It wasn't at all like the dream that had soothed me outside St. Louis, visions of bucolic farmland, pastures, a grand white house set back in a grove of oak trees, high-spirited, ridiculously expensive thoroughbreds gamboling in rolling meadows, noble heads held high in a gracious southern wind.

"This is it, bub," said the driver indifferently, making no effort to hold back a yawn.

When I looked out the window again, the town seemed like something out of a museum, a poorly done period diorama: life without motion. The bus driver disappeared out the door of the bus, jerked my duffel bag out of the luggage hold, tossed it onto the sidewalk. In front of Bates's store columns of feed and seed bags flanked the doorway. The doors were open and inside a single unshaded light bulb dangled from the high dark ceiling and a slowly oscillating fan kicked up tiny mists of grain dust and strands of spiderweb. A man in overalls and a straw hat stood just beside the bags of feed, spitting streams of viscous tobacco juice into an empty coffee can. At the café, a chalkboard hung from the screen door. On it someone had scribbled the day's menu: pork chops, lima beans, mashed potatoes, biscuits and skillet gravy, iced tea and cherry pie. $1.50.

The driver sidled back on board, took his seat, leaned back toward me saying, "Kinda brings new meaning to 'end of the line,' don't it, kid?" And he chuckled hoarsely as I climbed down onto the sidewalk. There was a gnashing of gears and the bus poked forward and down the highway, disappearing quickly as the highway dipped into the valley. At the edge of town, clapboard houses in various colors and sizes and in various stages of disrepair stood against the stark landscape. Above the valley, the old mountains glowed in the lambent evening sunlight with oblivious subtlety.

He touched me gently on the shoulder as I stood there in front of Bates's store. My grandfather. "Glad to see you, son," he said softly, his voice stronger than I expected. He offered a hand, the fingers stiff from decades of heavy, unyielding work. His grip was solid and firm, free of uncertainty or nervousness. He was of medium height and thin, with gray eyes magnified behind wire-rimmed glasses. Wide green suspenders held up a pair of blue work pants. He wore a bright red flannel shirt, sleeves rolled up to the elbows. In his left hand he held a weather-stained and battered cowboy hat fashioned in the low-slung style known as a Montana slope. Rather than a conventional hatband, the old man had sewn on a wide strip of lamb's wool around the hat's faded crown. Like insects stuck to honey, dozens of spent trout flies, colorful lepidoteran frauds of many kinds, descriptions, and fanciful colors, were hooked into the nappy wool. What hair the old man had left was silver gray and combed straight back. My great-uncle Albert stood just behind my grandfather's right shoulder. No words. We shook hands, exchanged cryptic smiles. The years had laid down layers of leathery calluses across Albert's palms. If you could have somehow straightened him out, Albert would have stood well over six feet tall. That day he was hatless. He had a great thicket of wiry white hair which had resisted all attempts at upkeep and management. Like ivy, Albert's hair set and kept its own course. As I got to know Albert better and to truly appreciate the eccentricities of his appearance, I thought he looked the way Mark Twain might have looked had he never traveled east of the Mississippi River. In a leather pouch on his belt, Albert carried a Brunton compass. It was, I learned, one of his many amulets, a talisman he liked to keep close at hand. Albert believed many things. One of them was that a man ought to know where he was, how he got there, and the paths open to him, no matter their point on the compass.

A wind came off the mountains, rattling high up in the trees, light and cool. It was a long and awkward moment, a clumsy homecoming at best, marked by stiff smiles, puzzled looks, amiable handshakes. Looking back, though, I think it was somehow fitting that our separated lives, our kindred blood should have met at last and mingled for the first time there in front of Bates's Hardware & Grocery in Mount Hebron, with the autumn dusk settling in, a soft purple light cascading down off the hills and forming pools of light around the old men's workboots.

I kept looking at them, looking for their age. They were old. God, I thought, really old. Albert had to be in his eighties, and Emerson wasn't far behind. And yet nothing in their speech or movements declared their age. So I just stood there smiling a goofy smile and thinking, Christ, they weren't anything like I imagined. I had bitten my lower lip for more than 2,500 miles thinking I was about to be handed over to two tobacco-chewing, brain-damaged hillbillies, old coots so senile they couldn't recall a day since 1920. Shiftless old apple-knockers who talked with glutinous accents that reeked of fatback, cane syrup, and clotted grits. But there was none of that. They were gentle-spoken, clean-shaven, handsome old men of great charm and dignified bearing. No tobacco drool on the chins, no wizened eyeballs. Neither had the countenance of a squashed armadillo or a rabid werewolf. Instead, happily, they appeared the opposite of all I had feared, Albert's smile broadened and my lingering sense of despair ebbed, fell away like a shield of useless scales, a protective armor that I no longer needed. There in front of Bates's store the soldier's son retired and the young boy I had never been dared to surface, genuinely thrilled not only to be alive, but just to be. The jungle and the war and Norwell's pink cloud were behind me. I was beguiled by the contented smile on Albert's face. I'd never seen an expression quite so profound or honest. I wondered what kind of life or what kind of magic produced that kind of smile, a look so serene in a world that liked playing chicken with the Apocalypse. The urge to race after the bus, to escape these mountains and their withdrawn close-mouthed inhabitants, disappeared. I was suddenly tired of running. I had finally come home.

Albert reached into his shirt pocket and took out a Hohner harmonica, its chrome plating worn dull as pewter.

"Play any?" he asked.

I shook my head as I watched him pour the remains of a bottle of I.B.C. root beer over the instrument, then shake it vigorously.

"Good. It's a terrible vexation, the harp is. Like fly fishing or root beer. Won't leave a man alone. So much sound from such a small thing. Hardly more than a toy. Yet sometimes I think I have the entire Vienna Symphony in my pocket."

Well, I thought, this was it: the spell was about to be broken. I was in for endless bars of high-pitched, twanging country and western yodeling. Sentimental folderol without rhyme or melody. Instead, what came out of that harp was the blues, low down and gritty, basso profundo, Albert bending the notes so that at once he was a bugler, an oboist, ivory thumper, hurdy-gurdy man, a minstrel, a balladeer of the down-and-out, the vexed, every troubled soul. The sound came deep and mournful, sweet and trilling, a roller coaster of musical tension and fretful resolution. A small crowd stood on Bates's porch, at the door of the café. A woman lugging a bag of potatoes stopped, set the bag down, tapped her feet to the steady gutteral backbeat.

Emerson rolled his eyes. "That's something else you can steer clear of," he said, jerking an accusing thumb at Albert's Hohner as it slid effortlessly between the old man's lips. "One gifted entertainer in the clan's enough. Too much." He put his arm around my shoulder and ushered me across the street. Albert followed, never missing a lick.

> *I felt bad this morning,*
> *Can't feel no worse no more.*
> *I felt so bad this morning,*
> *Going away for sure.*
> *Fields is dried up*
> *And I got this thirst,*
> *Felt so bad this morning*
> *Tonight can't be no worse.*

My grandfather threw my stuff in the back of a dog-weary blue Ford pickup truck, model and year unknown, at least to me. My duffel bag rested on a bed of deer antlers that were as smooth and white as soapstone. He drove and whistled gospel tunes while Albert sat by the open passenger's window tonguing a series of blues riffs, a crescendo of wailing sounds, the notes as pliable as wet willow. Like a boat snug at its moorings, I sat pressed between these two old men, watching the mountain highway flash by through a hole in the floorboard near Albert's feet. I closed my eyes and felt a great wave of relief, a great sense of refuge. My father had given me more than I had hoped.

This was more than a hideaway, more than asylum, more than a temporary cloister from a world gone mad. Even as we traveled the narrow road down into the valley below Mount Hebron, I let myself go; I let my mind drift from thoughts of refuge to images of home.

3. TRAIL'S END

This house is where I take my natural rest, but my home is out there, beyond the back door.

— *Albert "Salmo" McClain, 1965*

The drive from Mount Hebron to the farm took more than half an hour. The contest between the obstinate geography of the Ozarks and the jittery highway was an unfair one, with the old, worn-out highway avoiding every showdown with the intractable landscape. Climbing first to the rim of a sprawling plateau, the road dropped quickly into a shadow-filled, narrow valley. The edge of the mountains in the distance were dark, ink-black, veiled in columns of tremendous gray clouds, heavy with rain. The hills seemed in motion, rising and falling like the swells of an ancient turbid sea for as far as my eye could see. Moving quickly from the west, the clouds hung low over the hills, so low I thought surely I could reach out of the truck window and touch them. The road snaked along the thin lip of the plateau for a mile or so, the Ford poking along slowly, in no rush, the only thing in motion except for the illusion of the rising and falling hills, a small, unimportant, and only temporary intruder traveling upon that ledge of stone pinched be-

tween the valley and the sky. The Ford turned left off the
mountain highway and onto a county road heading northwest.
On a nearby knoll stood the remnants of a collapsed barn, a
tangle of gray and decaying boards dressed now in thickets of
poison ivy and maturing oak trees. A hole as black as a cave
marked where the barn door used to open wide, greet the
mountain mornings.

My grandfather slowed the truck and said, "The Woollum
place, what's left of it. Dave Woollum's children gave it up, sold
it to some St. Louis people that like the idea of owning Ozark
land just as long as they don't actually have to come down here
and visit it or live on it."

"Let's don't cloud the boy's vision of the mountains right
off," laughed Albert. "Anyway, this old place here is showing
real promise. No one's laid a plow or a chainsaw to it in years.
There's hope. Found two wild turkeys roosting up there last
spring. Best neighbors we ever had. Dave Woollum used to talk
to ghosts. Turkeys have the decency to hang around with the
living."

Emerson shifted gears and the truck jounced ahead. A good
truck, the Ford never got in a hurry, a characteristic that Albert
found wholesome and admirable. For as long as I knew him,
each time Albert got out of the Ford he would thump it soundly
on the hood. Albert had a habit of thumping things that stuck
with him, seemed to endure no matter the odds. Things like the
Ford he thumped with vigor, while things like his collection of
handmade, steadfast cane fly rods or his vintage L. C. Smith
double-barreled shotgun or his gathering of Remingtons and
Winchesters he touched gently, respectfully, with a sense of
deep and genuine companionship rather than restrictive reverence. Many a cold night he would sit in the big room near the
fireplace and wipe the rods again and again with a clean, soft
T-shirt, or rub a thin layer of oil into the aging wood and steel
of the L. C. Smith. His movements were slow, almost dream-
like, and you could see the fire reflected in his bright eyes and

you knew he was someplace else. Perhaps afield with Cody out in front of him, the dog's nose full of quail, or maybe down along the stream just at dusk hoping to catch sight of a fine trout on the rise. The two old men had a name for these spells when they simply vanished into some memory of the land they had stowed up inside them. "Journeying," they called it. Later I began to understand that when you have lived with the land as long as they had, if you're lucky, there comes a point when the land is part of you and you are part of it. The union, if not perfect, is inexorable. It's in you, all its rich bounty, its pain and loss, like blood and tissue.

The outdoor life pleased these old men so because they believed any properly obsessed fly fisherman carried rivers and trout inside him. The addicted angler, the only kind worth being, always had a place to cast his line, no matter how deep his longing or his misery, how twisted his misfortune, or how deep his pain.

Even in August, when the heat came off the land in visible waves, shimmered in cloudless skies and was a heavy, exhausting, inescapable burden, we would work from before daylight until noon. Workshirts and pants dark with sweat, hoes slung over cramped shoulders, we came out of the fields or garden bent almost double from the heat, drained, hobbling like harrowed convicts linked by heavy chains. Painfully we plodded back to the house and sat on the back porch, slumped down in the sticky yet consoling shade as we wiped our grimy, sweaty foreheads, arms, and necks with soaked bandanas, dragging them finally through our damp, matted hair, over our cracked and sunburnt lips. And for a long time every summer afternoon there was no talk, no sounds save those of complete exhaustion.

And every day Albert, at last, would crack the silence, gasping suddenly, "Root beer, damn it. Root beer."

Emerson would sigh deeply. "And the atlas, son. Bring the atlas."

I.B.C. root beer hissing and frothing over ice all around.

We rolled the cool glasses over our cheeks and I gave the old man the huge black atlas with the gold trim, the pages creased and dog-eared. We sat there in silence again, sat on the porch steps and the wobbly vegetable crates as Emerson leisurely flipped through the big atlas, that enticing catalog of the earth's known places, the land painted in rich pastels and the seas in tranquil, soothing blues. And the old man always wore an expectant smile, even during the last days of August when the heat sucked the air from the lungs, seemed as heavy as iron, something that was alive and callous and pitiless. But he called for the atlas each day at noon and took it carefully from my hands as if it were some sacred tome. And in a way it was, I suppose, for in its pages was a world of cool lands and cold trout streams, a world of adventure and beauty that delighted our senses and deepened our obsession for the cooling waters of Starlight Creek. On those hot and still summer days you could hear the sound of the stream in the hills just beyond the barn, the sound of riffles running against smooth stones. Although Emerson and Albert had probably not traveled more than five hundred miles in any direction from Oglala County, thanks to Emerson's atlas they were veteran world travelers, compleat anglers who had tested most of the earth's best angling waters, casting pure if imaginary lines over every stretch of classic trout water from Labrador to Iceland, to Norway, Britain, and Alaska's wild trout and salmon rivers.

Turning the pages of the atlas, Emerson would suddenly tap the bottom of his glass against the porch step, a sharp sound that brought the daily summertime meetings of the Starlight Creek Angling Society to order. With my arrival, the society had undergone a drastic growth in membership, its numbers swelling from four to five. Albert and Emerson were the founders and therefore the oldest members. Elias Wonder, who had a place up where Susan's Branch emptied into Starlight Creek, had gained membership in 1930. Membership held firm until the 1950s, when Cody was allowed full and undisputed admission. At first, my application was denied on the grounds that anyone who actually wanted to "fool around with trout" was insane and therefore unfit for the demands of membership. But since I was persistent and promised not to pester them on the subject of fly fishing or angling in general, the society decided to tolerate my presence, though unlike Cody's and Elias Wonder's my vote never counted.

Having brought the Starlight Creek Angling Society to order and with the immense atlas spread on his lap, the old man would mumble something about the record showing that it was still hot and that it was still August and that the weather was insufferable and that the society had assembled here on the porch of Trail's End in the Arkansas mountains to pursue, temporarily, a cooler destination.

"So, where to today?" the old man asked eagerly. "Give it some thought, fellas. Make it someplace cool. A chilly latitude laced with swift rivers and ornery trout."

Yes, Albert and I agreed, nodding wearily. Please, make it cool. Make it cold. Make it boreal, icy as the north side of a tombstone. A place where it wasn't August and where there were no weeds strangling the tomatoes, no insects chomping away at the bush beans. Albert's choice rarely varied. He wanted to head west, up into the wild country of Montana, fish the trout rivers the old Confederate had fished with the Sioux. He dreamed of perfect drift-free casts floating a tiny dry fly on the waters of the Madison, the Ruby, the Big Horn, the Yellowstone, the Kootenai, Grasshopper Creek. He thought it would be grand to fish these rivers all day and sleep near them at night, wide beryl-blue western nights, under broad skies, skies as immense as a sea and the night air cold against the skin as clouds drift overhead soaked in faded yellow moonlight. And there would be trout over a good fire, blue smoke rising, sweet to the smell, smoke that hung close to the ground and drifted like a fog across the campsite.

Emerson worked the atlas as if he had no idea where Montana might be, which only heightened our excitement, our sense of the wild and exotic, a land of unknown rivers and noble trout. On finding Montana, he carefully read the state's vital statistics that accompanied the map, read each sentence slowly as though each word was more than sound, was something beyond venerable, closer to ineffable, sublime.

Unlike Albert's, my imagination suffered from a great infection of wanderlust. One day I would suggest a sojourn along Vermont's Battenkill, the next a week floating the remoter regions of Salmon River out West. Often, I argued for an angling tour of Britain, thinking it might do our spirits some good to fish the waters that had spawned the genteel piscatorial genius of Izaak Walton. Since Elias Wonder spent each summer dozing in his three-legged chair in front of a table fan set out on the porch of his shanty, he neither voted nor participated in the midday adventures of the Starlight Creek Angling Society. In fact, he thought the whole thing smacked of foolishness. "I'm exactly where I needs to be," he said.

I had just brought Elias Wonder his favorite lunch, a sardine sandwich and hard-boiled eggs, and told him that on that day we had fished the great salmon rivers of Iceland. "Iceland, for chrissakes. Who needs that floating iceberg! I got trout as long as my forearm twenty yards out my front door. Why in the hell would I want to pack up my clean underwear and traipse off to some bleak ice-encrusted arctic wasteland where I'd catch pneumonia and die before I ever got a line in the water." And he would have, too. Died, that is. Elias Wonder was always on the verge of dying, a situation that tended to keep everyone at our place alert. The one time anyone could recall Elias leaving Starlight Creek he had gone up into Missouri to fish and it rained for three days and he caught cold and threatened to die for weeks afterward. Death and Elias Wonder held hands like lovers, unable to part, so death kept nibbling away at him, inflicting itself on him one disease or one hardship at a time.

He had unwrapped the sandwich and taken it apart. "Tell

that old fart Emerson it won't work," he said slyly.

"What?"

"Trying to slowly starve me to death. There's only three sardines on this sandwich." For emphasis Elias held up his left hand, on which there were exactly three fingers. A malcontent tractor had claimed the others years before. And he laughed and ate the sandwich and eggs hungrily, and washed it all down with a jar of the whiskey he made himself up along Susan's Branch. "Hell, don't make no difference anyway," he chuckled. "Three's plenty to fill up half a stomach, which is all I got." He had donated the other half to a sudden case of colitis more than twenty years before. Elias never let on that anything mattered much. He just sat on the porch of that shanty that was neither vertical nor horizontal but, like himself, slightly askew, and wiped his face with a handkerchief soaked in creek water. He kept his fly rod nearby and could, when he felt like it, flick the line and long 20-foot leader from his porch and settle a No. 16 dry fly on the smooth waters at the shadowy edges of Karen's Pool.

The hot days of August came and went and we sat there on the back porch, our sweaty faces half hidden under wide-brimmed hats as we pulled on cold root beer and thought of trout and shouted out the names of streams and rivers, any name that cracked like frost underfoot when you said it. Our daily lobbying, however, rarely mattered, because as the first and only president of the Starlight Creek Angling Society, Emerson always decided our final destination. It never changed. Flipping though the atlas with an eagerness that knew no ebb or temper, he would quickly turn the pages, passing by Alaska and Canada, the majestic American West, the splendor of Norway, the wildness of Labrador as he navigated about the earth to far-off New Zealand, a land that seemed to satisfy his passion for wilderness only slightly less fully than the Ozark hills of home. Emerson would hold up the atlas, showing us the salmon-pink illustration of the island nation surrounded by endless blue seas,

and he would sometimes chide us for our lack of creative vaga-
bonding. "Might as well dream big. What's the price of a little
harmless angling nomadism, anyway? Only a little time. Jesus
Christ, the tomatoes will wait, they're in no hurry." And Emerson would take off the big battered Montana hat, lean back
against the wooden vegetable crates, and invent luxurious lies
about trout fishing in New Zealand, intricate, captivating
stories of men and fish and a remote wild landscape. And what
grand lies they were. We sat there as in a trance listening to this
grizzled old angling cantor and hung on his every word as
though it were washed in truth. It was always easy in the back
porch's warm, soporific shade to slip into some pleasing dream
and for a time the day's withering heat would evaporate like
summer rain.

When he had finished, Emerson would slam the atlas shut,
tell me to take it back inside, and we would linger there like
lizards on cool concrete before heading back out into the hard
sunlight, the pitiless heat. Come late afternoon, at dusk, we
harvested the ripe vegetables, crate after crate of tomatoes and
the last of the summer corn and beans, and I would carry the
crates to the barn and wash the vegetables with buckets of cold
well water. Just the feel of the water would tempt me toward the
fly rods hanging appealingly in the workshop. I would stop my
work for a moment and could hear the sounds of Starlight
Creek, cool water splashing against smooth stones, just beyond
the fields and woods, and I knew the last of the day's light was
flaring off the creek's waters like little explosions of fireworks.

About three miles out of Mount Hebron, the road inter-
sected with an unmarked tumbledown, spavined, weather-
scarred dirt track that wandered aimlessly off to the left, into a
wide swale of tall grasses and hardwood trees. Standing like a
cairn at this unimpressive intersection was a tottering stump, a
three-foot section of exhausted hickory, onto which a milk can
had been mounted and painted blue. On just one side of the

can, the side facing east, the way the postman came each day in a 1947 Jeep, one of the old men had painted in thick turquoise letters, "Trail's End."

That's what Albert and Emerson called their place, all those rocky, woody acres of backbreaking aggravation and glory, the passageway to both heaven and hell. Emerson edged the Ford up to the milk can and Albert extended a long arm and plucked out the day's mail, three outdoor catalogs and the latest edition of "The Good News," the weekly newsletter of the Mount Hebron First Primitive Methodist Church.

"We almost settled on 'Dead End,'" quipped Albert as he slapped his harmonica in the palm of his hand, "but Emerson thought that sounded a trifle pessimistic."

"What's the news?" asked Emerson, pulling the Ford back onto the hard dirt road.

"The price of happiness is up," said Albert, riffling through the outdoor catalogs, then tossing them up on the dashboard, which was already cluttered with empty root beer bottles, Indian arrowheads, fossils, spent shotgun shells, quail and turkey feathers. Albert read through "The Good News."

"Nadine Chatam died. Age sixty-eight."

"Knew her mother. Made a damn good apple pie," said Emerson, and the words filled the truck cab, a terse yet caring eulogy.

"There's a revival meeting this coming Sunday. Down by the creek, weather permitting. Reverend Biddle will deliver a sermon entitled 'How Can You Die Right If You Live Wrong.'"

"Humph! Another harangue against the angling life, I bet," snapped Emerson. "Remind me to cut the good reverend's monthly trout allowance to three."

"Miss Dorothy Sue Ray, age twenty-one, needs guidance in her home, spiritual and otherwise, it says here."

Emerson sighed long and deep. "Don't we all," he said. "Don't we all."

The Ford veered hard to the left again onto a narrow drive

of packed red dirt. The drive curved lazily through a gallery of oaks toward a two-story house that sat well back among the trees, deep in shade. In the distance the last of the day's sunlight flashed from behind the dark hills. A single light glowed from one of the house's front windows.

In less than two thousand square feet, the house managed to emphasize comfort while embracing none of the architectural advancements or refinements of modern times. Much like its owners, the house and its furnishings were sober, unaffected, unembarrassed to flirt with insolvency. The house tended to embrace the practical rather than the needless, the theoretical, dispensable, or the visionary. Parts of the house were more than seventy years old and had stood firm against every press of weather and had withstood a wide sampling of misfortunes, human and natural, and yet, like the intemperate hills that surrounded it, the old house endured, survived. Standing there in the great expanse of front yard, in the growing twilight, I could see sections where the graying white paint had chipped away, revealing a rough-hewn skin of oak boards warped by time's inexorable touch.

It was, as I learned, not a home, but a shelter, a place to plan outdoor adventures, sleep some, eat some, read some. The thing the old men liked about it was the back door, a firm structure featuring a roof that seemed a vulnerable alliance of tin and wooden shingles, three small bedrooms, a bathroom, a kitchen, and just off the kitchen a large workshop, the only part of the original homestead still left, a room that smelled of gun oil and moist, rich earth. An old cast-iron stove dominated the workshop. The other furnishings included a long pine worktable where the old men spent endless hours during the winter months tying trout flies, an occupation neither had much aptitude for but both loved.

When it came to fly tying, neither Albert nor Emerson cared much for established fly patterns, no matter how classic, durable, or reliable. They thought of themselves as innovators, always trying to create the truly irresistible trout fly, a master of temptation instead of certainty. It made no difference to them whether their flies accurately copied true stream insects or terrestrials because according to the scriptures of fly fishing they followed, the scriptures according to Emerson, Albert, and Elias, fly size and presentation were always more fundamental and important to hooking trout than inflexible notions about fly patterns, of which there were thousands. Only when fishing with the dry fly did patterns become a matter of more serious interest. Between them, the old men must have created hundreds of trout flies, insect mutants as bizarre and seductive as any ever to drop from a fly tier's vise. With perhaps two exceptions, none of their titillating offerings ever stirred a trout's interest, a fact that didn't bother them at all. As long as there were fur and feathers and colored thread, there were hope and possibility and excitement—the chance of success. And they were two old men who thrived on chance.

Fly rods hung on the workshop's pine walls above shelves burdened with the mountains' treasures, all freely given. Rocks in all shapes, sizes, and colors; a rich collection of Indian artifacts, even a vial of sacred dust passed down from the Brulé Sioux; a buffalo skull, horns dull, decaying eye sockets so deep that there seemed to be something magical in that pitted gray bone, those empty sockets staring hypnotically from the high shelf. Above the skull a war shield fashioned from hides and festooned with eagle feathers. A stone club hung next to it, along with a good-luck amulet, a smooth pebble worn around the neck in a rawhide pouch. Elsewhere there were plants pressed and cataloged, armies of insects in tiny labeled jars, shed antlers in great stacks, even a note written on a strip of sycamore bark: "A—trout are rising.—E." Later the bark had been dated. 1900, Missouri.

On the other side of the small kitchen, with its small wooden icebox, the kind you had to put a block of ice in each week, rows of wooden cabinets, tiny two-burner stove, sink in-

variably clogged with unwashed pots and pans, and green For-
mica table and four cheap wooden chairs, was one large room
called the "big room" because it occupied nearly the entire bottom floor of the house. An enormous fireplace, flanked by
floor-to-ceiling bookcases, took up one side of the big room.
More bookcases stood along the other walls, each of them a rich
breeding ground for all sorts of adventure, intrigue, drama,
humor, tragedy. A little desk and straight-back chair occupied
the space near the lamp by the front windows. Here Emerson
spent as little time as possible not worrying about the things he
and Albert didn't want, couldn't afford, would never have. In
front of the fireplace sat a derelict sofa, threadbare and lumpy,
some kind of brown. Lying down on it was a unique experience,
because no matter how you worked it your feet ended up higher
than your head. No better comfort came from just trying to sit
on it, since the tumbledown couch bent under even the slightest weight, folding the occupant between slices of spongy foam.
Elsewhere around the big room was an array of hardbacked
chairs and a single oak rocker. This was Emerson's favorite
chair. Years before, he had tied a small blue pillow to its back so
he could doze in comfort while he rocked, keeping time to the
old house's rheumy inhaling and exhaling.

A cypress mantelpiece stretched the length of the impres-
sive fireplace. Here in simple wooden frames paraded the images
of the dead, photographs of remembered faces staring down
through foggy time. The frowning old Confederate at one end
of the mantel, then a photograph of my grandfather as a boy,
taken by a traveling photographer with a wagon for a darkroom.
The photographer sat Emerson, who was shoeless and wearing
overalls, outside on a cane chair. Emerson had a shotgun in one
hand and his first dog, named Stonewall, sat by him staring
blankly. Behind the chair you see the barn, listing to one side,
threatening even then to collapse. Next to Emerson as a boy,
my grandmother, a short woman with sad eyes. And then the
death march of Albert's wives, five in all, each photograph in

an oval frame, a necklace of heartache and inexplicable anguish strung out along the mantelpiece like some stream of never-ending melancholy. Karen in the middle. Smooth olive skin, dark haunting eyes, bright and kind. Waves of thick brown hair falling to her shoulders, hair lightened by the sun. You could see the streaks of light near her shoulders even in the old, heavily creased photograph. She had died just before World War I. Karen's Pool at the upper reaches of Starlight Creek, where the big trout lived cautiously and shrewdly in the deep water bordering the stone-strewn riffles, where the water was cold and blue-green and where there were boulders in the stream the size of Cadillacs, was named for Karen, for her timeless seduction. Albert, who rarely gave way to expressions of sentiment, said once that he liked fishing the pool because the light there reminded him of the way sunlight had touched Karen's long, lovely hair. Karen had died giving birth to what would have been Albert's only child, a boy. The child died as well. Albert named him Ian so there could be a name on the simple white stone.

Next to Karen, Diane. Diane with the perplexing half-smile and the white lace blouse buttoned primly at the throat. Her black hair worn straight and unadorned, not even a simple piece of ribbon to keep it off her neck. Dead at twenty of, the death certificate read, "a too delicate disposition and a failed heart." Susan, the last. Number five. Hair like a storm, windswept. Feral dark eyes and a thin, suggestive smile, the product of flawless lips. An eerie photograph, at once threatening and beautiful. Susan's Branch, an indomitable, unruly little creek that ran out of Bower's Hollow and into Starlight Creek near Elias Wonder's shack, carried her name, and wore it nearly as well.

Often I would find Albert standing alone in front of these photographs just staring and shaking his head, but there was no emotion in his eyes, only the reflection of the lamplight or firelight. When it came to women, Albert felt both blessed and vexed. If having married not one but five strikingly beautiful women was an accomplishment of note, so was having all of them die on you, a fact that naturally perplexed and troubled Albert all his days. By the time I arrived he had become convinced that he was a carrier of some lethal strain of virus that would likely kill any woman he loved.

Ten months after I came to Trail's End, Albert got sick, took to acting more peculiar than usual. He would pass out at the breakfast table, collapse head first into his bowl of buttered grits, and Emerson would take a wet cloth and gently wipe the clumps of grits off Albert's face. Albert's skin lost its color, not gradually, but all at once. One day he just turned jaundice. Finally, on a Tuesday in September we piled into the Ford and took him to see a doctor in Jonesboro. Albert had a temperature of 103. I held an ice pack on his sweaty forehead.

In the doctor's office, Albert looked around and said calmly, "They keep dying on me."

"Who does?" asked the doctor, a young man with prematurely graying hair and tiny pig eyes.

"All of them."

"All of them?" said the doctor with extreme lack of interest as he gave Albert a shot of antibiotics. Plainly, he thought Albert was nuts and he began to widen the physical distance between himself and his patient, as if old age and senility were as infectious as the common cold.

He scanned Albert's eyes with a penlight. "So tell me, old timer," he said cheerfully, "just who is it that's dying? Is there a wild dog among your chickens, perhaps?"

Albert regarded the doctor with a cold stare. "No, you idiot. Women. Especially all the ones that marry me." Albert had worn his fishing hat to town, the one with the wide silver brim. He fiddled with it nervously, like a man trying to nurse either an alibi or an imminent confession.

Suddenly the doctor perked up, took interest. "Oh, really, and tell me ... just exactly what happens to the women you marry?" he asked in a tone coated with more titillation than suspicion.

"They die," said Albert softly, the words heavy with confusion, remorse, regret. "They die. That's all. Cancer, consumption, childbirth. I seem to be stuck on death beginning with 'C.'"

While the doctor listened to Albert's shallow, quick breathing, Albert told him matter-of-factly that he had made five contributions to the Mount Hebron cemetery. Five deposits. Thanks to him the old cemetery's languishing population had grown considerably.

"You're fine," announced the doctor dejectedly. Obviously he had hoped to discover something rare, something different, something bizarre enough to catapult him out of Jonesboro and into the grateful arms of a stunned medical community.

"Liar," snapped Albert, unimpressed with the doctor's hurried diagnosis. "Check my blood again. I know there's something alien in it. I'm positive I'm host to some killer germ. A nasty one."

"Your symptoms are related to nothing more than old age," said the doctor, impatient now. To him, Albert was just an old man with a fever and a troubled conscience. And for the young doctor the waiting room offered no greater excitement. Just the usual crowd, the same old complaints, cases of hepatitis, nephritis, spastic cramps, anemia, piles, fatty hearts, rigid arteries, dysentery, farmer's lung, croup, bronchitis, runny noses and rattling coughs.

"Quack," said Albert as he buttoned his collar. He covered his nose and mouth as he stood in front of the nurse in the front room and paid the bill. She was young and gorgeous, as dark as an Indian, with soft brown eyes and brown, sun-streaked hair that fell to her shoulders. Albert fell instantly in love. He tossed fifty dollars on the desk, then fled out the door, deathly afraid that but a single word from him might do her harm, kill her stone dead.

Actually the young doctor in Jonesboro had a much more interesting case on his hands than he imagined, because Albert's fever never quite broke and the fatigue just got worse. It turned out he had a metastatic tumor in his brain that was gobbling up his memory and his life, emptying his mind, killing him slowly, slowly. But no one knew he was dying then, or that he would ever die. After all, Elias Wonder had been trying desperately to die for forty years and hadn't succeeded yet, and he'd tried nearly everything, including a direct hit by a bolt of lightning in 1956. "Didn't do a damn thing but clear my sinuses," said Elias morosely.

On the way out of Jonesboro we stopped for cold root beer. Albert put three aspirin in his and took out his harmonica, played some rolling delta blues as the Ford headed back into the mountains toward home.

Out beyond the chicken coop, with the sagging gate held fast by a piece of electrical wire, stood the barn, a nearly roofless building that leaned dangerously to the left. Like a boat caught in heavy seas, it always seemed on the verge of foundering. Built by the defeated Confederate, the barn had borne great responsibilities, stored many a dream. The doors were gone and it now stared dully across the garden like an ancient cyclops. The old men rarely bothered with farm animals because animals needed tending, usually just when the trout were rising or something more interesting or illuminating was happening up in the mountains or deep in the woods. So they avoided animals, for the most part. When I got to the farm they did have a cow named Judith, who stayed in the barn because she had a cough that wouldn't clear up. We nursed her day and night, feeding her hefty doses of castor oil. I had the night shift, floor nurse from midnight until five in the morning. Finally Judith got so she wouldn't take the castor oil. She moaned. She groaned. I read her Kafka, which depressed her, made her sullen. The night she died, Emerson was reading her selections from Thoreau and Judith hung on his every word. As cows go, Judith was a good one. We cut her into steaks, ground her into hamburger.

Besides Judith, there was Winslow, a hog of considerable size who used to stretch out in the barnyard as content as a sunbather on a tropical beach. In no time at all Winslow swelled into more than a year's worth of pork and bacon. Another gift from the earth, from which all our blessings came. Quarrelsome and belligerent chickens sauntered truculently in and out of the curious conglomeration of crates that made up the chicken coop, which Albert dubbed "as fowl a Hooverville" as there ever was. But we had eggs, plenty of them, even if they were laid grudgingly.

The vegetable garden sprawled like a lush green sea from behind the barn to the edge of the woods. Bountiful but undisciplined, the garden had a life of its own and more than once threatened to overrun the place, house and all. It was the most sumptuous and productive garden I will ever know, and it bore fruit through every season of the year. The garden was the farm's cupboard, a diverse and well-stocked open market that fed us, Elias Wonder, and a good portion of Oglala County with an almost embarrassing extravagance.

Much later, in a moment of weakness, Albert confided to me that the seriously afflicted fly fisherman needed an understanding provider, someone or something that would subsidize his folly, endow his passion, fund his piscatorial addiction. In short, pick up the tab. The garden was our unselfish benefactor, our generous financier, our emancipator. Because it flourished, the old men could nurse their obsession for trout along the waters of Starlight Creek, pursue exasperating wild turkeys in the thickly wooded sloughs, walk up quail that held as tight as grouse in the plum thickets at the edge of the peafields and cornfields that the old men worked by hand because the profit of having turkeys and wild quail was worth more to them than the profit of a land without them. In wild things, in the land as it was, the old men took comfort. Where there was wildness, there was possibility, chance, genuine life full of promise and risk and perplexing uncertainty.

The land the old men worked, this land they had lived on for more than seventy years, had little to recommend it. Judged by the standards of modern agriculture, it was at best hardscrabble in character, a commercial disaster. Only the immense vegetable garden defied the laws of farm commerce and made the old men a handsome profit. Indeed, the garden's fecundity mocked the rest of the farm's herculean poverty. Rocky and feckless and only slightly more agreeable to commercial agriculture than 10,000 acres of concrete, the land yielded little that anyone but the old men considered important or of value. From it they harvested solitude, contentment, peace of mind, a way of life instead of merely a living. Which is the way they wanted it. The land was theirs, free and clear, and they had evidently made a decision decades before to keep it the way it was, to work with it rather than against it. A decision for trout and quail instead of beans. It seemed to them the world had too many beans and too few trout and wild turkeys. Their life in the mountains became a compromise, a balance of giving and taking.

On a day in October, after we had taken two quail at the edge of the cornfield, I was standing behind Emerson and patting Cody on his huge dark head when I noticed Emerson hesitate as he put the second limp bird in his coat pocket and say to himself in a low whisper, "Be good to the earth and the earth will be good to you." He didn't say it out of sentiment or longing. It was an old man's statement of fact. A way of life given voice for a moment in an autumn cornfield when the air was cool and the sun was just rising and there was no sound but Cody who had left my side and was running in the thickets and the rush of quail on the rise. When he looked up and saw I had overheard him, Emerson quickly turned his back and called "Come, Cody, birds here now. Birds close." Cody raced out of the brush and both of them walked along the rows of spent corn, crumpled stalks that were the color of foxes in early morning light.

Emerson's words spoken in the cornfield came as close to an ethic as anything the old men had ever expressed. The land was not a theory or a principle; it was a belief, their religion, for these two old men were surely of the earth, their lives mixed and bound inexorably with it, as tied to it as snugly as a snail fits its shell. Their relationship to those ancient hills was hardly romantic or sentimental. Rather, it was practical, a daily experiment to see if they could take only what they needed in order to partake more fully of what they thrived on, the hills' natural wildness. Neither of them ever expressed any aspirations toward prosperity, a condition that would have, after all, hampered their way of life, upset the vulnerable compromise they had made with the land, one that allowed for the coexistence of old men, vegetables, quail, turkeys, trout, primitive hills, a nervous dog, and one unwary boy who fell into the wonder of it all.

Although the old men warned me that a life devoted to the land brought heartache and ruination, although they chided me for taking what they considered an unhealthy interest in their lives and especially the natural world, once exposed to such a life, there was never really any serious hope of recovery, thank God. And the poverty didn't seem all that bad; if it kept so much from their reach, they did not seem to mind. Indeed, they wanted it that way; doing without was the coin that had bought them the life in the hills beyond the backyard. Money, even in modest amounts, would have meant complications, and complications were something the old men had had enough of and didn't want any more of. Complications took time, and time, they knew, was running out. They wanted only the solitude the land freely gave. The solitude of Starlight Creek soothed them; it was not a self-imposed prison but a natural sanctuary, real and boundless along the shadowy banks of the swift-moving creek.

In the spring of 1966 a state agricultural agent named

Wayne Durham came through Oglala County appraising the farmland, offering advice to farmers on how to improve it and themselves by moving their farms into the twentieth century and the arms of prosperity. Wayne Durham had a thick neck, a puffy, flushed face, and a huge belly that hung over his belt like a bag of laundry. He came by the farm on a Monday morning and walked around the place for an hour, wheezing heavily, stopping frequently to mop the sweat from beneath his dark glasses. Every few yards Wayne Durham would stop, look about pessimistically, shake his head, and sigh deeply. Later that morning he and the old men sat around the kitchen table. Durham ate a plate of sliced tomatoes heavily salted, and drank glass after glass of iced tea. Thin beads of sweet pink juice from the tomatoes dribbled down his fleshy chin. In between bites of tomato and gulps of tea, Durham informed Emerson and Albert that their thousand acres were "an agricultural disgrace." Totally worthless, an eyesore and embarrassment to Oglala County. "You don't even own a tractor, for chrissakes," he said. He went on, greatly troubled, genuinely concerned. Why hadn't the place been logged, he demanded to know, or planted in something profitable? Why weren't there beef cattle grazing everywhere? How come the stream hadn't been dammed? Where was their sense of pride, ambition, profit?

Albert smiled broadly, as did Emerson. They had expected good news but nothing this good, so greatly uplifting. They had spent years and years trying to circumvent the tenets of modern technological farming and had often wondered at the degree of their success. When Wayne Durham told them he had never seen a less modern, less successful, more deplorable neglect of land that was dying to be cleared and plowed from highway to highway, they beamed with incalculable pride. In those days, making and keeping a small farm an unprofitable venture took skill and determination and intelligence. Both were happy to see that their hard work and sacrifice had paid off. Having the state of Arkansas proclaim them an agricultural failure only boosted their courage and resolve. Evidently they were doing something right.

Albert poured Durham another glass of tea. "Don't sugar it down, son," he said, grinning. "We're old men. We were brought up on bad news."

Albert's sarcasm rolled off Durham like rain down a windowpane. Durham pushed the plate of tomatoes aside. "Think of your neighbors at least," he said. He was almost shouting now, for he was apparently a county agent who believed vehemently in the future of high-tech agriculture even among the hard-luck, mostly worn-out farmers of the Ozarks. Wayne Durham had a mission, and that was to force-march every broken-down farmer in Oglala County down the road to high yields and enormous profits whether they wanted to go or not. "Think," he said passionately, "how upsetting and embarrassing it is for them to have this poor excuse for a farm in their midst, a blight in what could be a prosperous, modern farming community! Here they are trying to get with it and join the twentieth century, working day and night to subdue these rotten hills, drain the last ounce of productivity from this substandard soil, and you two have the unpatriotic nerve to sit here and not even clear-cut your timber! Some of these trees gotta be close to a hundred years old. Jesus Christ, what are you saving them for! Think about what you're doing, gentlemen, I urge you."

Albert did think about what he had said.

"They belong here," he said at last.

"What does?" asked Durham through a mouthful of tomato slices.

"The trees. They shade the creek, keep the trout cool. Hawks use them, too. And owls. And turkeys. Nearly every creature on the place, really. Why would we want to cut them down?"

Durham had a wide smile on his face. "Why, to make a

killing on the lumber, old man, that's why. Then you could plant pines, which grow like magic into telephone poles, and are worth even more."

Emerson spoke, almost musing to himself, "So it's trees and trout and Starlight Creek and turkeys and deer and quail—or telephone poles. Certainly the world isn't experiencing a shortage of telephone poles. Forget the trees, Mr. Durham, and the endless acres of beans and herds of cattle, and tell us how to better preserve our trout. You know trout are finicky creatures. Civilization upsets them. They'd rather die than have any part of it."

Wayne Durham got angrier, and the angrier he got the redder he got so that he quickly took on the aspect of some experimental strawberry gotten out of hand. He shoved another bite of tomato in his cheeks.

"Goddamn old hippie communists," he grumbled. "Men your age, too. You ought to be ashamed. What's wrong with modernization and advancement? It's the American way, and it's coming here whether you old farts like it or not. You'd better get on the winning team while you can, fellas, and get this place in shape. Chop, burn, disc, plow. That's today's agricultural formula for reaping big bucks."

Albert leaned over the table, close to Durham's plump cherry-red face, and said, "Care to go fishing? I know a good spot, place where a big trout hangs out near a rotten stump. Hits a dry fly at dusk like a runaway train. Of course, Wayne, if you hook him, we expect you to do the decent thing and let him go. If a man is careful and lucky, some of life's thrills can be experienced more than once."

Before Albert had flung out the last of his invitation Durham was heading briskly for the front door. You could hear his truck slinging dirt and gravel all the way down the drive.

"Well, now we've gone and done it," said Emerson without expression.

"What's that?" said Albert, motioning me to get his Orvis cane fly rod from the workshop.

"Why, let down the state, failed the nation, undermined the entire national economy. We'll hear from Reverend Biddle on this for sure. The only folks I know that believe in wealth more than county agricultural agents are Methodists." He turned and faced Albert. "Now let's get serious, old man. Let's hear the detailed, don't-leave-a-damn-thing-out truth about this mammoth trout. I want the truth, you old fool. All of it, and slowly."

With Wayne Durham went the last mention of scientific notions of the land, its commercial value and importance. Not only were Emerson and Albert not men of science, they were admittedly lousy farmers. They only knew what they had—wild turkey down in the cool, shady oaks; quail along the field edges and fencerows. Come the fall, waterfowl came to the flooded timber and ponds. Deer moved in the high country beyond the creek, and trout still rose in the cool waters of Karen's Pool and all along Starlight Creek, and up on Susan's Branch, where the water was warmer, there were smallmouth bass as beautiful as trout, just as cunning and tenacious. The garden bloomed without interruption; the chickens laid. To the old men, the place's worth was therefore immeasurable. The land was hard, true, but it had been kind and had included them in its bounty; the old men would reciprocate in the only way they knew how: they would not exploit the land, an obligation they were determined to keep until death took them. They wanted the hills more than they wanted material comfort, social acceptance, agricultural success, even religious salvation. The hills would provide; they always had. The old men would get by until there was no need to get by anymore. And getting by was good enough as long as the trout rose at dusk, surfaced like shadowy bathyspheres from the deep waters of Karen's Pool, spooky and primitive, ancient life struggling to endure. If fickle and chaotic, fortune had always been full of surprise, giving as much kindness as despair, and the old men, I learned, had always shouldered whatever fate dealt them with a mild and understanding temper.

Cody, my grandfather's Gordon setter, died the spring that Wayne Durham proclaimed Trail's End a toxin to the economic and cultural future of Oglala County. It didn't seem natural not to see the big dog there on the front porch lying on his side, his large handsome head, a mixture of deep blacks and soft golden browns, tucked into the deep fur of his heavily muscled chest. Cody had been there waiting that first evening when the Ford pulled to a stop in the drive. Nonchalantly, he had lifted his head, given me a long, curious look, risen slowly, and ambled to the steps. He'd sniffed my sneakers and jeans, pawed my duffel bag, yawned a wide indifferent yawn, then sniffed everything again as though he were a police dog pondering a difficult identification. Cody nearly always seemed to be in some kind of trance, but Albert assured me it was just ecstasy. Having yawned and sniffed to his satisfaction that first day, Cody strolled back to his spot on the porch, circled three times, and flopped down. He growled at last, a low, grating sound reminiscent of a rusty gate beating in a high wind. Albert patted me reassuringly on the back. "Don't mind Cody, son," he said. "Since he's a dog of highly questionable pedigree, he sulks. It's tough not really knowing if your blood's tainted, got a little Brittany or English setter in it. Just the thought makes Cody jumpy, irritable, even though he knows more than any wildlife biologist and botanist combined. You'll get used to him eventually. Should the matter of ancestry come up, though, you might want to make sure Cody's not around. It's a sore subject with him."

Like the old men, Cody was something of an outcast, a misfit, a dog of cosmopolitan interests in a region where rawboned, importunate, pointers held sway. A great many things besides the local canine competition troubled Cody. Albert believed he had strong evangelical leanings. "Cody's got plenty of abiding concerns," he said. "The old dog moves in peculiar ways. Fact is, Cody's about the only dog in these hills that I know of that is involved in an active crusade to save the world, or at least his part of it." As I soon learned, Cody's homespun plan was delightfully uncomplicated, based on the simple notion of denial. Whatever bothered him, from baseballs to skunks, he simply ignored. When ignoring something didn't work, which was often the case, he tried sleeping. If this too failed to bring him peace, he gave way to chasing, a strategy that rarely failed and helped keep his world and ours in a precarious yet pleasant state of equilibrium and unpretentious harmony.

Although world affairs often upset Cody, he had a fine sense of humor and he never bit anyone more than once, not even Elias Wonder, who annoyed Cody constantly, tormented him with innuendos about his father having been a shady, disreputable English setter from Missouri named Mugs who couldn't smell birds in an aviary.

From that first moment on the front porch until he died, Cody and I were rarely apart. If Emerson and Albert did not immediately take to the idea of having a boy foisted on them, constantly tagging along after them, intruding on their quiet hours afield as they went about what had always been a very personal and private relationship with the land, Cody unabashedly welcomed the company. He couldn't wait to introduce me to the hills, the fields, the creeks, the land in all its magic and glory, and to make me the benefactor of his outdoor skills and knowledge, which were considerable.

Inside the house the one lamp gave the wooden floors a soft cast of warm color. My grandfather laid down the big Montana hat next to a brass kerosene lantern on a round wooden table beside the door. He pointed to the staircase. "Upstairs. First room to the right." Shouldering the duffel bag, I headed up the stairs. "Supper's at six or so, usually," Albert shouted up the stairs. "Depends on who loses the toss and has to fix it. Don't dress formal. We don't."

And like the old man Albert disappeared in the dense shadows of the big room. Watching him I noticed he had a tendency to drag his left leg slightly, a condition that gave him a staggered, arthritic gait that so often marks rodeo bull riders.

Pictures and photographs hung on the wall along the staircase—some framed, others just tacked-up color black-and-white prints. A series of Plains Indians and upland birds—the hunters flushing quail, nervous grouse, half-hidden woodcock, magnificent pheasant hunkered down in snow-covered cornfields, even fall doves on the wing, clouds of blurred, khaki-colored wings. Other pictures featured trout on the rise, trout of every size and species—the wall a veritable homage to trout, a celebration of the beauty and primitive spirit of Salmo. There were portraits of hunting rainbow trout, sleek and shrewd, their flanks marked by an unmistakable ruddy pink stripe; beautiful little brook trout rising from deep, cold mountain streams, dark eyes fixed on tiny insects hatching by the thousands on the surface of the water. Above these brookies, an eerie close-up of a giant brown trout, with rampant staring eyes and slack rapacious jaws, an image of interminable patience, unappeased hunger, wildness that was at once captivating and haunting.

Near the top of the stairs hung a photograph of a lone fly fisherman, thigh deep in some nameless mountain stream, a shadowy figure in a low-slung hat. Bathed in a constantly shifting light, silver grays, and dappled browns, the angler stood among dark smooth stones, the camera capturing a nearly flawless back cast, the fly rod up, the line unfolding behind him, the loop smooth and tight, and, in the distance, a flashing dimple of broken water: a trout on the rise, rising from the pool like a shadow, rolling slightly in the day's fading light. For as long as I knew that old house, for as long as I enjoyed the company of those old men and the comfort and security of the room at the top of the stairs, this photograph was a part of my landscape, a soothing feature of my geography, one that both pleased and possessed me, punctuating each day's start and end, often even entering my dreams. It seemed to me to hold a nearly perfect moment, an uncluttered vision of grace and simplicity that never failed to ease my spirit. A few years later, after Albert had died, I would look at this fascinating old photograph again, one last time, and as always the light danced and the stream ran fast with possibility and the fly fisherman was inseparable from it all, as natural to the stream as the black stones he stood among. Then for the first time I took the old photograph from the wall and discovered the inscription on the back: "Albert, Missouri. December 1930."

Cody barked, waiting impatiently for me at the top of the steps. In the narrow upstairs hallway stood an immense oak hall tree festooned with hats of every kind. Hats for every season, every weather, every imaginable occasion. Baseball caps. Rabbit-fur hats. Beaverskin winter hats. Wide-brimmed cowboy hats with braided horsehair bands, slouch hats, sweat-stained outback hats, an ornate sombrero, even a handsome lonely gray derby for special events. It was the hat that Albert would wear to Elias Wonder's funeral.

The door to the room was open and thin traces of daylight spilled through the window, which looked out on the ramshackle barn, the fecund garden, the path leading down to Starlight Creek and the dark hills beyond. A high pine bed stood pushed up against the far wall, beside the window. A mattress as thick and unyielding as inch-thick plywood covered the bed; freshly washed sheets, a pillow, and a single blanket had been piled on top. On the small bedtable were a lamp and three books, novels by Hemingway and Flaubert and a thick work entitled *Camping and Woodcraft*, which had obviously seen years of hard use, for its binding was worn completely smooth. Above the bed, resting across two wooden pegs, hung a big

Winchester shotgun. Its smooth dark stock and twin carbon-black barrels smelled of oil. A simple wooden bureau stood against the right-hand wall.

I dropped the heavy duffel bag by the bureau, sat on the bed, and began laughing, a laughter brought on not by anguish or desperation, but because the walls of the little room were covered with yellowing cartoons, most of them clipped out of old editions of *The New Yorker*. My grandfather had been a loyal subscriber since 1929, which was a bad year for tomatoes and human beings alike and he needed a laugh, so he reached for *The New Yorker* because he thought Harold Ross, the magazine's founder and first editor, was a genius. He was a genius because he had the good sense to print almost everything writers like E. B. White and James Thurber wrote, even if he didn't get most of it. Nearly all the cartoons that had long ago been tacked to the walls were by Thurber. My grandfather admired Thurber greatly, especially his drawings of dogs. To Emerson, Thurber's dogs always looked perplexed, befuddled, mischievous, and up to no good, qualities that reminded him of Cody's own quixotic yet noble character.

I walked to the window and saw them outside, next to the back porch. Emerson had an ax in his hand and was working on a pile of stovewood. Albert had his Orvis cane fly rod and was playing out a long length of line, the reel clicking rapidly, sounding like a meadow full of jabbering cicadas.

Albert flicked his wrist and the rod shuddered as though it had been molded out of Jell-O; the line shot through the guides and lay on the damp grass like a strand of spun silk. Again his wrist twitched, a fluid, unbroken motion, all energy transferred in an instant from rod to line, and the line traveled almost in slow motion, moving up and behind Albert in a level, narrow loop until, at the instant it straightened out, the rod tip shot ahead and the line cut effortlessly through the air and back out across the yard gleaming in the dusk like a seam of moonlight. And though the whole cast had taken only seconds, to me

looking down at Albert and the rod and the grace of the disciplined line, it had seemed like a long, rhythmic reading of un-
spoken poetry, the union of angler and rod and line. I closed my
eyes and saw it all again and it seemed to me flawless in every
detail and I could not separate Albert from the limber rod or the
supple line. I watched until I could no longer clearly see Albert,
but only the thin leader and tippet of the line against the darkening sky, moving through the twilight like a comet's tail.

"Why is it that I always end up cooking and chopping while
you stand around casting?" I heard Emerson say. "I haven't won
a toss in twenty-seven years. No man is that star-crossed." I saw
the line shoot out again as Albert answered. "You dried-up old
sot," he said, "you've got bad luck, that's all. Whenever you call
heads it's tails, and when you call tails it's heads. Of course, it's
to my advantage that I always do the flipping and that Elias
Wonder slipped me a trick coin he got down in Memphis in
1930." And they both laughed, long and hard, and the laughter
drifted up through my window like ether on the night air.

The room was nearly completely dark. I stretched out on
the bed and now I could hear Emerson in the kitchen cursing
pots and pans and talking to Albert all the time, and there was
more chili to their speech than schmaltz, more humor than
regret, more resignation than longing. I reached down and
grabbed the pillow. It smelled of soap and fresh air. Cool air
filled the room through the open window and my eyes were
heavy. I lay there and thought of nothing but the night. Not my
father, not a single soldier, not even Norwell. Just the cool
night and how good the exhaustion felt and the image of Albert
and the fly rod. I felt light as a vapor and fell asleep thinking
things might turn out all right after all.

4. KAREN'S POOL

Perhaps I could just lease a place in heaven, in case there's no decent trout water there.

— Emerson Newell, 1965

Before the sun had climbed above the hills, Albert had taken two fine trout, both rainbows, strong and healthy, one thirteen inches, the second a husky, blunt-nosed fifteen-inch male. He released them both, easing the tiny fly and hook from their lips as carefully as a surgeon removing a stitch. And he watched each of them in the olive-green water of Karen's Pool until they regained their strength and slipped into the deeper, darker water where the morning's shadows still hung over the pool like a blue fog. Not until he was content that each trout had survived did Albert inspect his fly, a No. 16 March Brown, and cast again, placing the small fly upstream along the edge of the pool where it drifted as naturally on the current as if it had been a leaf or a stunned insect, helpless in the current, a morsel that Albert hoped would be too inviting for any trout to shun. In the gentle morning sunlight that came off the water, the fly cast a subtle glow, the way soft light sometimes does in a woman's hair.

I had been up since before daylight and had walked up the creek to Karen's Pool after stopping first at Martha's Chute, where I sat on a worn slab of stone the size of a respectable table. Its edge reached well out over the water which rushed unceasingly over smooth multicolored stones that cluttered the creek bottom. Long, thin alleys of light, gray smudged with pools of melon orange, drifted through the oaks that lined the far bluff. The creek whispered a chorus of sounds, a contrapuntal harmony of liquid trills that rose on the wind, sotto voce, as soft as a mist against the skin. I liked spending the mornings sitting on that great flat stone beyond the sweet gums and the slender mulberry tree on the near bank, listening to the myriad sounds of the creek, its liquid geometry, and watching the surface. Then, as the sun rose higher, working its way among the hickories and ironwood trees, among the hillside oaks and scattered elms, I would walk upstream along the bank.

There was extreme caution in every step, like a fat man trying his luck on a frozen pond and waiting for that first disastrous creak and snap. I took care because I knew Albert was nearby, thigh deep in the creek, enjoying its solitude. The old men fished for many reasons, I suppose, but angling gave them no greater reward than solitude, the priceless pleasure of spending unemcumbered time along a cold stream in the presence of trout. No other bounty they had known matched these moments of quiet during which they desperately tried to smuggle themselves, in spirit if not in body, back into the natural world, the place where they were most at ease, truly at home.

There was an old river birch tree on the west side of Karen's Pool and here I sat in the early morning hours and watched Albert and Emerson work the pool with their willowy fly rods. Sunlight shimmered off the pool's smooth surface in rising waves, rose up toward the stark bluffs, dissolving the blue-black shadows that lingered there, exposing the craggy face of ancient stone.

Through some brand of indefinable financial wizardry, some

economic alchemy I never quite grasped, the old men had somehow managed to work the farm just enough to allow them to spend the bulk of their days as they wished—that is, afield, along the creek, in the cool shadowy hollows, up in the hills. Whatever profit the farm generated went toward this end and few others. As far as I know, they harbored few wants or desires that the land would not satisfy. Neither longed for much of anything. Oh, there was the endless wishing and grumbling about new fly rods and reels, about shotguns and good dogs, but it rarely came to anything. Neither of them truly pined for other places, the great remote wildernesses beyond the Ozark Mountains. After all, Emerson had the big atlas and it took us wherever we wanted to travel, and at reasonable rates. While Emerson and Albert certainly wondered about other trout streams, other wild country, and read of such places with tireless enthusiasm, they never ached to visit them personally. It was enough for them simply to know that such places existed, still hung on, survived. These mountains, the land they lived on, the cold, swift waters of Starlight Creek, were never an escape from life, but life real and immediate, life beyond the artificial, life intensified. The solitude they sought was a natural part of their lives, something they cultivated and cherished, longed for rather than struggled against. Solitude was their profit, more valuable to them than a fat bank account, and they determined to spend it wisely and well.

Karen's Pool held magic and mystery, both of which the old men hungered for. To them, the waters of the Ozark mountain streams, which were really no more spectacular than other streams (and some were a good deal less), were as worthy as any of the world's great trout water. Like anxious, spiritually ravenous pilgrims, they traveled to the creek each day, in every season, as much in pursuit of solace as trout. It was their presbytery, their mosque, their basilica, their bethel, their sacrarium.

Near the river birch the bank was shady and cool and it was

there by that old tree that I began my tutorial in trout angling, studying the fine art of fly fishing with a child's rabid devotion. Here I sat for my daily piscatorial classes, observing the old men as they fished for hours on end, day in and day out, until I could close my eyes and clearly see and copy their every motion, no matter how meticulous. Here near the river birch, a cool wind off the mountains, did I pass my angling apprenticeship, always watching, listening, observing. I memorized everything, even how Elias Wonder always bit his lower lip when he hooked a trout and how the sunlight came off the water after a thunderstorm in a rose-colored vapor. I had to remember everything, keep it all in my head, every detail. There is a special joy in such dedicated concentration: the days do not seem to pass as quickly.

Running down over a long staircase of submerged gravel bars, the creek entered Karen's Pool just yards from where the river birch stood. Starlight Creek began modestly, in the high country north and west of the farmhouse, a latticework of small springs, thin capillaries of icy water as transparent as thin slices of moonstone filtering up from underground creeks and caves carved out of ancient layers of limestone, forming pools of cold blue-green water that eventually overflowed, spread, joined, grew in power and moved inexorably downhill, over slippery stones and damp roots, through narrow ravines and hollows. By the time the creek reached Old John's it had become a stream of consequence and unique character. Old John's was actually a stone chimney left standing in an orchard of gnarled fruit trees gone wild on a knoll just above the stream. All anyone knew was that years before a man named John had built a cabin there. He had come and gone without fanfare or notice. The mountains had a reputation for swallowing men whole, leaving no trace, not even a shard of bleached bone. The old men could remember little about Old John, except that he had one gray eye and one blue eye. No one knew just when Old John left, if he did. He just disappeared and his cabin went to ruin and his orchard went wild and now only a crumbling stone chimney stood to mark his having existed at all.

Below Old John's, the creek rushed over wide beds of burnished stones covered with slick moss, cascaded over a series of small rocky falls, and made a slow, rattling sound like a heavy rain against a tin roof. Trees hung over the creek, shading it, giving it a deep moss-green color. Up along the higher reaches of the creek, the part known as the Peaceable Kingdom, the trees arched nearly to midstream, a vaulted cathedral swaying in the wind. Reflections played off the creek's surface, countless images of light and shadow. Come the fall, when the wind blew cold out of Oklahoma and Colorado, sometimes the narrow upper creek became completely covered with fallen leaves, glowed like a quilt fashioned from brightly colored thread. On a blustery morning in November, after a fierce storm had howled through the valley, bending saplings to the ground and twisting them into grotesque poses, I walked along the creek above Old John's. Huge rafts of dark, flat-bottomed clouds moved northwest on a scudding, damp wind. Strangely, the creek was free of debris except for a lone sumac leaf that was pressed flat against a stone and glistened in the dull light like a fresh splash of blood.

Below Old John's, Starlight Creek erupted violently out of a narrow gorge, then widened, moving lazily over shoals of worn, crumpled stone. As all mountain streams do, Starlight Creek took its character and moods from the mountains. Like them, like the natural world as a whole, it was in a constant state of flux, ever restless, falling ever changing, not just day to day, but moment to moment. There is great allure to swift water, its headlong rush, its conquering of obstacles. For me, much of the endless attraction of cold, rushing mountain streams is their ambiguity, the way they hold their secrets close, refuse to be predictable. Much like the cunning trout that lived in its waters, Starlight Creek remained largely inexplicable, always fresh and full of surprise. I sometimes sat by it for hours and thought of it as a magician's trick, one that you never tire of, that forever exhilarates you though you don't understand why. Albert and Emerson had lived on the creek all of their lives and yet neither man professed to know it, understand its moods. Instead, they thrived on the creek's limitless ability to astonish, beguile, enrapture, startle. It heated their blood, filled them with anticipation. Each day on the creek meant new journeys, fresh introductions, different discoveries, one heaven lost and another found.

Perhaps half a mile above Karen's Pool, Starlight Creek turned slightly to the south and onto the farm. The only boundary marker was an old water oak with a smooth notch cut deep into its bark. Suddenly pinched between an alley of great slabs, rocks the size of old Buicks, the creek became a series of swirling rapids, a cataract spewing sheets of cool mist into the air as it sped over the rocks, before finally flowing into the deep calm of Karen's Pool. There it mingled with the water of Susan's Branch, which ran down the south face of Lost Mule Mountain and traveled insouciantly past Elias Wonder's place, which clung precariously as a loose stone on the north side of Karen's Pool.

Below Karen's Pool, the creek journeyed into the long stretch of water the old men called Martha's Chute for reasons only they knew, and which they kept to themselves. I did later learn that it had something to do with a trip they had taken to Memphis in 1910, the same trip on which Albert fell in love with the blues and bought his old Hohner harmonica for a dollar at a pawnshop in the city. More than once I asked them about Martha's Chute, which seemed an odd name for a sparkling run of mountain trout water. Their answer never varied. "Boy, some matters just aren't your concern. All you need to know about Martha's Chute is that you ought to smile broadly when you're there. That's all, because if you did know the facts, the lovely details, you'd smile from ear to ear." In the summer months, all along Martha's Chute the blend of cool water and air formed a perpetual cloak of frail mullioned fog that hung just inches above the surface, a nearly translucent shroud.

Martha's Chute gradually gave way to Cervantes' Shallows, a rough section of water only inches deep where Emerson said only old fools and dreamers, people like him and Albert, dared try to hook the small, wary trout that leered from beneath dark stones, their noses pointed upstream as they fed hungrily from the current. Coming out of Cervantes' Shallows, the creek passed below the farmhouse, bent south again, and ran into a series of three small pools we called the Trilogy. From here it emerged as a wide, slow stream moving languidly through the bottomlands and the thick oakwood sloughs until it left the old men's place at Woollum's Stone, an immense sand-colored stone worn almost perfectly round that marked the eastern boundary between Trail's End and the old Woollum place. David Woollum had taken to talking to ghosts in the winter of 1944. He died in 1959 saying that death wasn't any big deal since he'd been conversing and living with the dead for so many years anyway.

To the old men, Starlight Creek was more than water and trout, more than fishing; it was life itself, immediate, volatile and vital, and they were singularly devoted to it and its well-being and to the trout that lived in its cold waters. The creek, the valley it flowed through, and the high country it seeped down from provided whatever spiritual nourishment they needed. There is nothing like a swift, cold trout stream to clear a man's head, raise his temperature and blood pressure. No matter where we were on the place, we could always hear the creek on the wind, the mollifying sound of rushing water, a generous palliative, freely given.

Albert and Emerson were strict monogamists, devoted solely to the trout in Starlight Creek. The trout, mostly rainbows, were not all that big or spectacular, as trout go. Indeed, they weren't even native trout. They were western trout that had been stocked in the mountains beginning in the 1940s after the big dam projects in the region changed the nature of so many of northwestern Arkansas' streams, transforming them from warm-water bass rivers to cold-water trout habitat. All this mattered little. All that mattered to Albert and Emerson was that there were trout. Being bachelors, though, allowed for some lapses of fidelity, especially in the early summer when they would spend weeks along Susan's Branch casting their fly lines into the warmer water, hoping to get the attention of the stream's abundant but spooky population of smallmouth bass. And then they would come back, as always, to Starlight Creek, for as much as they admired the beauty and fight of the smallmouth bass, it wasn't a trout.

Trout did not simply fascinate the old men; they obsessed them. Everything about trout perplexed and delighted them. Any creature so graceful, powerful, and secretive, so unwilling to adapt to civilization, was a creature worthy of respect. And trout were such likable fish: recalcitrant, intractable, defiant. Everything spooked them, sent them swimming for cover, for survival.

"They're doomed," said Albert one afternoon as we sat on the big flat stone by the river birch at the edge of Karen's Pool.

"Who is?" I asked, somewhat startled because Albert rarely talked while he was on the creek and even when he did speak, it was never about angling.

"Trout," he said, his voice low and sullen. "Bring civilization within a mile of them and they turn belly up. It's wildness for them or nothing. No compromises. They believe in the simple life. Cold water, plenty of food, and clean oxygen. Wildness. Dumb bastards don't know any better, I guess." He took another bite of his egg sandwich and a long pull of cool creek water and shook his head. "Doomed. Poor dumb bastards. Doomed, and me along with them, thank whatever gods there are."

There was nothing snobbish about the old men's affinity for trout. They were drawn to trout and the fly rod not out of any need to be among the sophisticated anglers associated with the sport, but rather to associate more fully with trout. Trout appealed to Emerson and Albert because trout seemed to lead a life as precarious as their own, awkwardly balanced on the edge of extinction, the complete emptiness of oblivion. Too, they admired the trout's wariness, its unwavering suspicion that something was out to get it, to do it in. The trout had gotten to be such an ancient fish, they believed, because of its prudence. Trout trusted nothing, not even other trout. All they knew vibrated in their instinct, their primordial blood. All of these qualities intrigued Albert and Emerson. Such wildness captivated them, drew them irresistibly into the waters of Starlight Creek, fly rod in hand, an act, an effort, however feeble, to immerse themselves in the trout's world.

The hold trout had on them and ultimately on me was nearly absolute, like a spell, some kind of vexing yet delightful piscine voodoo. Trout simply cannot be figured out, no matter how much technology they are exposed to or bombarded with. Trout are steadfastly ornery and beyond reform, and the old men admired, even envied, their unyielding tenacity.

Such a fish demanded, of course, special attention, certain considerations, a method of pursuit as finicky and fastidious as their own behavior. A curious fish insists on a curious form of angling, one heavy with respect, tradition, skill, and challenge. If there was only one fish in the lives of Albert and Emerson, Elias Wonder, and soon me, so was there only one correct way to fish for it—with the fly rod. And not just any fly rod, but a subtle, willowy, handmade bamboo fly rod, a good line, a trustworthy reel, tippets as delicate as gossamer, and the smallest dry flies possible. Albert and Emerson had no spare time for hobbies or sports or insignificant moments of recreation. To them fly fishing transcended all of these pastimes. It was a personal and private act of faith between angler, stream, and trout. Fly fishing did not come to these two poor subsistence farmers as a right of birth, but as a blessing in what was an otherwise hard and often despairing life. Consequently, what little theology they held to rested firmly in the waters of Starlight Creek and the trout that struggled there for survival. Indeed, as Albert said on more than one silver-gray morning before daylight took hold, trout and streams and lithe bamboo rods were as close to the divine as he and Emerson and Elias Wonder, that irascible malcontent, were likely to come. Starlight Creek whispered the gospel, the good news, loud and clear, and every trout that rose to their flies was an unforgettable sermon of color and motion, resolve and urgency, grace and the elusiveness of life in the present where it throbbed with such compelling and enthralling power. Standing in the waters of Karen's Pool, the old men worked the supple bamboo rods, limber as relaxed muscle, and waited for the trout to rise and draw them to what was a nearer and more immediate, more accessible, more forgiving heaven.

Fly fishing absorbed them, touched every aspect of their lives on and off the creek. To say that it was all just a matter of catching fish would be like saying that astronomy is nothing more than noticing the stars. Fly fishing, like the noble trout, had character, a tough eloquence about it. Despite the simplicity of its mechanics, it demanded that the angler become truly involved with trout, even get in the water with them, become, if only temporarily, part of their ancient and wild lives. Once an angler took up the fly rod, he became heir to a sturdy body of opinion, belief, and notions, all of which tended to bind the angler, the fly rod and trout together for a lifetime. Albert and Emerson had fished with the fly rod for more than sixty years and never tired of its magic, never stopped seeking its untouched potential. Fly rods in hand, they entered into the natural world, a world of risk, chance, raw energy, adventure.

Given the erratic nature of trout, it seemed somehow fitting to Albert and Emerson that fly fishing should employ as its chief implement a humble little rod made of bamboo. Yet it is a deadly instrument, as lethal and efficient in the hands of a trout fisherman as a sharpened ax is in the hands of a lumberjack.

The fly rod is at best a curious thing, fitful, moody, chameleon-like. Depending on the skill of the angler, handling the bamboo rod can be as simple and effortless as knotting a tie or as complex as brain surgery. Whatever an angler's skill, the fly rod is an outstanding companion, a welcome conversationalist because it speaks not in words but in motion and energy.

No one at Trail's End, not Emerson, Albert, Elias Wonder, or me, fit the image of the dapper, genteel, sophisticated fly fisherman who frequents the outdoor catalogs and so much of outdoor literature. We hadn't a tweed coat among us or a wicker creel or a handsome Leonard or Payne rod. The old men believed earnestly that the principal ingredient of fly fishing was a good sense of humor, while avoiding anything that smacked of pretense, technology, or just plain foolishness.

Albert and Emerson owned many fly rods during their lifetimes, but admired none so much as the bamboo rod, which was the rod of their youth. It was the only rod they truly trusted, a rod not yet burdened with the false reputation of being a flimsy and expensive artifact, a plaything of the rich, something to collect rather than use.

By the 1960s technology had come to fly fishing and there were new rods appearing, made of fiberglass, fast rods, powerful rods. Albert tried one not long before he died. He wiggled it in Bates's store a few times, a frown on his face, his motions stiff, forced. The rod was nine feet long and threw a 6-weight forward line. Again he wiggled it, then cast the line through the entire length of the store and into the street beyond. He set it down. "I just don't feel it," he said. Again, he looked at the big, imposing rod, shook his head glumly. "Don't feel anything, really, except a kind of cold, clammy feeling."

I touched the rod, studied it closely, thought of the beautiful cast Albert had made with it. Why, the line must have traveled at least one hundred feet. To me the rod seemed a thing of great power and even greater temptation. I nudged the old man and asked, "What don't you feel, Albert?"

"Trout," said Albert abruptly, a tinge of disappointment in his voice, as though he had expected that I would grasp the rod's failings as quickly and surely as he had. "That subtle finesse that will put a No. 18 dry fly on a quarter at forty feet. This rod is all right, I suppose. It's got power, but power alone won't catch trout. I'll stay with bamboo. It has grace, a soothing touch."

Unlike the new glass rods, bamboo rods demanded regular attention and care. There developed over time a loyal bond between the bamboo rod and the angler as one ultimately became the extension of the other. All those long days and cool evenings sitting by the creek watching the old men fish, I knew that with each cast there was also a building sense of excitement and exhilaration because they believed that in hooking a trout the hook not only brought the fish to them but drug them deeper into the trout's element, the remnant wilderness that surrounded them.

The old men collected fly rods the way small boys collect marbles or baseball cards. Emerson had ten rods. He looked after them as though they were his children. Even cleaning them in the evening boosted his spirits. He and Albert never considered bamboo rods as things. No, they were the inanimate creeping toward life, wands as full of excitement, chance, fortune and agony as the natural world. Supple, malleable, like the passage of life itself, something capable of giving without ever giving up or giving way. Albert owned three good rods and two reels. The workshop off the kitchen held the usual assortment of leaders, lines, hooks, tippet material, waders, dry flies, wet flies, and nymphs, all of which they had either made or smuggled into Oglala County from the outdoor catalog companies by mail. Not much really, when you consider they were up against trout. It was their desire to keep angling a simple art and therefore they aspired to put as little technical wizardry between them and the trout as possible.

While the old men fished every day, through every season,

they kept few trout. Trout were too special, too precious a part of the natural world to kill. Releasing them back into the cool waters of the creek unharmed stood as the central axiom of their angling epistemology. They clung to the notion, whether true or not, that once released, left to live, a trout became that rarest of possibilities—a part of the natural world that might, with luck, be experienced more than once, a wonder that could go on to reproduce itself, keep populating the creek's inexorable and delightful chaos, its ever-present portrait of life.

So, to Albert and Emerson and Elias Wonder, fly fishing seemed life's most reassuring constant. It got them out of the fields, away from the house, put them into the creek's waters, let them feel that perpetual tug against their flesh, the measure of life immediate, real, and deep, and it put them, sometimes, eye to eye with the vigor and intensity and elegance of trout.

Often, as I watched from beside the river birch, every cast seemed to me almost purposely designed to slow time, to suspend the present moment for as long as possible. Only the creek mattered and the presentation of the fly, how it behaved on the water, and the way the light came off the surface of the creek in bursts of orange and yellow and white, and how good the wind felt on my face, and the cold water numbing your calves and thighs, and, always, the wary trout. This was what mattered—not yesterday, not even tomorrow, not last year or anything from the past, which the old men refused to be shackled to as fiercely as they avoided being haunted by any vision or portent of what seemed to be a troubled future. What mattered was the momentary certainty of the hills, Starlight Creek, and trout. After that, all they were sure of was that their continued existence, like that of the trout, was a matter of considerable doubt.

The intricacies of fly fishing intrigued and fascinated the old men. After all, the serious fly fisherman had to depend as much on his skill and intelligence as on blind luck. The way Emerson saw it, fly fishing had saved them from the dreary life of subsistence farmers, given them a way to participate in the rhythms of the natural world other than by shouldering a hoe. Too, fly fishing was great therapy. It kept them nearly sane, out of trouble, usually sober, and allowed them to pursue a life that, in imagination at least, had no limits or boundaries.

For as long as I knew them, they never worried once about actually landing a fish. Like every seasoned trout angler, they knew they were, in the end, no match for trout. The contest was unfair from the start: the trout held all the aces. Curiously, it was a comfort to them that they would never get the best of Starlight Creek or its uncanny trout. The challenge never dulled; the thrill never faded. The reward was angling itself, just meeting the trout in its world, on its own terms, feeling the tenuous nature of its life and suddenly understanding the tenuousness of your own.

Of the trout's many excellent qualities, it was its uncompromising refusal to accept the world on man's conditions that enticed Albert and Emerson, lured them to Starlight Creek day after day. How they doted on the trout's piscatorial petulance. No other fish they knew was as irascible, churlish, disagreeable, temperamental, or provocative, loyal only to its own survival. Elias Wonder's passion went deeper still. Like him, trout seemed to have a bilious, splenetic attitude toward life, and a man could experience no greater satisfaction than pursuing an ancient fish that just didn't give a damn about anything but itself. It seemed a puzzling relationship. Trout fishermen revere the trout; trout, on the other hand, unaware of their sublime standing in man's world, revere nothing, including man, a creature they seem to view with special contempt. Nihilism is a rare trait in fish but trout are full of it. The old men liked that. Trout were estimable companions, saying not a word, but speaking instead in motions, wrinkles of water, mystery and surprise.

Whenever I watched the old men on the creek, a feeling, odd yet comforting, swept over me like a chill that settled in my spine and spread, touching every nerve, a feeling that I was witnessing a poignant, intensely private drama, a catechism of life, tension and resolution, played out in an intimate struggle between man and trout. A passion play, a mystery, an extravagance, a morality play, a telling tableau, all of these at once as each of the old men cast, trying not so much to hook a trout as to immerse himself in the trout's wildness.

On a day in March, Albert got up before daybreak and, as usual, took his rod and walked down the worn path to the creek. He walked downstream and stopped finally at Cody's Rock, where he knew there were some fine trout and a mammoth grizzled brown with a scarred lip that he had been trying to catch since October. Albert fished for hours. He moaned, said his luck had gone sour. He waded out of the creek, his patched, faded waders looking shiny as ebony, and sat on the big rock. He began wiping the moisture off his rod, a 7½-foot two-piece Phillipson that was as smooth and dark as wild cherry bark and as limber as a length of willow. He began to talk, which was unlike him. All his life Albert had been a man who liked angling for trout more than he liked talking about trout.

"A good rod," he said, laying the Phillipson across his lap. "Hooked into many a dream with it." In a soft voice he told me he liked fly fishing because it had backbone and character. It was a noble way of life. And if fly fishing provided the angler with humbling doses of misery and disappointment, so too did it yield adventure, elation, glorious isolation enough to ease a man's troubled heart. He figured he had cast a line for sixty years at least and still it thrilled him, filled him with expectation, drained away the tedium of the farm like pus from a wound. He found it hard to put his feelings into words. "It's more than excitement," he said, looking out over the creek, down into its clear, clean water. "It's more like an alliance of enchantment and exuberance, a pleasing delirium that at last distills down into a sense of real peace, absolute and perfect." He turned back to me, laughing. "God, that was a mouthful of rambling mush. I need to take a course. My language is too prolix. But I hope you get the core of what I'm saying about angling." I nodded and returned his smile.

He stood at the edge of Cody's Rock and cast again, letting the fly rest upstream, about midway in the current. I found myself thinking that each cast carried with it not only the hope of a trout on the rise, but a sense of renewal as well. He cast again and I could tell from his eyes that he was deep in concentration and that the rod was an extension of his emotions, as real and genuine as any he had ever experienced, including love, which he had embraced and lost five times over. Later that morning, he confided in me that trout anglers overcame their misfortunes by developing selective memories, a portion of the mind where all the good days, all the good trout water, the good rods, the good trout, were stored, ready to surge through every cell and muscle, a rejuvenation of body and spirit. And then Albert took a hard-boiled egg from his coat pocket, peeled it, and put the shell back into his pocket. He ate it leaning up against Cody's Rock, staring at the day's fading light coming off the creek in clouds of soft yellow vapor.

After fishing nearly all day around Cody's Rock, I walked upstream to Karen's Pool, and saw Emerson fishing there along with Elias Wonder, who stood on the far side of the pool. I took my usual seat up against the birch tree, took long gulps of warm root beer from my canteen. I remember thinking on that late afternoon that the great lure of fly fishing is that it is more of a journey than a quest, a journey with unlimited beginnings and no definitive end. The angler hopes for nothing and prays for everything; he expects nothing and accepts all that comes his way. And although he knows all along that he will never sink his hook into a trout stream's true mystery, the desire to try, to cast once more and once more again, is never quenched, for there is always that chance that one more cast will carry him beyond skill and luck and bring him untarnished magic.

For me, there was never any question that some kind of

magic mingled with the waters of Starlight Creek. Sometimes as I fished the creek at dusk when the light came off the water soft as velvet and blue shadows lengthened in the woods, I would suddenly feel lightheaded, dizzy, for an instant having no more substance than a cloud of cool mist on the stream. A cleansing feeling, beyond fear or confusion. For that moment the world around me was sensible and full of purpose, soaked in reason and resignation. A boy's clumsy attempt to dismantle himself into the elements, a pool of molecules mingling with the creek and the air, the light overhead, the trout deep in the cold, translucent water. Of course, it never happened, but I never doubted that it could, for I knew that where there was cold trout water there was hope, of a kind.

Trail's End was no paradise, though. Emerson, who had a soft spot for Milton's poetry, often mumbled that the only paradise was paradise lost. The only certainties about the farm were work and hard luck, both of which arrived regularly and by the bucketful. Even so, the old men took it all with good humor and went on turning their backs on the questions of profit and production, settling instead for a way of life that offered no frills beyond simplicity and unadorned satisfaction. The Reverend Biddle kept telling them that the poor would inherit the earth, but the way Albert and Emerson saw it, it wasn't something that was going to happen anytime soon. "By the time we get it," snapped Albert one Sunday, "it'll be like inheriting last month's fish!"

They were firmly harnessed to the earth as it was and they took the land, its beauty and its blind treachery, a day at a time. Inconvenience and poverty were as much a part of their lives as hailstorms, tornadoes, bountiful harvests, drought, good trout, plump quail, plagues of insects, and deer moving up in the high country. They were satisfied. They never prayed for help, for a change in their luck, for anything, although I did hear Emerson ask the Great Mystery once to bless a No. 18 dry fly he had just tied on in hopes of tempting a huge rainbow trout that stalked the deep water of Karen's Pool.

Each morning, even before he put the coffee on or began the biscuits, Albert would stand on the back porch and listen to the purling of the creek, the rush of water over stones. It was as if he needed to hear the creek, that sound of life ever on the move, running irresistibly downstream, before he could commit to another day of exhausting labor and the back of fortune's hand. I often thought that should the morning come when he could not walk down the stairs and hear the creek, he would die. As long as the creek filled the wind with its gentle roar, that was enough; the old men were content. If the land yielded great harvests of doubt and perturbation, it also comforted them endlessly with fortuity, prospect, sanctuary, not an escape from life but an immersion in it, complete and uncompromising. They had the creek, the trout, the shadowy hills. They were satisfied. The land defined them and they were its image, tough and unyielding, intolerant, cryptic, hypnotic, possessed of beauty and misery, ruthlessness and benevolence, cruelty and absolution.

Living in the belief that the natural world was the product of life and not some eternal adversary, they did not despair, for every wind brought change, chance renewed. Of course, they knew too that Wayne Durham had been right, that his predictions would in time come to pass. Progress and prosperity were on the move, headed straight at them. They could not stop it and did not intend to try. For decades they had known that their way of life was ending and that something else, something different, something they knew nothing about, would take its place. Change happened. Nothing could deflect it, stop it. They heard it moving closer. Even above the sound of the creek they could hear down the mountains the high whine of chain-saws and the growling coughs of bulldozers.

They did not bewail their fate and damn the human race.

But neither did they see what harm it would do to posterity for them to live out their years exactly as they had always lived— alone on the land, on the creek, just yards from the place where they had been born well before the turn of the century. Neither of them harbored deep feelings about many things, but this they did believe: they were as much a part of Trail's End as the river birch, the oaks, the trout, the quail, the few remaining turkeys and deer, the hawks overhead. They and the land were insepa- rable. In death they wanted to rot there, be part of it forever. Not totally in jest, Albert once burst into the kitchen and made me swear that when he died I wouldn't let Emerson plant him in the ground. Instead, he wanted me to haul him out to the compost heap, bury him there, and turn him regularly like last autumn's leaves.

That was the same day they argued over which of them had the earlier memory of hearing the creek for the first time. Both claimed it was the one sound that crept through every year of their lives, even into infancy. Albert claimed he'd heard it while he was in the womb. "That was your mother's indiges- tion," said Emerson. Both agreed, though, that the creek was life's voice and they wanted, when it came time, to die at home with the windows open wide and the sound of rushing water filling the room. Beyond this, they asked nothing, not even to leave a single footprint along the muddy banks of Starlight Creek. Endings were good, necessary; they knew that change would sweep over their graves without so much as tipping its hat. The prospect of death never troubled them, although Al- bert did once worry that if something like the resurrection came to pass, would he be properly dressed for it and would there be a fly shop nearby.

They kept their minds on the here and now, and let the good Reverend Biddle worry about the hereafter. On the day that Wayne Durham lectured them on their "primitive and wasteful farming practices," Emerson shrieked, the veins at his temples throbbing madly, "You think *we're* up to no good, for chrissakes, what about Tolstoy?"

"Tolstoy who?" asked Durham, his face suddenly blank as rolled dough. "Who or what in hell is a Tolstoy? What kinda name is that, anyway? Sounds Indian maybe, or Jewish. You trying to tell me there's a Jew Indian living in these hills?"

"He's a genius," said Albert reassuringly. Albert's lips were visibly trembling from the effort of holding back the huge guffaw that was building in his throat the way pressure builds in a pinched garden hose.

Wayne Durham wiped his face thoughtfully with his bandana. "Wait a minute! He's not that foreign rube down along Miller's Run who's trying to grow grapes, for chrissakes, is he?" he bellowed, his hands shaking with fitting patriotic rage.

"Naw," said Albert coolly. "Tolstoy lives up the mountain on five hundred acres of virgin timber, on land that's never felt a plow's blade. He makes shoes. Damn good shoes, too. The fellow on Miller's Run is Billy Hayes, the amateur taxidermist, the one who has the stuffed squirrel posed like an eagle in flight. Thing's even got gold eyes."

Wayne Durham looked confounded, just sat there shaking his head and feeling sorry for himself because nobody else would and because he had to deal with these mountain lunatics who didn't seem the least bit concerned with profit margin or prosperity. The hell with them, he decided, and stormed out of the house determined to head back to Little Rock just as soon as he stopped by Tolstoy's for some shoes and at Billy Hayes's place to get a look at the soaring squirrel with the golden eyes.

For a month, every morning before school and every afternoon when school let out, I sat by the river birch at Karen's Pool and watched, and listened, never saying a word. I watched every cast and every dimple on the surface of the water that signaled a trout rising, and every fish took my breath away. Infatuation matured into longing, deep and abiding. I ached to hold a fly rod, stand in the creek's cold water, cast a line. Surely, I thought, the old men knew of my yearning, saw the pain and the desire on my face, knew the depth of my sincerity. Yet neither of them talked much of fly fishing except to comment on the mood of the creek, the character of a certain splendid trout, whether luck had stood fast or abandoned them.

Late spring had spread across the mountains before I found the courage to ask them one morning at the breakfast table. I spoke up just as they were piling their dishes in the sink, getting ready to head for the creek for an hour's fishing before the sun topped the hills—the sign for them to exchange fly rods for hoes and wheelbarrows.

"Could you show me?" I said weakly, my voice struggling to break the bonds of a whisper.

"Show you what, son?" Emerson asked, pulling the wide, flat brim of his Montana hat down over his eyes. The hat was the dull silver color of a trout's belly.

"You know, teach me—" I stopped short because I was shaking badly and I wanted to sound serious and mature, someone worthy of instruction.

Certain that something of consequence was at hand, Albert took off his hat, sat back down, and poured himself another cup of coffee. His hands trembled slightly, sending tiny waves of coffee over the lip of the cup onto the tablecloth. Albert looked at Emerson, his face a mixture of confusion and incredulity. Emerson returned a similar look, only his face was more distorted, as though he had just bitten into a sour grape.

"Teach you what, exactly?" said Emerson in a low voice, the same voice he fell into whenever he felt a catastrophe was at hand.

"Fly fishing," I said.

Silence, for a long moment. Canyon deep and cave perfect. It was as if all of us had stopped breathing at the same instant.

Emerson took off the big Montana hat and scratched his head thoughtfully. His bright eyes fixed on me.

"Teach you fly fishing!" he roared, a thundering sound that caused Albert to fling what was left of his coffee straight up in the air. "Why—why, that's criminal. Tell him, Albert, for chrissakes. That's criminal. Why, I'd get a lighter sentence lacing your root beer with paregoric. Teach you fly fishing, for chrissakes. Better you should ask me how to pick up eighty-year-old women. Fly fishing!"

He sat back in his chair and the red drained slowly from his face. He and Albert were old washed-up mountain farmers, he told me. That and no more. Not teachers or scholars, and certainly not your typical old pipe-smoking, rocking-chair patriarchs, dispensing homespun wisdom to their kin, boring them with memories of the "good old days, which weren't all that damn good," and old folkways that were as suspect as they might be virtuous.

Albert nodded. "Yeah, we're a couple of old farts who want to see the younger generations screw up all on their own, with no help from us. Though we probably could steer them to disaster a good deal faster."

Emerson embraced a more serious tone. "We have nothing of lasting worth to teach you, son. That's what it comes down to," he said earnestly. And he told me coldly that he and Albert were of the belief that an old man, and especially a relative, should never teach a child how to fish—unless, that is, the old man had something against the child and was out to get even.

Then Emerson leaned forward in his chair, so that his face was but inches from mine and I saw that there were endless flecks of blue in his gray eyes and that the lines that spread like dried-up creek beds in his face were cut more deeply than I had realized. "Why, to anchor you with what paltry knowledge the two of us have of fly fishing would make as much sense as a second-rate con man trying to teach his kid the ropes, the same crap that put the old man in the slammer in the first place." He sighed deeply, as if searching for the next turn of his argument.

Pools of sunlight began to fill the kitchen. Albert looked

nervously out the back door toward the creek.

"I'm fumbling about for the words," Emerson mused out loud. "We barely know anything about angling ourselves. That's it, that's what I'm struggling for. Why, we'd just saddle you with a cartload of bad habits. Trout fishing is worse than alcohol or women."

"Well, maybe alcohol," Albert said, smiling.

"It's a ruinous thing, an addiction more destructive than Albert's habitual need for I.B.C. root beer. Fly rodding will consume your life. You'll transform, become absolutely piscine. Look at Albert..." Emerson pointed his long, bony index finger at Albert, who dropped the smile and took on the grim aspect of a man about to be hanged. "...that salmonid smile, the cold, indifferent eyes, the constant pucker of the lips."

"The indomitable spirit," said Albert, coming to his own rescue.

"And he's only been at it sixty years," concluded Emerson. "Imagine what kind of pisciform monster a lifetime with a fly rod might create! The thought is frightening, son. Frightening. The rod and reel. Don't ask me to damn my grandson to a life as a maladjusted piscator." And he took a long pause, then added, "Anyway, your father did not send you here so that you might immerse yourself in fly fishing or quail, or mountain streams, or wild turkey, all of which are frivolous to him and to most of the civilized world. Save yourself some grief."

As he talked, I was thinking. About trout. About how the morning was getting late and how we should have been on the creek an hour ago. From my chair I could look beyond Emerson, out the back door. Sunlight cut into the forest in great shafts like faults through stone. Albert, too, had his back to the sunlight and he became a shimmering silhouette with a pompadour of ungainly hair.

"Have you really thought this through?" Emerson asked, his words thick as though coated with molasses. "Again I say, look at us." This time the bony finger went to Albert and then into his own chest. Albert squirmed in his chair, a man unable to keep a tight grip on neutrality. "Look at the way we live. Take a good, long look. These are the rewards of the outdoor life, son, sad and paltry as they are. Take up the fly rod and the shotgun, and before you know it, you're an outcast, a social leper, rejected by your family, despised by your neighbors, mistrusted by your community. Unaware that your soul is quite safe, in the best of company, your church will pity you, pray mightily for your redemption from hideous sin. The final question is, should any man turn his back on ambition, profit, security, and a parking place in the city, just to pursue a fish!"

Albert jumped up, shook his fist at the ceiling. "And look at Elias Wonder. Yeah, take a gander at that buzzard. Forty years ago he was happy, generous, charitable, tall, dark, and handsome. Then he took up the fly rod. Now consider him. Uglier than a fresh road kill. Evil-eyed, cantankerous, sullen, mean. An antisocial misfit that causes a groundswell of spleen wherever he goes. Consider him well. Should a man abandon success just to pursue a fish?" Then he bolted for the door, yelling, "Yes, but only if it's trout!"

Emerson's face was turned away from me, but I could hear him chuckling under his breath. When he spoke again, it was only to say: "Amen. That's the spiel, son."

I smiled at them both. Soon we were all on the hard-dirt path leading down to Starlight Creek and we were all laughing, sinners together.

We fished only a little while, because there were fields to tend. I thought I understood it now: even if the old men had no interest in being my angling mentors, they would not try to stop me from following my own interests, no matter how foolhardy, whether it be trout fishing or nuclear physics. If they had never actually invited me to go with them to the creek each day to fish, neither had they seemed to mind my company, the hours I spent watching them. Perhaps it was their way of testing my devotion to the trout of Starlight Creek, the depth and veracity of my new convictions.

"Better get things cleaned up," Emerson told me after a dinner of venison steaks, fresh-baked bread, potatoes, tomatoes, field peas, and iced tea. "See to the feathered ladies out in the coop. Tuck them in cozy. Get your mind off trout, if you can. I know they've got you. I can see it. Every fraternity of sufferers knows its brothers. Trout hook men; men don't hook trout. Better try and throw the hook while you can. By the time you're a grown man there probably won't be a pure trout healthy enough to fiddle with."

Albert yelled from the big room, where he was stretched out on the couch, "How's that for wise, soothing, elderly counsel, son? Words of succor from the ancient and learned. It must be humbling to eat at the same table with Emerson, the Exalted Sage of the Ozarks, and St. Albert. Ah, yes, a path lighted by guidance from the dim past, exhortations from the doomed! Now, if you two boys will excuse me, I'm off on a moonlit walk with Mr. Hemingway, who wishes to persuade me that when it comes to sports afield, it's quantity that counts rather than quality or experience. Forward, then, good brother Emerson. A double amen to your orations."

And I heard the front door close and Albert's harmonica playing "Little Walter," deep and mournful.

At breakfast the next morning Alert said brusquely, "I suggest we dismiss all piscatorial conversations this morning and get down to the creek. You know how the trout pout when they miss a day of humiliating us."

Emerson looked at him hard. "Onward it is, then," he said. "Son, you clean up the dishes, fetch the eggs."

Albert was up and walking toward the back door when he turned and winked and I knew my incipient conspiracy had enlisted its first confederate. On that morning I had determined to baptize myself completely in the life of Starlight Creek.

From that day, every spare moment went to walking along the creek, studying the water. Cody joined me on these expeditions, shared his ample knowledge of trout with me with unbridled enthusiasm. I had no rod, no reel, just an unquenchable curiosity. In trying to figure out the vexing nature of trout, I became something of an amateur hydrologist, limnologist, entomologist, and possessed ichthyologist. No event along the creek, no matter how seemingly insignificant, escaped my notice. I kept detailed scientific notes, formed sweeping new theories on the lives of trout, even though all I ever really knew for certain was that trout were the most puzzling of creatures.

Cody accompanied me everywhere. His interests were more practical than scientific. After all, there was a trifling chance that I might stumble onto a trout. If so, Cody wanted to be there to catch it. That chance came on the same cool afternoon when Emerson informed me that the only grandfatherly advice of any worth he could pass along was always take root beer over ice. The ice seemed to give it a good, frothy head. On that afternoon, under a sky of dull gray clouds, Cody caught a handsome rainbow trout just below Karen's Pool. I had been at the pool's edge turning over rocks, studying the insects and insect larvae the trout might be feeding on, when suddenly I heard a great commotion just behind me, a sound like someone had just dumped an ice box into the creek. Expecting some kind of new and terrible disaster to be staring down at me, I turned slowly and saw instead Cody prancing madly about in the shallow water, a leer on his face like a madman's. Just moments before, he'd been on top of a large rectangular slab of stone that reached almost to midstream. Like a thief, he'd crept to the edge of the boulder and lain there, so he could see down into the clear water curving around the stone. Stretched out there on that massive stone, the old dog had looked like a sphinx cut from ebony, motionless, waiting, infinitely patient. And I had gone on looking for insects aquatic and terrestrial, that the trout of Karen's Pool might be feasting on.

Then came that loud splash and the water beside the rock began to boil as though it were on high heat. Cody's tail beat wildly; hunks of wet fur slapped the surface; then there was Cody's big head with a handsome rainbow trout grasped gently in his mouth. Cody brought it to the bank, thrilled at his angling prowess. Like the old men, Cody rarely kept trout. Normally, he would have nudged the exhausted trout back into the water and waited until it regained its composure and swam away. But on this day Cody's high sense of scientific duty overwhelmed his desire to get the trout back into the creek as fast as possible. We had been looking for a live trout to study and Cody had determined to provide one. The resulting speedy drama lasted just long enough for me to note the trout's sex, length, weight, and overall general health. But by then the trout had ceased to flop about on the soft bank, a condition that upset Cody, made him nervous. Seeing that our scientific observations were completed, Cody reached down, gently took the trout into his mouth, and placed it in the shallow water at the edge of the pool.

Consumed by guilt and shame, we both knelt there watching, fearing we had killed the trout. It lay on its side in the water, motionless, as though it had no more life in it than a twig floating on the current. Still, we watched. I walked into the water and stroked the trout's muscled flanks. It flicked its tail and I knew it had not given up, that there was still life in it. Minutes later, it righted itself, rose in the water the way a wind rises out of a canyon, full of renewed strength and power. In a blurry instant, the trout snapped its body like a whip and quietly disappeared into the pool's deep, dark waters, thus easing Cody's conscience and mine.

On a May morning shrouded in darkening clouds and a constant drizzle, Albert stole into my room, came almost on tiptoe, silently, as though he were a man on the run. "How much money you got?" he whispered. Down the hall, Emerson lay naked on his bed reading Loren Eiseley. He was naked because he had gotten into a patch of poison ivy while trying to outsmart an old hermit gobbler down in the oak sloughs by Woollum's place. As always happened, the turkey got the best of things, leading the old man right into the tangle of poison ivy, and Emerson got the itch, which he deserved, he said, for fooling around with wild turkeys. Albert scrubbed him down with so much calamine lotion that Emerson took on the aspect of a body freshly laid out at the mortician's, just waiting for something eternal to wear.

"Well, how much?" prodded Albert.

"About fifteen dollars," I said. That included all my wages at $1.50 a week, plus what was left of the $25 my father had given me.

"Okay, that's plenty," said Albert, his voice registering a hint of excitement and intrigue. "Get it and meet me by the truck. We're going to town."

Albert said nothing as we drove. He had this sly grin on his face, the same grin he wore each time he outfoxed Emerson or got the best of the good Reverend Conrad Biddle of the Mount Hebron First Primitive Methodist Church, or each time Elias Wonder threatened to die and didn't. Between us on the seat was a thin piece of quilt, folded in half, rolled up and tied loosely at each end with a length of torn sheet.

In town, he parked across from Bates's, then gingerly carried the parcel into the dimly lit store. Mr. Bates looked startled, as if he'd never seen Albert in town on a weekday.

"What's up?" he asked with some urgency. "How's Emerson? Everything all right with you old fellas?"

"Emerson's down with the itch," said Albert. "Just as cranky as ever, more temperamental than a two-legged dog." As he spoke, Albert set the package on the counter, untied and unrolled it. It was the old Orvis cane rod and some nameless worn, dull gray-steel reel already packed with line. In the store's diluted light, the old rod took on the color of soft sunlight, pure, comb-fresh honey. A thing of beauty.

Albert coughed slightly, cleared his throat to get Bates's full attention. "You know, Bates, a man can use only so many rods. Really, any more than one is a wasteful luxury, seems to me. Any more would be too many dependents for a man of my years, so I'd like to sell this one. It's been a good rod, devoted, trustworthy, more dependable than most things a man hooks up with in life. I'd like to get what I gave for it, if possible. That would be five dollars. You think I could display it here in the store?"

Bates's face took on a suspicious and confused look. "Albert, you haven't sold a rod or reel or shotgun since this place has been here. Why now? Look, if it's credit you need . . ."

"No, no, Bates, thank you anyway. I'm still solvent. The simple life keeps a man away from many things, including debt. No, I just got a special urge for five dollars. Now, can I leave the rod with you?"

"Certainly," said Bates. "I'll put it in the front window with a large white tag on it. Bet it sells in less than a week's time."

"Good," Albert said, smiling. "That's good. Many thanks to you, Bates. I appreciate it." And the two men shook hands.

Throughout the entire transaction, Albert had not turned to me, looked at me, acknowledged me in any way. Now, he simply walked out the door. But I knew my part. My hands were already deep in my jeans pocket, fishing out one-dollar bills.

"Wait, Mr. Bates," I cried. "I'll take it." My hand trembling, I slid the money, five crumpled dollar bills, onto the counter.

"Take what?" asked Mr. Bates, now genuinely perplexed.

"Why, the rod and reel there, the one for five dollars," I said, my eyes locked firmly on the little rod, the worn-out reel. Sunlight coming in through the wide doorway flashed off the rod's polished ferrules.

I laid another dollar bill on the counter, and said confidently, "And I'd like four dry flies, sir. Two No. 16 Adams and two No. 18 Quill Gordons."

Bates looked out the door in Albert's direction and then

down at me, then out the door again. He scurried down the aisle to the long glass case where he kept the trout flies, along with the watches, pocketknives, cigarette lighters, and cheap costume jewelry. He put the flies into a brown paper bag, took the money and, leaning down close to my face said, "Boy, you just spent six dollars on fishing. That's six dollars down the rathole, boy. There ain't a fish in this whole county worth no six dollars," he sneered.

"Yes, sir," I replied politely, and reached out reverently for the rod.

I found Albert at the café, nursing a bowl of soup and a glass of iced tea. He sat in the back corner, his pale skin standing out like a slice of moon on a stormy night.

"What'd you buy, son?" he asked, crushing a handful of crackers into his soup, stirring them in until they got soggy and drowned, white pulp floating in a stream of bright red tomatoes, string beans and corn, and a dash of Elias Wonder's stump juice.

"Why, the rod," I said proudly.

"What rod?" asked Albert, a seemingly genuine pall of ignorance spreading over his face.

"Why, the rod you just left at Bates's store to be sold," I said, as a tight ball of bewilderment knotted in my stomach.

"Couldn't have been me, son," Albert said flatly. "I've struggled to encumber my modest life with few canons, but I must admit to warming up to a few principles, one of which is that a man never willingly parts with a fly rod, especially if it has been a loyal rod, steadfast and reliable, any more than he should part with a faithful dog or a truck that always kicks over, even in harsh weather." He paused for a moment to wipe a glop of cracker from the corner of his mouth. "Let's have a look at this rod of yours."

I handed him the rod that Mr. Bates had wrapped for me and he unwrapped it with great care, as though the contents were as fragile as porcelain. He fitted the pieces of the slender cane rod together and gave it a shake. "Could have trout in it,

THE EARTH IS ENOUGH

son," he said. And I saw how he held the old rod, how he looked at it, his eyes all but glowing, his mind, I knew, conjuring up every trout the rod had taken. "Sure, it might have trout in it. I guess it really depends as much on the angler as the rod. How much did you give for it, anyway?" he asked as he rolled the rod back up in its cotton cocoon.

"Five dollars," I said incredulously. "Exactly what you told Mr. Bates to sell it for."

Albert kept working on the soup and tea, then whispered darkly as he looked about the empty café, "Leave me out of this, son. You want your poor old uncle locked up for contributing to the moral collapse of a child? I didn't give you the rod. Such an act would be worse than a drunk spiking his baby's milk just to give it a taste of its future. No, this is trouble you purchased of your own free will, with no help from me or Emerson or anyone else. And it is trouble you've latched on to. Just ask Donna when she comes around for the dishes. She'll tell you straight that you've gone and hitched a ride on the Devil's tail."

But Miss Donna said no such thing, although she did tell me in a chiding voice that any man who eats at the table with his hat on is "sure nuff eatin' with the Devil."

"You sure about that?" said Albert with an amused grin.

"Albert, you know I don't kid around when it comes to Satan," Miss Donna snapped as she gathered up Albert's dirty dishes.

"True," confessed Albert. "But you know how we mountain people are. We're not choosy about our company, don't care about the condition of their soul or the length of their tail."

Miss Donna winced. Albert chuckled. I just sat there thinking about that Orvis rod, how it had shone so in Bates's store.

After Miss Donna had strutted away in a huff, Albert asked me again, "What did you give for that rod?"

"Just what I told you. Five dollars."

"Kinda pricey, don't you think. I mean, for such a beat-up old rod. Thing might not have five dollars' worth of fly fishing left in it. Perhaps you should have talked Bates down to four dollars. Shit, maybe three." But he was smiling as he put seventy-five cents on the table and got up to leave.

The next morning I clutched the rod and felt almost faint as we walked out the back door into the morning sunlight. I remember thinking what a great deal I had made, how modest the admission fee to heaven really was. Just $5 plus a couple of flies. Just one cast, I thought. Just one cast as I stood thigh deep in Karen's Pool and the trout would rise, a moment not of ascension but assumption. A flick of the wrist and I would slip into another sense of time and place: apotheosis.

I practiced with the rod in the mornings. I practiced in the evenings after school. Often, I skipped the drudgery of school altogether and stayed on the creek all day and well into the evening, especially during the first cold days of autumn when we would ease quietly into the water after dusk to stalk the monstrous browns, shrewd, deadly, beautiful, the supreme hunter, coming out only in dim light or at nightfall so that it became a shadow among shadows, a killing phantom, a spooky apparition flashing more colors than an artist's palette. Night, another world; nights so black sometimes it felt as if the very atmosphere coiled about us. I fished from memory, feeling my way over muddy lampblack stones, the stream, black as a raven's eye, tugging at me, and often I thought how easy it would be to slip, let the dark waters fill my waders, sink slowly to the bottom of the pool, nudged there by the great browns, their huge jaws agape.

At night we moved in the creek like crawfish, scuttling around the rocks, casting to places we knew were there, masked in the night, bathed sometimes in lutescent moonlight. Casting nymphs into the soothing darkness, the interminable blackness where flashed the eyes of bobcats and raccoons, where the owls in the deep woods howled like dogs, where the deer moved through the high country. At times it was so cold my hands went numb and my jaws shook uncontrollably and my thighs and calves ached from the cold and still I did not give in, but stayed in the creek cast after cast, each one an act of faith, a communion between me and the cold and the night and the stream's great trout. Hooking one was like being hooked to a runaway truck. Its courage and power seemed endless.

Slipping into the creek after dusk, casting for the big browns, I crossed into another world, dark, sublime, both frightening and glorious. Each moss-covered rock seemed a primordial step backward, back, back until sometimes I was there utterly alone in the darkness and it suddenly was ancient time, the creek a Devonian bog, and I had no voice, no recognizable shape. I was just something different and alive, rising up out of the coal-black water. Starlight Creek at night seemed altogether different, a stream of brooding, limitless, inexplicable contingencies. On such nights even my mind drifted as a black stream full of the mystery of fish, flowing on and on without end.

My practicing paid off and in the blink of an eye I became with every feeble cast an expert at hooking trees. Even when I did manage to get the fly line forward, it inevitably landed ten feet in front of me in a wadded mess that looked something like tossed spaghetti, a clump of frustration and dismay. In the evenings, I worked on knots, knots with names like nail knot, blood knot, surgeon's knot, which suggested to me that perhaps they'd been handed down from some more vulgar vocation such as that of a hangman. Fortunately, since I received no instruction, was under the tutelage of no master, I never really knew just how unsightly my efforts were, otherwise I would certainly, out of respect for the grace and tradition of fly fishing, have stepped aside, laid down my rod forever. Indeed, there are many who still think such a decision would restore much of angling's former irreproachable reputation.

Along the far side of the pool, up above Elias Wonder's dilapidated cabin, whippoorwills called, the song seeming a litany for the fading light. Farther up the pool, near the cascading riffles, I heard a trout break the surface, eager for the night and its bounty.

Elias Wonder's single lantern glowed in the cabin doorway, a smoky light curling in broad charcoal circles, drifting on the evening breeze. And there he sat on the three-legged chair by the door, light glowing off his dark Indian skin, making it look discolored. He had been watching me for hours. I could feel those eyes on me, measuring my every motion with the fly rod. Those eyes black as fragmented obsidian.

I heard a small slosh at the pool's distant edge below the cabin, felt thick waves which lapped against my thighs as he moved easily, quietly through the water. Elias Wonder's small, compact, powerful shadow moved closer, cutting through the water with an almost elegant grace, until he reached the great raft of dark stones that rose up out of the middle of the pool, a massive staircase of rock. Moving among them as skillfully as a lizard, he worked his way to the shallower water where I stood, stopping perhaps three yards downstream of me. I heard the clicking of his reel as he worked his line out. I saw the line; it seemed lighter than the air, something that threatened to escape gravity's hold. He brought the line back in quickly, checked the fly, then cast above the slow current that moved around the first of the rocks.

In the moonlight I studied the deep wrinkles in the old lunatic's face. The light softened his hard features. In a voice as faint as a feathering breeze, he began to talk, still working the rod, the long length of line he had worked out. "You can feel it, can't you?" he said, and the words lingered on the wind. He waited for a moment, not wanting to interrupt the chattering whippoorwills on the hillside or the groaning frogs on the banks. "Rhythm," he said, drawing out the word. He moved deeper into shadow, became, for a time, ephemeral, a bodiless but soothing voice. "Ever notice how everything out here has a rhythm to it? Creek's got a rhythm all its own, just as the trout have one they move to, a rhythm in the blood. Seems there's a rhythm to the wind, even among the rocks. That's true. Believe it. Out here the so-called lifeless things only appear dead. Don't discount the rocks. Look closely. Geography. Geology. Water. All part of the land's rhythm."

He cast again, each movement slow, almost exaggerated, exposing every detail of his wrist action. *Rhythm.* The word echoed in my head, distilled into my blood, and I watched the old Indian and knew, finally, he was teaching me, sharing a secret: rhythm. The blending motions of stream, trout, rod, line, drifting fly, and man.

I moved closer, watched him intently, trying to memorize everything about him as he stood there in the pool, the night closing fast, insects coming off the creek, the trout rising hungrily. Like the old men, Wonder filed the barbs off his hooks. This prevented the hook from needlessly tearing up the fish's jaw, the soft tissue of its mouth. He could do something I have seen no other fly fisherman do since. Upon hooking a trout, getting a look at it, he would bring it no closer than seven to ten feet, then he would flick his rod sideways, instantly dislodging the hook without harming the trout.

"The way I see it," Wonder said, changing flies, tying on a subtler pattern, "you're hooked. Trout have you. Another soul lost." He paused for a long moment, looked down at the cool, deep water. "Or maybe found." He cast the handsome new fly up above the rocks, at the edge of the riffles. "Maybe you ought to know the code," he said.

I followed his lead, putting a little more snap in my forward cast and the backcast, transferring more power to the line. "Code?" I asked, thrilled that I had progressed far enough not only to be accepted by the old men, but asked to take some secret fly-fishing oath, perhaps some prayer uttered by Izaak Walton himself.

Wonder kept his eyes on the tiny fly skating on the surface of the pool. "Oh, it's nothing official," he said. "Nothing binding. I just thought, you being young and the rest of us so old, and there not being that many of us foolish trout men left, you might remember us from time to time, as you grow, as you travel, as you cast a line over different rivers."

"What exactly am I supposed to do?" I asked. My confusion wrecked my concentration, causing me to hook a fine fifty-pound stone.

Wonder took my rod, flicked it down, then up, in one quick snap, and freed the hook. "Nothing all that special, really. Here's what I've been doing for many years. I just raise a good drink by the creek, offer a toast to Albert and Emerson, even that old bastard dog of theirs. And now to you as well. There are so few of us left. That's all, just a toast to trout men, one and all. There are so few left, so few who believe the earth is enough."

And then he hooked another rainbow, played it till it leapt, flashed in the moonlight, a burst of luminescent light. Then Elias Wonder twitched his rod and the trout swam off, a silhouette of beaded light just inches below the surface. He told me of the time a carnival came to town and set up in Miller's pasture and how there was a bearded lady in it who sat on the back of a humpbacked dwarf and shot a .22-caliber rifle at sheets of cheap tin making accurate portraits of the Presidents. "You just don't get that quality of entertainment anymore," he said with deep regret. Then he reeled in his line, began moving quietly across the pool. He stopped and turned, and his face, caught in moonlight, startled me. He looked so old and tired. "There is a serious side to this code business, too, you know. No worms. No salmon eggs. Not even the pretty pink ones. And no tender, sweet niblets of corn. You don't bait what you love. You tempt it, lure it, get under its skin." He waded downstream, crossed over, walked up to his cabin.

I watched him as he shed his waders and hung them up to dry. Then he sank wearily back into his lawn chair, reached inside the cabin doorway and picked up a large jar of his homemade whiskey. The stuff had a violent smell to it—unique, unmistakable, combustible. I always suspected its chief ingredients were ground-up Mexican peppers, cheap after-shave, a hearty dose of Tabasco sauce, a lacing of kerosene, and a pinch of burnt rope. The old men called it "Eternal Nectar," on the assumption, I suppose, that if one drank the stuff and survived, his chances of making it through eternity were considerably increased.

Wonder took several long pulls from the jar, leaned back in the wobbly chair, and stared aimlessly at the moon, the immense gallery of stars overhead.

I walked to the bank, reeled in my line, and started downstream toward the house. Specks of starlight came off the surface of the creek like swarms of fireflies and I could still hear Elias Wonder, his voice rising above the stream's persistent hiss. "Rhythm . . . there's a rhythm to it all."

The next morning when I woke up I took my rod and ran to the stream while the light was a harvest of grays and waded out among the rocks at Karen's Pool. I cast my line, and felt the tug of the cold water against my thighs. Always that tug, that urgency of motion, of life ongoing, resolute. I lost all sense of time, of place, of everything. Concentration absorbed me. Never had I felt such a consoling aloneness. There in the dark, cold water, the sun creeping up the far side of the mountains, setting the sky on fire, was the first time I felt it, that gripping chill that sets every muscle jumping, that shuddering that separates one moment from the next, that signals the passing from one kind of life to another. Even though I was but a boy, I knew standing there in the stream that, from then on, things would be different. It was not that the world had changed, but that I had changed in some fundamental way that I could not understand or undo. I felt, too, a sense of actually becoming, belonging. If my life as a refugee was not over, at least it had changed in both direction and purpose.

Just as the day gained the mountains, poured over them like

a flood of warming light, the trout hit, not a violent strike, but a delicate tug, a suspicious bump. Until I felt its weight on the line, bending the rod tip, I doubted that I had a fish at all. I saw it clearly and was in awe of it, a small rainbow trout, but tenacious as the Goliaths of its tribe, a creature of beauty and power. On taking my small No. 18 black gnat, the trout ran downstream toward Cody's Rock and suddenly jumped, its supple body arching in the morning sun so that the light flashed brilliantly off its iridescent flanks, displaying a stripe the deep strawberry color of fresh salmon flesh. Another run, across and farther downstream, and I gave it more line because I wanted the moment never to end, wanted never to be separated from the trout, the stream, the endless range of morning light. Just as I knew that my life was changing, so too did I know at that moment that no matter what became of me, whether or not I caught a thousand trout or never another, nothing would ever quite compare to this trout, the way it hauled me so easily and humbly into its world, into the chaos that is the natural world, at once terrifying and thrilling.

Its energy spent, I brought the exhausted trout close to me, let it swim into Albert's old landing net so I could remove the hook from its mouth without touching it. The trout lay motionless in the net just below the surface of the water, its gills straining for air, for life, while a single dark pupil stared up at me, full of light, full of mysteries I could never know, be part of; then it slipped away, disappeared into the deeper water down by Cody's Rock.

I groomed the little fly and hoped it was tempting enough for another trout to sample. I took two more trout that day, both bigger than the first. Yet that night I dreamed only of the small trout's dark, brooding eye and all that it saw and knew, not in its mind, but in its blood.

After the evening ritual at Karen's Pool with Elias Wonder, my grandfather, with great reluctance, allowed me to accompany him and Albert to the creek, with the understanding that we would all keep to our own stretch of water and leave one another alone.

Emerson led the way down the path toward the creek, saying over his shoulder, "Son, you're nuts for getting into this, and that's all I'll say of it. Just remember, I'm not your damn mentor or your baptist. I'm family. Refuge of a kind."

While other seasons celebrated quail or deer, Starlight Creek and its trout were with us year-round, through every adversity or stroke of good fortune, the waters and the dark-eyed trout moved with cold indifference. And every morning at five o'clock Albert moved about noisily in the kitchen, putting on the coffee, making the biscuits, frying the bacon. No one spoke at breakfast, not even a grumbled "Good morning" or an idle word about the weather. The sound I recall is that of spoons clacking against coffee cups as we waited for the first streaks of sunlight to come down the mountains, across the damp fields and garden. That was the signal that sent us on our way, lunch in our coat pockets, carrying a canteen of root beer and a Thermos of Elias Wonder's nectar. Dew lay on the tall grass and a mist hung close to the ground, and the sound of the creek, the rush of swift water, filled the narrow valley like an anthem. Once at the creek's edge, beneath a gum tree, we drew lots to determine who would fish where. Karen's Pool. The Peaceable Kingdom. Cody's Rock. Martha's Chute. Susan's Branch. Cervantes' Shallows. Cody, being the best-tempered among us, fished wherever he wanted. And each morning I watched as Emerson and Albert walked along the creek, disappeared in the fog and thick woods. In the fog they looked ephemeral, specters walking on pure air. We fished alone, each of us out of sight of the others. We entered the creek quietly, slowly, as if entering a church for morning prayers.

We all met for lunch precisely three hours later at Karen's Pool on the big outcrop of stones below Elias Wonder's place.

By the time I arrived, Albert was already opening his inevitable can of Spam, which he shared with Elias Wonder, even though Wonder suspected that Albert was secretly trying to poison him. Often Emerson would still be across the pool, still fishing, and I would sit on the flat stones and study him, trying to memorize his every movement, even the look in his eyes. Soon enough, though, he would reel in his line and wade over to the rocks. After standing his rod safely against an old oak tree, he would unwrap a biscuit stuffed with bacon and pour a long shot of Elias Wonder's whiskey. The root beer was for me. As the old men drank and ate, Wonder would sometimes tell us about the time in France during the First World War when he got caught in a cloud of mustard gas and came out as Robert E. Lee and spent the next six months in various military hospitals in France trying desperately to surrender to every officer he saw, dead, dying, or alive.

Elias Wonder told such wonderful stories because he was as mad as King Lear. I loved to lie on the warm stones by the edge of Karen's Pool and listen to him and watch the morning sunlight on the water.

After an hour's rest, we would walk back to the house, wipe down the fly rods and reels, hang up our waders. Taking up hoes and shovels and wheelbarrows, we headed for the garden and the fields and worked until dusk and did not mind the work or the exhaustion or the pitiful status of our economy, for we could hear the hissing waters of the creek and knew that the trout were there and waiting.

5. DAYS AFIELD

A bird gave me a message once. No, damn it, I don't mean that no damned bird spoke or anything like that. It was an old crow and it was in the middle of the highway, just sitting there black as hell, just glaring at me, those eyes drowning me in their blackness. No matter where I moved, it moved. Then it just took off into the trees, leaving a single black feather on the highway. Finally I understood it was a messenger. This is what it told me. "There is common ground. There is common ground."

— Elias Wonder, 1966

That familiar touch, as light and feathering as a small wind; that touch on my shoulder, the long, bent fingers gently shaking me while I came up from under the stack of warm wool blankets and could tell by the inky press of the night against the windowpane that it was still hours before daylight.

The light from the hallway cast Albert in blue shadow, a drifting form, one with a tender voice. "Moon's high and full." Although said in a whisper, the words had a jolt of power to them, a feeling of high importance, acuteness. I nodded my head and Albert turned toward the doorway. He had put on a massive coat, and over his outrageous hair and wide ears sat a rabbit-fur cap pulled down tight. Klondike gloves now covered his long, spindly, yet strong hands. It was early November and cold. Just hours before, after supper, the thermometer outside the front door had read 38 degrees. The night promised only a deeper slide into the cold. Emerson expected frost by morning.

We had spent the whole morning repairing the barn roof. For every hole we fixed, two more appeared, as if the old building refused to be mended, cured, wanted only a quiet and final end. Then there had been the long hours gathering collards, the leaves full, chilly, crisp. Hour after hour on bended knees among the furrows tying the collard leaves together and piling the bundles into crates and onto the truck. Emerson took them to town and Mr. Bates bought the whole load.

Now it was after midnight and the moon was full, a great cream-colored moon, high overhead. After supper, Emerson had taken a walk into the backyard, stood there for a long time craning his neck, looking intently up at the sky. He returned to the kitchen, stood there by the table with a look of boyish glee on his face. When he smiled, his thin, white flesh, pulled tight across the bones of his face, seemed always in danger of ripping. "Things feel right, look right," he'd said. Even in the dim light of the kitchen's single light bulb, the old man's eyes had glowed. "A fine moon. A good cold wind out of the north. And the temperature's falling. A good night, perhaps the night the geese will come." At that, Albert had dashed out the back door and down to the barn, brought out an old wooden ladder and propped it against the flat tin roof over the workshop. Then we'd all headed for bed.

Now Albert had woken me tenderly at midnight. We dressed warmly and went outside, carrying armloads of quilts and pillows. Albert tucked a Thermos of coffee laced with Elias Wonder's magical brew under his arm. I toted another full of scalding tea cut with milk and sugar. And up the ladder we went, the disaffected ladder threatening to collapse. Three of the bottom rungs were cracked. Emerson first. Then me. Albert brought up the rear, protecting the warming mix of coffee and whiskey under his arm. We laid the thick quilts—red, blue, white, and burgundy—over the rippling tin roof. In the silky moonlight they looked like an enormous Japanese fan.

"Put yourself in the middle there, son," said Emerson, shaking out the blankets. In less than five minutes we were packed under our cargo of covers, as snug as rabbits in their warren. My back relaxed, settled into the roof's pleats, and I could feel the old men's breathing, the rhythm of it. Everything had its rhythm, Elias Wonder had told me. And I believed it, too, especially on such nights when I lay with the two old men on the roof in a small mountain valley looking up at the November moon, studying the stars, saying nothing at first, just searching the skies for the first sign of them. Geese. That first wailing noise, that ragged dark line against the moonlight, like a strand of black thread stitched across a soft yellow cloth. And on those nights, I thought that maybe there were not many rhythms, but only one and everything was part of it—the mountains, the land, the creek, every night sound, all part of the autumn night, a tapestry of light and wind, a primordial pulse you could feel wrinkling down your spine, inexplicable and inexorable.

Wrapped in our cocoon of colored quilts, we lay there, our eyes fixed on the wide mountain sky. To me the night seemed vital, vivid, in motion. It pressed on my chest and if I closed my eyes I thought I was adrift on a great black rolling sea. I moved through its black waters like a great chambered nautilus and the old men and Elias were with me, always with me, a part of me, my ballast, that by which I kept my direction, set my course. And there was no room in those spiral chambers for nostalgia or regret or remorse, but only for the truth of things, in all their grace and joy, defeat and tragedy.

I liked closing my eyes and feeling all these things, wishing them so. Long after the old men had fallen asleep on the roof, I would lie there between them and continue my dream journey through the night, through its sea of obsidian-colored light.

The old men snored loudly on both sides of me. I felt their heat and closed my eyes.

That first night, the geese did not come. They did not come for three more nights, although, according to Emerson, both the time and weather were ripe. We had first heard them in October, a shocking, inspirational cacophony above a layer of wild gray clouds moving southwest. It was just at dusk when the sounds came, as suddenly and unexpectedly as dry summer thunder. A clarion call, unmistakable: the herald of change, life on the move. *Whongk. Whongk. Ga-honk. Ga-whonk. W-hongk. W-hongk.* We all leapt up from the kitchen table, rushed out into the backyard, scanned the heavy clouds. And the geese kept up their clatter, sounding as if they were directly overhead, calling to us, us alone. Albert said in an almost reverent voice, "It's a sign, son. A sign sure and inevitable. Tomorrow will be colder."

Almost every night thereafter the skies seemed crowded with winged travelers, thousands upon thousands of waterfowl moving south, taking the ember of life with them, hauling behind them the future, the hard winter ahead.

Albert began lugging the ladder from the barn to the house each evening, and if conditions seemed right, we would wake up at midnight, climb up on the roof, up toward the autumn skies. The old men's humble need was to reach into those skies, it seemed, to be among the ducks and geese, let the changing season sweep over them. But most nights the sky remained empty and we would talk in hushed voices to stay awake. Emerson thought the Reverend Biddle needed a night on the roof, "inside the great cathedral, on his back looking up, feeling the Great Mystery on his skin like ice water." Emerson thought it was a great pity that Reverend Biddle did not believe in the God we did not believe in. "For chrissakes, look what Conrad's missing. God? Here's whatever god or gods there are. In attendance here, now. Of the earth." And so it seemed. Earth as God; God as earth, its bones, flesh, stone, wind, and water. Here was

God's aim writ large. Life. One way or the other. With man or without him. And then Albert would change the mood and tell me about the time it rained ducks.

His big hands were tucked behind his head and in the sooty darkness his wild white hair shone like a cloud of dense fog. "No lie," he said. "Ask Emerson. Ask Elias Wonder. Ask anyone. It rained ducks. Not ordinary ducks, mind you, but frozen ducks." Emerson muffled a laugh and Albert rolled on his side toward me, propping his head on his elbow. "Was in late December of a hard and early winter. A Saturday, as I recall. Saturday, right, Emerson?"

"Saturday," Emerson agreed.

"About noon or so. Had been sleeting hard since before daylight. We were in town to store up on some beans and matches, fill the kerosene can. Elias had come with us and after reaching town had drifted into that other world of his, the one inside the mustard-gas cloud. He walked up and down the street introducing himself as Robert E. Lee and trying to give himself up. No one would accept his surrender. Anyways, just as he was assuring Mrs. Mabel Grath that he was indeed Robert E. Lee, poor Elias was knocked unconscious by what turned out to be a duck. A mallard. And it was frozen. Looked like one of them ice sculptures I've heard of. Perfectly preserved in ice and dead as dead gets. Hit Elias with the impact of a Joe Louis body punch.

"Mrs. Grath let out a curdling scream and in an instant the sky let loose with a whole barrage of frozen ducks. Dozens of them, each one iced-up in a different pose, and all of them with a look of surprise on their faces. One knocked a hole in the roof of the café and landed in one of Big Joe Dunklin's big pots and Big Joe ran like a madman out to the blackboard and changed the soup of the day from vegetable to duck gumbo. Two of them, their wings frozen straight out, as if they'd been iced in mid-flight, put a spectacular dent in Hupple's truck. Cost him nearly a hundred bucks to have the hood and roof pounded out.

"It rained ducks for at least five minutes. A hail of frostbitten waterfowl littered the street. Everyone went nuts, began stuffing the ice-blasted carcasses under their coats, in plastic bags, flinging them into the back of their pickups. I tell you, it was a banner day in Mount Hebron. The only disappointment was when Elias Wonder came to. He wasn't Robert E. Lee anymore. He was Elias Wonder and he was one pissed Indian. He felt the swelling lump on his head, took one look at the stiff duck at his feet and the screaming Mrs. Grath, balanced the apparent equation and with a great surge of energy began chasing Mrs. Grath down the road, swinging that frozen mallard over his head. He'd have caught her too if he'd had shoes on and didn't keep slipping and falling down. Then he dropped the frozen duck and like cheap pottery it broke into a dozen pieces.

"Meteorologists came to town, along with state wildlife biologists, all of them tossing about scientific explanations and logical reasons for the phenomenon. And everyone smiled and nodded and knew they were crazy as hell, because the day it rained ducks was a day of genuine wild portent and mystery."

Emerson had to admit he would never abandon the image of Elias skating precariously on the highway's sheet of ice, the duck held high over his head like a mallet, his eyes fixed on the nimble-footed Mrs. Grath, wailing, "First you give us blankets full of smallpox and diptheria, then you take our land, and now you bring on us a plague of frozen ducks."

We had started our vigil on the roof three days after coming down out of the high country, where Emerson had been tracking a big buck since spring, sometimes staying up in hills for days at a time. Emerson had recruited us to accompany him, and so, bedrolls packed, canteens full, we set out for the dark distant ridge before dawn. Emerson led the way as we crossed the creek below Cody's Rock, began moving across the rocky face of Tavern Ridge. Dead leaves swirled on a strong, stinging wind, and the land smelled of rot, more sweet than putrid, a heady smell that clung to our boots and coats. Past the ridge, we hiked to Bluff Mountain, then up Mount Bethel, rising more than seven hundred feet above the creek. Below, the farmhouse looked so distant, so tiny and insignificant.

It got colder, and the cold became a pain as sharp as shattered glass, numbing our faces, throbbing in our hands and feet. By noon we had gained the summit of Big Horse Mountain. Turning slightly west, we descended the other side until we came to the right branch of Elk Creek. There we camped against a huge outcrop of stone that sheltered us from the wind and ate cold bacon and beans and waited out the night huddled together, no one sleeping, each of us longing for the first smudge of smoky gray light in the sky. Emerson said the deer was too close for a fire.

The next morning, Emerson slipped away from the rocks, moved down the creek through floating columns of fog, and reappeared like a ghost high above us, signaling us to join him. Once on the ridge, we hunkered down behind a fallen tree, decaying, a withered gray corpse. No one spoke. The forest seemed without sounds that morning. No wind among the trees, no owl bewailing the building light, no birds along the creek; the creek itself moving as silently as rising mist. Below our hiding place was a small oak sapling as thick as a fencepost whose trunk the big buck had rubbed raw with its antlers. The bark had been peeled away, exposing the tree's soft tissue, pink as young flesh.

Emerson had seen the deer, watched it, tracked it. More than once, he and Albert had talked well into the night about this deer, whether it was the right deer to take. Emerson put its age at three years. A mature buck, one that had had time to mate, to put the grace and power of its genes among the deer of these mountains. Taking it for our meat, enough meat for the year ahead, would leave many others that would carry its traits of beauty and survival, endurance and cunning. The deer, they thought, had seen its best years. Soon time would overtake it, if they did not. Emerson was certain the deer would not last another winter.

And we waited. An hour. Then another. The fog thinned, began to dissipate under a hard gray sky. Suddenly a slight noise, a rustle, as if a wind were rattling among the dying leaves. Emerson nudged Albert. Slowly, following Albert's movements, I turned to the right, saw it at the edge of a small opening in the woods near the creek. It was obscured by thick brush, only its massive head and muscular neck visible. So huge was its head that at first I thought it was a feral mule. I strained to focus the hazy form and saw the great dark eyes, keen, cautious, weary, reluctant. It moved out a step. One step only, then raised its head into the wind, dissecting the smells, suspicious of them all, even the wildest of them. Slabs of muscle rippled beneath its somber winter coat. The creature was poised in a moment of exquisite tension, ready to bound back into the safety of the dark woods.

All these years later, I cannot say much about its antlers, the size of it, the number of points. Such things did not matter to us. We were not there above Elk Creek as trophy hunters, sportsmen out for a hunt. To us it was like all of its kind, a beast of great worth and beauty, raw wildness, as enviable to us as the creek's trout, the field's quail, the slough's turkeys, the bobcats which moved down from the hills at night and moved among us, noiseless as shadows.

How quiet that moment seemed, as if the whole earth had suddenly held its breath. Even when the deer dropped its head to feed, its dark, alert eyes took in everything that at that moment was its whole world, that small clearing along the creek.

Albert eased the barrel of the big .308 onto the trunk of the dead tree, his movements like those of a mime, every muscle straining in silence. The wind blew from across the creek and the deer did not smell us, that distinctive, dangerous odor of human beings. Albert put the rifle's sight on the deer's neck, just behind the head, held his breath, and squeezed the trigger.

The deer slumped to the damp ground, as if gravity itself had suddenly raised up and grabbed it, pulled it flat against the creek bank. A long moment of tension, fear of a wound instead of instant death. Albert kept his arms steady against the dead tree, his eyes narrowed, looking straight down the barrel of the .308. Then Emerson stood, jumped the fallen tree, ran down the hill. Albert retrieved the spent shell, put it thoughtfully in his coat pocket.

The shot had killed the deer at once, snapping its neck. A surprisingly clean hole, I remember thinking, for something that was so deadly. We cleaned the big buck there along Elk Creek just up from Turner's Hollow, its warm blood spilling onto the moist, cold ground. We butchered the meat, salted it, put it in bags, then wrapped the bags in large squares of leather. Since the deer had not been chased, had not run terrified, the meat lacked that sorrowful taste of defeat, that taint of panic, a last run for survival. The rest of it, even the great antlers, we left there in the woods, a winter offering to the high country for its bounty.

While we often went into the high country that winter, we never took another deer. The big buck had filled our larder and for that we were grateful. And for the rest of that winter we would spend many an hour beyond Big Horse Peak watching deer, admiring them, enjoying them, their character like that of the high country, indomitable. The big .308 stayed at the house, locked away in the gun cabinet, replaced on our hikes by a pair of cheap binoculars Albert had ordered in the 1930s through the Sears Roebuck catalog.

That was the same winter we spent nearly a week in the mountains beyond Cracker-Jack Creek on the far side of Blue Top Mountain searching for a mountain lion. Leaman Swertz, a hog farmer at the far end of the valley, claimed to have spotted one at his place. We drove over to Leaman's farm and looked at the tracks out behind one of the slopping pens. Albert knelt down, touched the tracks lightly, as if too much contact might ruin them, erase the wonderful excitement of a big cat being spotted in these hills after so many years. When man had come, the big cats were hunted down or driven out. Or so everyone assumed. But it seemed every year someone would rush into town, announce that he had seen a mountain lion, heard again that piercing, bone-mashing scream, the sound of "death itself," a sound that, everyone knew, would eventually drive a man mad. And a group of men would go off into the hills and find nothing and kill deer and drink gallon after gallon of Elias Wonder's whiskey.

These tracks were different, though. I knew that by the way Albert kept touching the imprint, the crusted, caved-in ground that had recorded, for an instant, the creature's size, its weight, its direction of travel. Albert brushed away the crushed leaves, nodded his head, and grinned. The next morning we left, heading north, toward Blue Mountain and Henry's Peak, toward the Missouri line. Almost immediately Albert found another set of tracks, along the main fork of Judy's Creek. Again, headed north, which puzzled Albert because he thought the big cat would have changed direction, turned west toward what Albert called *mauvaises terres*, the badlands of northern Oklahoma, a country still rugged and isolated enough to suit the cat's sullen disposition.

The days in the mountains were bright, clear, cold, the sun almost flat on the horizon by midafternoon and the valleys dark chilly vaults of cold stone and earth. On the third night we made camp along a beautiful creek above a place Emerson called Abram's Gap. The night turned bad, gloomy, the stars hidden by ashen-gray clouds moving on strong winds from the west. Before dawn it began to drizzle, the mist gradually changing to ice that stuck to our hats and coats.

Albert heard it first, knew it at once. The sound came just as the coffee reached a boil over the fire. At first I thought it was a peal of distant thunder. Calmly, Albert walked up to the rocky precipice above the camp. Once more, that sound, a cry from deep in the hills, far back out of the light, a sound of the night, as if the night itself had shrieked, let out a scream that was more hypnotic than frightening. A primitive sound, one that stirred the imagination.

Albert walked back to the fire, stood close to its heat, the flashing orange light highlighting his face. I remembered seeing Elias Wonder's face captured in the light of his lantern, how tired that peculiar light had made him look. Now, by firelight, Albert too seemed weary, the years finally showing on him. The big cat screamed again in the far distance. Albert smiled and took a cup of coffee from Emerson. "Big one," he said at last, the words registering no great enthusiasm. "Probably on the far side of the knob. Finally moving west of north. Knew he would. Couldn't believe he'd set foot in Missouri, not with the open lands of Oklahoma so near. He might make it there, maybe."

And he sat by the fire and I put the biscuits on and we ate and packed our bedrolls and started the walk back toward Trail's End, back home. On the north side of the Blue Mountain it began to snow.

By the time we had started our vigil on the roof, looking for the first great migration of Canada geese heading for the rice fields of central Arkansas, east Texas, and Louisiana, the ducks had already been on the wing for some time.

The old men had a small and mostly unimpressive duck blind down in the flooded timber of the oak sloughs. It was a homemade wooden johnboat painted drab green. Advocates of proper waterfowl fashion, the old men had decorated the leaky boat with massive bundles of winter grasses, cattails, and corn stalks lashed to its sides. Tied securely to a nearby oak tree, the boat was more platform than vessel. Emerson first heard mallards—greenheads—overhead in October, and their calls, like trout breaking on the surface of the creek at dusk, sent his temperature soaring. His cheeks went flushed, turned the faded burgundy color of beets just dug from the earth.

The presence of waterfowl meant the onset of change, one season's passage, another's arrival. The old men believed that ducks, like trout, served as testimony to the land's health, its vitality, life's continued endurance. The sound of ducks on the wing: the message of renewal, revival, diversity. These predictable natural rhythms signaled the earth's trust, which seemed absolute and unconditional. Only men doubted the earth, because they could calculate the damage of their lives, imagine the consequences of their actions, wrap their future in the same tragedies as their past.

Ducks brought the old men all this, not only pleasure but pain, the pain of memory. Two nights before we went down to the duck blind, they told me how as young men they had hired out as hunting guides in the duck country down around Stuttgart. In those days there were so many ducks on the autumn winds that sometimes the flocks all but blocked out the sun. Thousands upon thousands of them. And the two young men from the hills would take the eager hunters from Little Rock and Memphis, Dallas and St. Louis, out into the rice fields before dawn and show them how to kill ducks. The hunters fired their big shotguns until the guns felt like solid iron in their freezing hands, until their shoulders ached, throbbed, jumped in painful muscular spasms, and by day's end were tattooed with painful purple bruises. Kill ducks they did, and no one worried over it because it always seemed that for every duck they brought down another five took its place. Winter skies had been black with migrating ducks for as long as the young men could remember. They led the hunters out and shot from dawn until twilight when the light rippled at the horizon, and the men filled strings of johnboats with the day's kill. Hundreds of ducks, of every kind, so many that they could hardly move the johnboats through the shallow water.

That had been more than forty years ago. So very long ago. And now fewer ducks came. Each year their numbers grew smaller. And while the reasons for the decline in the duck population went far beyond the old men's youthful overkilling, they blamed themselves for the loss; it haunted them, plagued them, ate away at their hearts. Those years when they had killed so nimbly, efficiently, feeling no concern, no emotion at all, seemed, I thought, their greatest shame. In the fall, sadness glossed their eyes and the first sound of ducks overhead was like a choral prayer, a visible sign that perhaps, after all the passing years, the earth had forgiven them. And every year the ducks returned and life went on and the old men were thankful and reassured, hopeful, because they believed that nothing was in-finitely fixed, but was as fluid as time.

Their invitation to join them in the duck blind was deliv-ered with grudging reticence. "You don't really want to go down there and sit for hours in the cold, do you?" asked Albert, handing me a box of shotgun shells.

Emerson, sitting at the kitchen table, brought up a great sigh from deep in his old chest. "I've never seen a body so determined to take on so many of life's agonies at once. Trout, ducks, quail, turkeys. All of it. You're playing the dead man's hand, son. Give it some thought."

I did, and took the shells, and the shotgun, and got my coat. Cody scratched at the back door impatiently, then paced back and forth, whining and yelping. A seam of light, no thicker than a thread, marked the worn peaks of the mountains. Cody knew it was time. If Cody delighted in trout and was confused by quail, he was overwhelmed by the mere possibility of ducks, all they entailed: the cold; the long, cramped hours in the little boat; the prospect of icy rain or snow; the rattle of wings on the wind; the coal-black silhouettes soaring above the trees; almost floating on the wind like ragged bits of dark con-fetti; the bite of the autumn wind; ducks calling wildly from behind pale gray clouds. Cody trembled, he shook, he fought, usually in vain, to temper his eagerness to leap into the slough's cold, dark water to retrieve a downed duck, this winged creature that so troubled his dreams and excited his blood and had a wildness to it that set off something wild and primitive in himself. Cody never got enough of ducks, and long after we had left the blind he stayed behind, the passionate hunter.

The ducks would fly low over the slough, just above the trees, dipping near the water to consider the handsome decoys the old men had carved and I had painted, six of them, floating contentedly on the water, obviously safe, fat, at ease. My paint job was hardly art. I had strived only for the temptation of greens and browns, a touch of white, and every one with calm brown eyes. Each decoy had cost us only the price of the paint. The old men had always carved their own decoys. Twenty years later in Charleston, South Carolina, I would watch a man happily pay $11,000 for an old, crudely made decoy. The thing looked like a hard-luck rooster. "Why?" I asked him, looking again at the decoy, doubting not only its beauty to a duck, but its worth as a collector's item. "A work of art," the man boasted proudly while writing out a check. "Grand primitive art. Notice how the low-grade, uneducated backwoods hunter managed to capture the essence of duckness."

The essence of duckness. Perhaps that's what Cody was after, what he never tired of.

Auctioning our antique duck decoys would have tickled Albert, made him laugh, just as he laughed when I told him that his L. C. Smith shotgun had become something of a collector's item and was worth a good deal of money. I gave him this good news the day the doctor looked at his X rays and saw the tumor in his brain that was not only killing him but erasing his memory, gobbling up entire decades of his life. Every morning afterward, the dying old man sat weakly at the kitchen table as Emerson held a cup of coffee to his cracked white lips, whispering all the while, "There, there, Albert. There, there."

When I told him about the shotgun, he said he had bought it from Bates for $22. "That's all it is, son," he said firmly, unimpressed by what he saw as the gun's illogical increase in value. "Just a twenty-two-dollar shotgun that shoots high."

Before going down to the duck blind, Albert would count out nine shotgun shells. Three apiece. Gone were the days of waterfowl slaughter, at least on their little piece of land. Our passion was not the kill. There was no joy in squeezing the trigger. The joy came from the season and from all that the ducks were, their image and their reality. Like trout, the old men saw their lives as important, precious, of worth. The season's greatest pleasures lay in the lives of the ducks, not in the deaths of those few we took to help feed us. Each morning's trek down to the blind had little to do with sport; rather, it was yet another attempt to be not only on the land, but of it, one more tendril of life along the creek, a life whose fortunes were our fortunes, whose future was no more secure than our own. Perhaps that is why we spent so many days in the blind not shooting, but just watching. And each day was one of great enthusiasm and adventure. Just the distant sound of wings coming off the water at dawn, a rustle like wind blowing through tall grasses, brought a childlike glow to Albert's fading old eyes.

Nine shells for no more than six ducks, the shells so old that their casings were solid brass. No paper. No plastic. Six ducks. Makings for hot gumbo, the sharp, spicy taste of winter skies which we would still be sipping in the cool, rainy days of March or the last sultry days of July. The past as nourishment; the sweet taste of memory. Nine shells. Cody knew by the sound of them in our coat pockets how his fortunes were faring. When the clicking stopped altogether, he knew our hunting was done and he no longer waited for us at all, but raced out the back door in the early morning darkness and sat alone in the johnboat, barking ecstatically at the sky. On those mornings when there were shells, I sat in the rear of the boat, my arms tight around Cody's neck, feeling his muscles ripple with impassioned anticipation. Hunkered down in the front, the old men, dressed in drab greens and browns, called the ducks by mouth. Neither had ever owned a duck call. If pressed, the human vocal cords could do the work, and they were free and much more reliable.

As he called, Albert's Adam's apple bobbed, twitched, shook, waged, pumped, wavered, oscillated, warbled, conjured up sounds that faithfully imitated each species of duck he spied— the small whistling teals, the big mallards with their hoarse cough, the canvasbacks, the disappearing black ducks. And each time Albert called, Cody lunged forward and I held him tight, digging my hands into his long fur, certain he would at any moment drag both of us overboard and into the slough's raw, icy waters.

"Keep a hold on that upstart, son," Emerson said in a scolding whisper. "He'll announce us to every duck west of the river if he sees the opportunity. A character flaw. One we share, I suppose. Ducks tend to overexcite us both, fog our reason."

I imagined Albert as some odd caricature of a mockingbird, a living symphony of the most curious, enthralling, atavistic sounds. There seemed no wild utterance he could not mimic: the fox circling the chicken coop; the hawks taking quail at the edge of the cornfield; the crows socializing along the highway, a black-cloaked fraternity gathering there to wait for a good feed, a fresh road kill. They had learned that pickup trucks were efficient killers, but incomprehensible, because they always left their prey behind with coldhearted indifference. Albert could counterfeit the scream of the bobcats that came down out of the high country at dusk; quarrelsome chickens; a big buck grunting in a foggy November wood; bobwhite quail calling at evening, a high, lilting whistle; Cody growling in his sleep; geese sounding like the brass section of a mediocre high school band; the eerie, tumultuous, uproarious caterwauling of spring turkeys.

How Albert enjoyed the earth's sounds, true and pure and so wonderfully chaotic. He had learned to duplicate these sounds on his harmonica: nature as the blues. It was wonderful: the life of the mountains in wailing, mournful riffs of Sonny Terry, Little Walter and Big Walter Horton. Listening to him, I would close my eyes and imagine that the Creation had taken place in the middle of Clarksdale, Mississippi. Blues country.

"I don't think these ducks will shimmy or boogie on down to a chorus of Little Walter," Emerson scoffed, and Albert, laughing under his breath, put the Hohner away and called again. In time, four greenheads came in low over the trees from the east, took shape gradually in the day's dappled gray sky. "All males," whispered Emerson. Cody shook terribly, rocking the boat. "Steady that beast, son," Emerson said, his voice barely audible. The greenheads made one pass, never slowing. The decoys, wearing a fresh coat of paint, bobbed temptingly beyond the hidden boat. Circling quickly, the ducks came in lower, this time from the west. On cupped wings they seemed almost to float down toward the water. It had begun to rain, an icy rain. Cody buckled and strained, his adrenaline boiling.

In one simple, graceful movement, Emerson shouldered the double-barreled shotgun and took the two lead ducks. Cody launched into the water before the sound of the second barrel had dwindled to a meek echo in the thick, dark woods beyond us. Emerson tucked the expended hulls into his shirt pocket. And we watched Cody smiling a toothy grin, swimming joyfully in that frosty water, finding the first duck, taking it into his mouth as gently as he did the trout.

All too quickly the nine shells were spent. With his fine ear, Cody could distinguish between the dull clink of loaded shells and the hollow rattle of spent hulls. As the hulls grew in number, Cody would mope about, knowing that his yearly adventure with ducks was ending.

To lift his spirits, the old men hunted quail one day a month beginning in October. As with the ducks, the quail too had suffered greatly from loss of habitat and the inexorable press of civilization. Like Albert's memory, the quail too were fading away, disappearing, victims of cancer of another kind. That the old farm still had quail at all was a wonder, a miracle as divine and bewildering, Emerson thought, as the Reverend Biddle's holy touch, the hand that had raised Haysberry's milk cow from the dead.

"Thank the gods we're old and at death's door," said Emerson as we walked the north edge of the fifteen-acre pea field. "So much of what has been our life seems headed for the same fate. Better we go ahead and die than be around on a piece of ground with nothing wild for company." Albert nodded his agreement.

Fall was census time. We walked the hedgerows, the fallow fields, the thick cover along the fields and old paths, flushing coveys, counting birds. Quail had been on the land since before the old Confederate showed up. The old men had known quail all their lives. Once the birds had ranged throughout the valley. No more. For some inexplicable reason a handful hung on at Trail's End, though for years their numbers had been dwindling. While we walked, Albert explained his theory of "natural" versus "unnatural" extinction. "See, now Emerson and I are old and used up. We are examples of natural extinction—not of a species, but of a certain time and a certain manner of living. But these quail, they are evidence of unnatural extinction, in that their value as a species has not naturally run its course. Rather, they are being hurried on into oblivion by ruinous outside forces."

Emerson came to a stop, huffing. "Come out and say it plain and clear, you overinflated sack of skin. Quail ran into human beings and that was it for the quail."

"That's about it, brother Emerson," Albert agreed.

Emerson walked up close to the rear of the barn, where a rack of aged firewood backed up to an immense pile of limbs and brush, the longtime home of Ian's Covey, named for Albert's son who died at birth and whose name Albert's tumor had now completely erased.

By then Cody had got the scent of the birds and drew up short at the brush pile, his head so low that his nose nearly touched the ground. As usual, his exuberance got the best of him and his front paws began to inch forward.

"Steady, beast!" Emerson said. Cody knew the serious tone

and held. "Let me get into my counting position."

My job was to back up Emerson's count.

"Scatter them!" Emerson cried suddenly, and Cody vaulted forward and the quail burst into the air, a blur of feathers, shapes speeding off in all directions in dizzying roller-coaster patterns of flight, wings whistling through the still air. Rather than climbing for height, they flew close to the ground; these quail trusted their safety to the ground cover, the endless wrinkles of topography, rather than to the blank openness of the sky.

"Nine males, six females," Emerson said confidently, watching the last bird land at the edge of the woods. It hit the ground running; you could see the winter grass tremble as the bird raced into the trees, to the safety of the dense shadows.

"Fifteen," said Emerson, and turned to me. "Is that right?"

"Right," I said, though I had actually stopped counting at six so I could give myself completely to watching the quail in flight, listening to them on the wing.

In a week's time the quail count was done. Emerson brought out his quail log, a frayed and yellowed notebook that contained the details of the farm's quail population and genealogy back to at least 1900. In 1902 there had been twenty-nine coveys scattered about the farm. In the fall of 1966 we counted but ten. In 1906 the coveys averaged nineteen birds each; in 1966 they averaged less than twelve. In 1903 the family had taken 110 birds; in 1966 we would take less than fifteen.

Albert lay on the lumpy sofa chewing aspirin. I put a blanket over him and he nodded his thanks. Emerson sent me for more wood. I piled the thick logs high in my arms, determined to haul in enough for an entire evening's fire. As I stacked the wood on either side of the hearth, Emerson started reading off the list of coveys that we had not found, that had left or died out over the last year. He read the list of names the way a man might read a list of dead friends, gravely but, too, with a touch of remembered pleasure at having known them, been among them at all.

"Oak Tree Covey... Clinchville Covey... Mailbox Covey ... Woollum's Covey... Yankton Covey... Faulkner Covey ... Wonder's Covey. We will miss them," Emerson said, closing the log. "And the world they took with them."

"Wonder who?" asked Albert, popping another handful of aspirins into his mouth and tucking the blanket under his chin. "God, but it's freezing in here."

The next morning, Emerson opened a box of old 20-gauge shotgun shells—four for me, six split between him and Albert. Cody waited anxiously at the back door.

That season we took eight quail: I had missed two birds, wasting two shells. Despite our efforts at conservation, the quail fared poorly; nature treated them as it always had. The hawks took their share, as did heavy weather. And in the winter the quail appeased the deep, gnawing hunger of many a predator. It was the way of things, and by spring there were two fewer coveys. Those that had made it moved farther into the woods, higher into the hills, there to await the spring, the sun's warmth, the stirring in their blood to mate, breed, carry on.

On the third cold night of that week in November, after we had climbed the ladder to the roof and spread out our quilts, the geese finally came. It was well after midnight when we first heard them, way off above the hills, low in the sky, their calls a rollicking, vibrating sound, irascible and blaring as diesel horns. Moonlight shone on the damp grass, glimmered for an instant on the wings of the big, dark birds as they flew overhead, not in elegant, precise formations but in tattered lines, reminiscent of an apprentice tailor's first stitched seams. No perfectly straight wedges, but a weave of birds, their grace individual as well as collective.

The night pressed so hard against my chest I thought I would lose my breath and pass out. The geese came on, moving like wisps of dark clouds in a heavy wind, moving in and out of the moonlight, calling madly. And I began to think of all the books I had read of late, all the biology and astronomy, all the chemistry and physics, yet, staring up at the geese, I knew that they had not prepared me for this. They had taught me so little. I wondered why God would secret himself away from such creation. I thought of Elias Wonder telling me that God, the Great Mystery, was creation. On such a night it was hard not to believe the old madman.

The geese were overhead, dancing to the music of the earth, the ancient movements that thickened their blood. On that cold night atop the farmhouse roof, it seemed to me that life evolved with the earth, not in spite of it. The old men lay there looking up, saying nothing, just looking and smiling and seeming young again, expecting nothing of the earth and accepting everything. Suddenly I felt drained of thought. I was moving with the geese, a life of instinct, and I remembered the eyes of the dying deer, and the trout, and thought then that looking into them I had somehow stared deep into the earth's dark, uncompromising energy. I remembered what Albert had said to Elias Wonder at Karen's Pool. "When I want to check the health of the universe, old man, I look into a trout's eyes. I have never known them to lie."

"Well, the messengers have come," Emerson said from beneath the mound of quilts.

"Amen," said Albert.

Emerson sat up. "Bless them for coming," he said. "For giving us another year, another chance."

I slept little that first night before going into the oakwood bottoms. A cool, soft wind blew limply through the open window, filled the room. Sometime after midnight the wind changed direction, turned to the north, blew across the creek and smelled of rain and pungent molds and the sharp sweet odor of wild onions. My shoulders ached, every muscle feeling as though it had been bound by tight knots of rope. Although it was only early April, my shoulders tingled from sunburn. Each day's heat stayed with me through the long night, a dull persistent pain. The daily work in the fields and garden seemed endless, a struggle without promise of outcome, but I did not mind, for it brought a kind of forgiving exhaustion and eroded the boundaries of time. The days blended one into another and I did not rue their passage. Indeed, I let them go willingly, let them go as though they were the cold swift waters of the creek flowing effortlessly through open fingers.

Leaning against the bed's smooth pine backboard, I felt and listened to the night, watched its festival of subdued light and shadows. No matter the hour, how apparently quiet the moment, the valley never truly settled into either complete darkness or complete silence. From the window, I saw billowy clouds moving across the sky, tracking northeast. Pools of mottled moonlight flashed across the greening fields and vanished into the thick woods, the trees heavy with new leaves. Where the moonlight reached the forest floor, the light looked muted, yellow-green. On the surface of the creek tendrils of light played on the moving water as though they were something alive, journeying with the water, moonlight and creek mixing with one another.

Although I had been with the old men but six months, I had already found comfort, even security, in many things, including the supple, sonorous nights, their reassuring hush broken by barred owls calling from the oakwood sloughs, the sound more like the rattled growl of a wary dog than an innocent hoot. Some nights, out near the woods, I could hear the brittle leaves cracking like thin sheets of ice, a sound that told me coyotes were near, ears erect, noses to the wind, eyes wild and dark. And each night an old gray fox came around, announced his presence boldly scratching and banging at the chicken coop's shaky gate. The gate was held closed by a twist of frayed electrical wire. So far it had held fast, but the fox's blood knew patience and determination, and his pinching hunger lusted after corn-fed, lazy, spoiled chickens. The frequency and ferocity of his nightly attacks never lessened, as if he knew that fortune favored his future more than the chickens.

Raccoons traveled with the long shadows of twilight just as the horizon blurred into a panorama of bruised purples; they checked the big yard for edible delicacies, then waddled into the garden for a quick salad before sojourning down by the creek, where they sat like a clique of squat, furry Buddhas nimbly angling the shallows for crawfish, a meal they especially relished. The snap of the small crustacean's body between a raccoon's teeth produced a distinctive sound that reminded me of the sharp snap made by a bone violently popped from its socket.

No night passed that Cody's snore, a high-pitched whinny followed by a slow, restful sigh, did not permeate the room. Always a dog of high aspirations, Cody had a fertile and prolific dream life marked by conviction rather than whim. The subject of his dreams remained a private matter, but each night, without fail, he would stretch across the foot of my bed and slip immediately into his uneasy snore, his feet twitching, his legs jerking. Before long, his breathing accelerated, and he was gulping air like a long-distance runner. Then, abruptly, he began wheezing, coughing, groaning, and his breathing became so shallow that his chest seemed hardly to expand and fall. Emerson had a simple explanation for Cody's career as a somnambulist. The dog was crazy, mad as a hatter, loony as Chester, a rooster he had had on the place who spent his life hiccuping every time he meant to crow. Albert harbored a different theory about Cody. Once fast asleep, he believed, Cody chased the things in dream he couldn't catch while conscious. No, he didn't conjure up rabbits or quail or trout. These quarry were plentiful enough out the back door. Cody, declared Albert firmly, closed his eyes and set about chasing love.

One night as we stood by the fireplace in the big room looking down at Cody, who was lying on his back with his four legs stuck ramrod straight in the air, Albert turned to me, slowly shaking his head. "Look at that, boy. Ain't it dowright pitiful. He's got it bad, real bad."

"Got what?" I asked. I studied the old dog for a long moment and decided there was the smallest trace of a smile on his handsome gold and black face.

"Girl troubles. Women have been driving him to distraction for years."

I grunted, disguising my confusion. As far as I knew, Cody had led a life of unswerving celibacy. Like Emerson, Albert, and me, he was but one more male in a household bereft of women.

"But, Uncle Albert," I said, "Cody doesn't have a woman —you know, a girlfriend."

"True, son," said Albert. "Still, that's what's doing him in, haunting his dreams. Bachelorhood can be a crippling condition. Look at what it's done to me, five times over. And the old man. Christ, we're as mopey and dyspeptic as that old wretch Elias Wonder. Hell, I've tucked that old maniac in enough times to know. Ten seconds under the sheets and that wrinkled, suety appendage he's still lucky enough to have for a leg is pumping away. You can hear all the ill-mended bones creaking." Albert patted me sorrowfully on the shoulder and disappeared, a long, thin shadow drifting down the dark hallway leading to the stairs. A lonely sigh punctuated his fading mumbling.

In my room at night, I rubbed the shiny pink scars that rippled over my hands and forearms like freshly raised welts. Months before, Emerson had cut the stitches out with his Barlow pocketknife and the flesh still itched and pinched. I traced the scars in the darkness, purls of swollen flesh. In the corner the old dream crouched, a permanent resident, always ready to nuzzle at my pillow. No longer a frightening nightmare, a thing with fangs and cold hands leaving me cringing in the morning light, tangled in the bedclothes like a corpse in a death shroud. No, it was too familiar now; it came too often. I felt it each night, alive and waiting in the shadows of my room. Even before I closed my eyes, I knew it would come and drag me again into that icy stainless-steel room doused in a harsh white light. Every inch of the room was metallic, slick, cold to the touch. A white sheet lay over a drab green stretcher. No air stirred within the icy room and nothing moved. Even though I knew what was beneath that crisp sheet, I always looked, irresistibly drawn to it, its black, haunting secret. Night after night, I pulled back that sheet and my throat tightened again upon seeing there on that green canvas stretcher a single blot of dark crimson blood. From floor to ceiling along the room's four walls were aluminum vaults shut inside metal drawers. In the dream, I rummaged through these boxes like a madman. I yanked them out of the wall, tossed them desperately to the floor. There were hundreds of boxes. The work took hours: a nighttime. There was no point, it seemed, no conclusion. In that world of antiseptic steel, that mortuary of confusion and terror, my search yielded only that single drop of accusing blood.

When the dream first came, I would wake up soaked in sweat, muscles cramped, hands trembling. The dream seemed an unfinished game of hide-and-seek. Obviously, I was searching for something. What I could not figure out, though, was exactly what I sought in that shivering morgue. Finally, I constructed an answer: I was looking for Norwell, any trace of him, what he had been, that boy of flesh and bone the moment before he vaporized in a hot shower of exploding grenade fragments. I wanted irrefutable evidence of his existence. Despite my theory, my desperate interpretations, the dream continued.

It still comes, though less often as the years pass, and I am no longer certain what the steel room, that metal table, those tiers of metal boxes and that drop of blood mean or portend. Norwell? All those dead and gone? Or perhaps something harder to comprehend or recover—innocence lost, forgotten, forever lamented?

The only night sound muting Cody's dreamy antics was the ancient house's incessant creaking. Like a floundering ship, it seemed to list regularly. Each lurch produced an unnerving chorus of grating, scraping noises. My room, normally cathedral quiet, became a broken-down carnival organ, all the stops wide open. And all in an unsettling instant. Everywhere, wood—old, warped, decaying—wrestled with its burden, its hopeless struggle to remain intact, an inviolable asylum. While this ever-impending architectural collapse failed to disturb Cody or the old men, it terrified Horatio, a ragged, one-eyed cat who looked as though he'd been dragged over a painter's palette, ending up a motley gold and brown, black and white, orange and tiger-striped. Horatio padded gloomily about the place, his one good eye peeled for the telltale signs of catastrophe. He expected bad news the way other cats looked forward to fresh milk and fat mice. He adored sitting on the front porch waiting for night, when his vanishing eyesight no longer mattered. In the darkness he was just another motion among motions, a sound with needle-sharp claws.

All of this, and so much more, stirred in my mind, wiggled like a catfish drifting in dark slow muddy water, until I saw the streak of lamplight shoot across the dark hallway. I heard the sound of running water and knew Albert was up and in the bathroom already, getting the water hot for his morning shave. The leather razor strap cracked like a whip as Albert worked the straight razor against it. Because of the strawberries and the garden, the constant attention both demanded, he and Emerson hadn't shaved all week.

Before dawn we walked into the wide rows of strawberry plants clogging the field west of the barn and labored through the day, mostly on our hands and knees. Although strawberries were ill-suited to both the ground and the climate, every year the old men managed to coax fat, juicy berries out of the weary soil. Emerson was especially attentive to the plants, seeing to their every whim, watering and cursing them with equal vigor. When in late fall the first cold winds filled the valley from the north and west, he moved nimbly among the young plants, gently wrapping a muffler of pine straw around each plant's delicate throat.

Emerson believed in plants, though he never completely trusted them. After all, nothing could turn on a man with such cold, merciless indifference as a plant. A curious blight, a virulent plague, a sudden storm, an unyielding march of insects could sour a man's agricultural fortunes with woeful abruptness, lance his emotions, eviscerate his always desperate accounts. Even so, when it came to strawberries, Emerson defused his usually thick-coated cynicism. Strawberries only rarely let him down and their hardiness bought him rich returns. He liked them. They had pluck. They endured, put some spare change in one pocket and handfuls of free time in the other, time to let the land rest while he and Albert mended a fence or pursued a trout, repaired a shingle or walked up a covey of quail along a ridge of tangled wild plum, painted the barn or hiked the valley along the banks of Starlight Creek. Strawberries funded all of these comforting celebrations.

Holidays at my father's house were mandatory observances. Flags got raised and appropriate hymns, strongly patriotic, were sung off key as suitable toasts were raised in excited enthusiasm. If a holiday called for the exchange of cards, then cards were dutifully exchanged. Since Christmas carried with it a ritual of gift giving, gifts, inexpensive rather than necessarily useful or desirable, were given ("I ain't no goddamned general," he'd say as he dropped me off at the PX with a crumpled twenty-dollar bill in my hand, that to cover presents for at least ten family members).

When I first came to the mountains, it was nearly December, a tireless procession of cold and rainy days. For days, thick columns of stone-gray clouds choked the valley. The wind blew icy and hard, threatening snow, and Christmas got closer and closer. I awaited the first signs of celebration. None arrived. The old men went on as they always had—working, eating, reading, dreaming—and hours gave way to days and days to weeks. No time was put aside to fell a Christmas pine as perfect as anything from a print by Currier & Ives. No cheerful decorations came down from the attic, no guests arrived at the door brimming with gifts and brotherly love and eager for a jar of Elais' homemade whiskey to warm their stomachs. No one raised a cup to hail in the festive season. Outside, no big red bow was wrapped around our mailbox, no tiny bells jingled merrily above the front door. Nothing changed, in fact, except that the work got harder and the weather got colder. Days became colors, shades of gray, clouds of soot swept together as if in a storm. Finally, it began to snow, and it snowed hard for days. The pond froze and the mountains became a monotonous topography of white. Outside, in the barn, the chickens trembled, too cold even to manage a respectable cackle.

Three days before Christmas, Albert came in with a long, skinny pine bough graced with one sagging brown cone. Smiling wildly, he placed the bough on the mantel in the big room, stood several paces back, and admired his skill at interior decorating. In spite of its gloomy look and emaciated character, the pine bough, in a day's time, would soak the room with a delightfully sweet smell. The whole ritual had taken no more than five minutes, then Albert tapped me on the shoulder and we returned to the woodpile outside the back door. He swung the ax as though it were weightless, neatly splitting the heavy logs into halves, then quarters. He split each log with a single stroke that ended in a raspy sigh. That winter, Albert turned eighty-five. As he worked the ax, his breath formed small white clouds of exhaled warmth that rose on the icy wind. Late that night, we all sat in the big room and delighted in the sweet smell of the pine bough and no one spoke a word.

That simple pine bough lifted my spirits. It seemed there might be cause for celebration after all. The next day, during a trip to town, I smuggled $10 my father had given me before leaving Okinawa into Bates's store and wandered the long narrow aisles stocked with canned foods and cloth, dry goods and work boots, tools and shotguns, colognes and wallpaper. Unable to decide, I walked and walked, touching everything as if it held some wonderful mystery. Albert and Emerson had gone to the café to split a bowl of chili. Albert liked to spike his with hefty doses of pepper and Tabasco sauce. He washed it all down with a pitcher of ice water. Of a more cautious nature, Emerson took his chili, like his whiskey, straight.

When I passed the first aisle for the fourth or fifth time, Mr. Bates eyed me wearily, like an old bull trout sizing up an insect floating helplessly on the surface of the stream above him. Finally, he took to following me around. In a voice vibrating with annoyance he asked if he could help me. I went on looking, my search unrelenting until I came to the big glass case that ran nearly the length of the store and which held Bates's special treasures, an array of old watches, cheap costume jewelry, pocketknives, and a modest but meticulous collection of tiny fraudulent trout flies: a dapper-looking Royal Coachman; a No. 16 Quill Gordon, an elegance of thread wrapped around such a small but deadly hook; a smaller Royal Wulff with a delicate bouffant of gently teased browns and whites set off by a red dot on the abdomen, a mark of character as distinctive as that of the black widow spider; and a No. 20 Adams looking like a gray-winged creature forever poised to lift off the surface of swift water. Such a display of temptation hypnotized me, held me firm. Behind me, Bates cleared his throat loudly and spit out the door into the road, shattering the spell.

"Something for you today, boy?" he said, not looking at me but staring over my head to where Mrs. Irene Wencell stood by the fruit bin squeezing apples, examining each one for imperfections, any sign of a texture, a spreading bruise, unhealthy discoloration. Mr. Bates knew she'd fondle every apple he had, dimming its shine. She'd spend all morning standing there studying his apples and driving him insane, chiding him endlessly on the shame he should feel for selling decaying produce.

"Too ripe," she'd say in that reedy voice of hers. "Mealy, squishy, every one rotten." According to Mr. Bates, Miss Irene hadn't bought a piece of fruit from him—not so much as a single apple or pear—in thirty years. Even so, she thought it her solemn duty to stop by the store daily to examine the quality of the produce.

"These trout flies, Mr. Bates," I said. "How much?"

"Mushy!" muttered Miss Irene, vigorously thumping yet another apple.

"Two bucks for the bunch," said Mr. Bates in a distracted voice. As he watched Miss Irene, his face tightened, the jaw muscles twitching and what had been a lazy half-smile deteriorating into a cynical sneer.

I peeled off the money, two wrinkled dollar bills. He put the tiny deceptive insects, little creature of feathers, fur, and thread, into a small paper bag. They fell so softly you couldn't hear them hit bottom. Then he pushed past me and headed for Miss Irene, eased up on her like a cat creeps up on a suspicious lump under the carpet. I tucked the bag inside my coat pocket and walked out of the store toward the café.

Albert was talking to Miss Donna. She was up to her elbows in a sinkful of steaming soapy water that smelled of lye. She nodded wearily at the sound of Albert's voice.

"Been tending berries, Miss Donna. A week on my hands and knees. Got a prickly poison ivy rash up to my armpits. Working berries takes it out of a man soon enough. Sore legs, scraped knees, fingers so stained it looks like you dipped them in red ink, a permanently twisted back, a neck stiffer than a rusted hinge. Yeah, all that's what a strawberry patch bequeaths a man. God bless 'em, though, because were it not for those berries we wouldn't be sitting here warming our insides with good hot chili and dreaming of those sly, vexing turkeys down by White Oak Slough."

Miss Donna wiped her sweat-covered face tiredly with a cloth, nodded, slid another tray of silverware into the dish-

water. Her thin forearms were the bright pink of freshly slaugh-
tered meat. Albert left a dollar on the table as we left. Miss
Donna, stacking dishes now, didn't notice.

On Christmas Eve, I worked frantically to get my outdoor
chores finished. Done, I wiped off the kitchen table, scrubbed
the dull white sink transected by cracks that zig-zagged across its
surface like rivers across a barren desert plateau.

The old men sat in the big room. A fire of hickory logs
crackled and glowed in the fireplace. Albert was stretched out
on the couch, flipping through the latest outdoor catalogs.
Emerson sat at the little oak desk chewing on the stub of a
pencil. I sauntered cheerfully to the center of the room.

"Say, boy," said Albert, "you got two hundred dollars?" His
face remained hidden behind the pages of the Orvis catalog and
his voice sounded childlike and far away. "For two hundred dollars I can be a fulfilled and happy man. Says so right here on
page twenty-eight. Two hundred bucks gets me a dandy new fly
rod and matching reel that'll catch anything with fins and gills
and a fishy smell. Satisfaction guaranteed or my money back.
Hear that, old man! Imagine that—mail-order contentment.
Happiness posted only slightly damaged through the U.S.
mails."

Albert's unwavering optimism clearly depressed Emerson,
and he had learned to avoid it by tuning Albert out, ignoring
most of what he said. Like Miss Donna at the café, Emerson
simply nodded whenever he heard the first highstrung notes of
Albert's annoyingly gleeful, buoyant voice.

"We're broke," said Emerson. The words came easily, as
though they were frequent visitors, old friends. He chewed
harder on the pencil, grinding it between his teeth.

The announcement struck Albert like a gripping cramp. In
an instant he had bolted up from the couch and was pacing the
floor, rubbing his large hands nervously through his hair.

"Broke, but not busted, right?" he said. "Just the regular
poverty." He stroked his hair with greater urgency. "Old man,

every month you cast financial ruin in my face. If we weren't loosely related, joined by blood, I'd think you were deliberately trying to upset me."

By now Emerson had put the pencil down and started massaging his temples, kneading the skin on his face as if the muscles there were jammed tighter than cable on a pneumatic winch.

Only the fire's hissing and crackling interrupted the heavy silence.

"Merry Christmas," I said, trying hard to coat each word in some kind of holiday spirit.

"Huh?" grunted Emerson incredulously.

"Eh?" echoed Albert, his bushy silver-gray eyebrows beetling up and down.

Taking the paper bag from my pocket, I carefully shook its contents into the palm of my hand. The little assortment of trout flies glowed in the firelight.

"Merry Christmas, fellas," I said again, and extended my hand first toward Emerson, then toward Albert. They exchanged befuddled stares.

I heard the pine chair scrape across the floor and Emerson leaped up from behind the desk. Scraps of paper, bills, bits of fishing line, receipts, a crumpled dollar bill—all scattered like a hail of confetti as he grabbed me by the hand and jerked me toward the front door. Untied at the waist, his old green bathrobe flapped behind him like a flag in heavy weather. Behind us, Albert sank to his knees and crawled hectically on the floor recovering the spilled trout flies. He stopped to examine one more closely, looking like a medieval monk caught in the humble act of prayer.

The old man and I bolted out the front door, down the porch steps slick with a new glaze of ice. A wind had come up, cold and hard out of the west, gusts as sharp as needles that stung the flesh, numbed the lungs with every breath. A slice of moon outlined the dark and distant hills in a pale translucent yellow light. Dragging me toward the barn, the old man began howling, running faster and faster. As we twirled, jumped, scampered, strutted, loped and vaulted beyond the barn I noticed he was shoeless. Each time his feet touched the cold ground he cringed and yelped; his lanky body seemed to constrict in one huge puckering motion. Even when he quit running down past the barn, he continued jumping, a pogo stick with shining eyes and a trembling smile.

"L-l-look," he said, stuttering from the cold. His lips had turned blue.

"Where?" I asked. I reached out to draw his robe closed, tie the sash.

A disheartened, troubled look spread over his face. He leaned against the wind, forced out another word. "Down!" he shouted.

I looked down and discovered that we were standing at the edge of the strawberry field. Young plants, tender and vulnerable, crouched snug beneath their quilt of pine straw. A feeling of awkwardness swept over me, a tide of uncertainty. Obviously I was missing something, something of importance.

"Straw-ber-ries," the old man said with some effort, the syllables stumbling out of his mouth in single file and frozen solid in shrouds of icy mist. "Th-th-they thrive on adversity, just like zin-zin-zinnias." He had said it, all he had to say, and now he began flapping his arms up and down in a ridiculous motion. That failing to heat his blood, he tucked his hands under his armpits, his body's last pockets of warmth. His eyes watered and bulged; his nose ran; his teeth chattered, clacked like wind chimes. Without further explanation he fled back toward the house. Reaching the porch steps he called out, "Ha-ha-happy Christmas, boy."

It snowed that night and when morning came we tossed snowballs at one another out by the barn. I remember the three of us red with cold, skin chapped, laughing long and hard in the dim, gray morning light.

All of these thoughts tumbled through my mind as I sat quietly on the edge of the bed and watched a steady funnel of steam float languidly from the bathroom. I could hear Albert humming and knew he was busy lathering up his face, the skin tanned, tight, smooth. For Albert, a good shave required an equally good song, a chorus of some gritty blues tune, the tone low and bent with tension, laced with as much portent as pain.

Walking quietly to the open bathroom door, I watched him shave, how he methodically pulled off glops of lather and flecks of gray beard with long, measured strokes of the straight razor. He bent over the sink, stripped to the waist, his skin pulled snug against his ribs and hard belly. He wore his tan like a shirt; it covered his neck, face, arms, and ended abruptly like a border between two lands. Freckles stood in cramped legions across his nose, under his eyes. He splashed handfuls of warm water over his face until the skin glowed. There were two glasses on the shelf above the sink; one was for the set of teeth he planned to get one day. Like a sunken treasure in the second glass was his Hohner harmonica. In the dreamy light of the room's lonely forty-watt light bulb, it looked like a silvery fish helplessly trapped in a shrinking pool of water. Albert soaked the instrument regularly. The practice, he believed, made for liquid music, trilling, longing notes that hung tragically in the air like tears. He picked up a comb, which like Albert himself had but half a dozen rickety teeth, and pulled it through his wild thatch of hair, a thicket of grays and dull silvers.

For a long time Albert watched me in the bathroom mirror. "Morning," he said finally, and winked.

He returned to the nagging problem of his hair, telling me that as a boy he had once attended a lecture given by Mark Twain. The year? Couldn't recall. Maybe 1900, maybe 1903. He remembered that Twain was an old man, a wild-looking creature whose appearance made more of an impression on him than his words. Twain told glib stories, fractious jokes. Joining in with the rest of the audience, Albert had laughed and applauded. Even so, all he could recall of that evening in any detail was Twain's outrageous looks.

"What a great head of hair the man had, boy," Albert said, turning to wipe his face with a wadded-up blue towel. "Looked like he had a fright wig on. He was slightly stoop-shouldered and reminded me of an old peddler who had toted a heavy bindle for too many years. He had dark, gloomy eyes and a voice as precise as a scalpel. I spent the evening just staring at the old comic, hypnotized by that unruly hair, that irreverent moustache. From that night on, I always wanted hair like that —completely irredeemable. Well, I got it, and damn if I know how to handle it. Never appears any more appealing than the leavings of a brushfire."

He put his hands under the warm water, then smoothed them over his head, that undisciplined hair. Immediately, the water transformed the silver hair into a landscape of lead gray. The water did no more good than the comb.

A layer of dripping moisture covered the mirror. Albert turned to face me. A new seriousness etched his face. "You're up early," he said.

"Yes, sir."

"Problems? You sleeping okay? That dream still upsetting your natural rest?" He flipped the towel over his shoulder.

I lied, and did not tell him the dream still stirred in my room at night, hung in the corner like a bat. Then I told him straight out that I thought maybe I'd go with him that morning.

"You mean turkey hunting?" he said. His nearly always gentle voice dropped half an octave and took on a tone of grave anxiety.

"Yes, sir," I said.

"Jesus!" He put on a T-shirt, then a green workshirt. "Turkeys. Jesus. You can't really want to mess with turkeys, boy. They'll ruin you. They're worse on a man than good bourbon and a harem of well-meaning women. No, don't get involved with turkeys."

Sitting on his bed, tying up his boots, Albert talked on and on, desperate to keep me out of the woods, away from all the fascination it held. Fascinations couldn't do a man any good, not anymore anyway.

"Listen to me," he said earnestly. "Goddamn it, I'm trying to save your soul."

So he revealed to me the tragic story of turkey hunters. They were shiftless ne'er-do-wells, laggards despised by decent hardworking folks worried about profit and progress, important matters. Men lured to wild turkeys ended up leading lonely, desperate lives. Their selfish, shameless quest for turkeys eventually cost them their jobs, their families, everything. Chased from the woods after turkey season, they hung lifelessly around town. You saw them on street corners, moping, pouting, crippled by their affliction. Only the sound of some vexing tom turkey gobbling madly on a cool spring morning excited their blood, thawed their senses, caused their fatty hearts to race again, their tired nerves to dance like downed power lines. They suffered from an obsession that Albert found difficult to explain. Couldn't be defined. Mostly, he said, it's all about that sound. Evocative, thrilling. Primitive. Raises the hairs on a man's neck. Gives a body goosebumps. Dooms the listener to a bewildering and enchanting version of hell. The fortunate turkey hunter ends up a harmless psychotic, haunted by delusions of turkeys looming everywhere, sitting next to him at the breakfast table, hiding under his pillow at night. Oh, it's a pathetic sight, what a turkey can do to human reason, that mushy terrain called sanity.

I nodded.

Albert went on, deciding that I needed the whole sermon. "Melagris gallapavo sylvestris," he said glumly, his body shuddering. "What is it the French say when they're not sampling wine? Patience passe science. Patience is greater than book knowledge. A motto the disenchanted turkey hunter hangs on to."

Try to understand, Albert said emotionally. Turkey hunters

are ornery because no one understands them, no one except other turkey hunters, who know they're just as crazy as they are and keep the hell away from them. No one appreciates that turkey hunters aren't hunters but pilgrims, serious men devoted to an honorable quest, the pursuit of the world's most cantankerous bird: the wild turkey, that blue-headed, evil-eyed, exasperating, beautiful son of a bitch. Wild blood, every bit as wary and suspicious as the wolf and as temperamental as the grizzly bear. Wild blood, a wildness that reminds a man of his own long-suppressed wildness, his frayed link to the natural world. Longing, that's what turkey hunting is about, a longing for that disconnected past. The turkey hunter seeks the company not just of turkeys but of wildness. Pulling the trigger has nothing to do with it unless a man's got an empty stomach. Turkey hunting is first of all a drama, life lived completely and totally in the present, with no memory of the past and no worry of the future. On entering the woods, the turkey hunter becomes different, something else, becomes, like the bird he's after, not thought but feelings, sensations, undiluted instinct. Come life's end, the turkey hunter still doesn't understand turkeys, but has lived a handful of memorable moments in their world.

Stay clear of turkeys, boy, and lead a happy, normal life. Sleep nights. Have a regular family life. Enjoy a rational future.

My face felt flushed. The words had come as hard and fast as a freight train. I had been wearing a smile for so long my cheeks ached.

Albert hadn't finished with me, though. This is all true stuff, he said. No fooling. After all, just look at what a lifetime of turkey hunting had done to him and the old man. They were pitiful specimens. Just husks of humanity, worn out. Grizzled anachronisms living off remembered gobbles, the stored electricity of primordial sounds. Irritating old misanthropes, community eyesores foolishly leading the kind of life that no serious modern man would think of embracing.

Albert stopped to catch his breath. "This isn't working, is it?" he said with a grin.

I returned the smile, only broader.

Lamplight highlighted Albert's face, his deepset eyes. "You know," he said, "this isn't supposed to happen. You know that, don't you? The colonel didn't pack you up and send you halfway round the world so you'd end up spending your time messing with turkeys. He wants something more for you. More than he's got. More than we've got. Emerson keeps telling me we're to keep you out of trouble, not immerse you deeper into it."

He reached over and shut off the light.

"I'm an old fool, but my eyes are still good. I've seen the way your eyes shine when we're on the creek, when the fat trout are rising. And when we're in the woods and I'm close to you I can almost feel your young heart hammering."

He sat there in the dissolving darkness of his room and I could sense in his low, gentle voice that he too still knew and felt that special excitement, that inexplicable wonder of feeling, suddenly, so completely alive that it frightens, thrills, and overwhelms you.

Albert shook his head. He took a blackened key from his bed table, rubbed it thoughtfully, tossed it to me.

"The old man'll have our asses for this," he said. "What the hell. Yeah, what the hell. He'd do the same, the sanctimonious old fart. He's got the turkey fever worse than any human I know. A regular high-spiked swamp fever, incurable variety, the kind that stews the mind. Emerson talks to turkeys and expects an answer. That's peculiar. This wild turkey business will put you back in your right mind, get you back to your studies."

Emerson had left the previous afternoon to deliver strawberries to town. From there he went to spend the night at Elias Wonder's place up on the creek. Elias was threatening to die, again.

We have this day, said Albert. The dark oak sloughs. Wild

turkeys. Luck. To have luck you had to believe in luck. And the floor of the woods was littered with fallen dogwood blossoms. Luck, too. And a sign. A truly good sign, a turkey hunter's sign.

He told me to hurry down to the kitchen, get breakfast on. The sun was coming up. Breakfast in that old house stays in the memory, mostly a lingering sweet breath of smells. Hunger and the emerging sunlight, a new day, chilly and fresh, mixing like smoke with the hissing sound of sausage frying up in the big black skillet, the rich aroma of coffee and rising biscuit dough. Sweet jellies, thick molasses, fresh butter, hard-boiled eggs.

Albert came into the kitchen, poured steaming coffee into the Thermos, wrapped four warm biscuits and sausage patties in tinfoil, put the whole package in his coat pocket, the permanently wrinkled brown coat with the gaping hole in the left pocket where the quail he took for dead had come to life, exploded from the pocket an hour after sundown as we emptied the day's quail from our pockets on the back porch. The bird fell limp to the wooden floor with a thud and when Albert reached over to pick it up, it took wing, a blur of earth colors and beating feathers, a spontaneous whirring sound like that of a difficult tractor motor trying to catch on a cold morning.

I slipped the key into the lock on the gun cabinet, opened the heavy door and was briefly overcome by the smell of wood and metal coated in heavy oil. I took out the L. C. Smith and the Winchester and slipped four 12-gauge, No. 4 shells into my pocket. They were from a box the old men had bought six years before. "Just four shells," Albert had told me emphatically. "Just four. Only takes one to put a fine meal on the table."

Albert moved quickly out the back door. He didn't speak again until almost mid-morning. In the dark woods words were a nuisance, an encumbrance. Albert moved effortlessly, gliding over moist, glistening grass, cutting through banks of heavy fog that hung in the swales. He moved with the land instead of against it. He wore it as if it were a suit of comfortable clothes. In those dark moments before the full morning light, the sensation was of being truly of the land rather than apart from it; for that brief time I was no longer the alien, the misfit, the orphan.

I walked behind, duplicating Albert's steps. A vague, diluted light edged across the fields, slipped nervously toward the woods. In the sky, a wide band of pale yellow light encapsulated a waning moon. We moved on, the moon over our left shoulders. We crossed Starlight Creek, Albert balancing like a ballerina on the slick stones, then followed a narrow path into Wolf's Slough northeast of the creek. Back across the water, dogwood blossoms lay scattered on the damp ground, looking like a delicate dusting of snow.

Where the woods thickened, Albert stopped and knelt by a gnarled oak. Behind us, daybreak climbed the hills. Shadowy crevices became flooded with light. Albert did not move, kept still and silent. Of a sudden, a loud, groaning tremolo began deep in his chest and rattled in his throat—the distinctive sound of a barred owl, elusive, bold, wild. Albert's guttural hoots rose on the moist air like musical notes. They drifted into the slough, penetrating every secret place. Albert called again, keeping the hypnotic six-beat rhythm, the last note rising dramatically like the sting of an insult. His challenge did not go unanswered. The retort came at once, assured, belligerent, a sound unique in a place of curious sounds, a vocal diatribe, a territorial imperative, ancient and merciless. Albert owled again, this time letting out a sound deeper, more resonant, more threatening. Again, that incomparable gobble: melodious spleen, lilting warning, an aria of invective. What was it Albert had called it once? "The lovely music of the damned." Yes, that was it.

Soft, rosy light fell on Albert's cheek. Morning. He held his index finger to pursed lips and we moved on into the tangled slough. The woods became a roofless cathedral about us. Albert moved like a thief, not even upsetting the fallen leaves under his boots. I could not hear his feet on the ground. He seemed suspended in the mist like a ghost. The woods on this morning seemed foreign. Every sound, smell, gesture, no matter how in-significant, was the turkey's ally, confederate. These woods were its, not ours. Albert stopped, owled again. Again, bitter gobble, closer, a booming noise like a quartet of fugel horns. Albert pointed to the north. After another two hundred paces, he sig-naled me to stop. Ahead was a rise topped by an immense oak tree. Using hand signals, he motioned me to sit against the back side of the tree. He sat on the opposite side. The rough-edged bark cut into my back. The morning was cold.

Gradually, soft gray light filled the slough and the world developed like an exposed negative. Inky images focused into clear, sharp details. The gobble came again, but different now. Less angry, less hostile. There was a sense to it at once of ur-gency and caution. Out of the corner of my eye I could see Albert, the L. C. Smith shotgun across his lap. I saw his right index finger move slightly, a twitch I followed to its end. The turkey was standing at the bottom of the rise. Its bald head, a mix of soft blues, rose reds, and milky whites and no bigger than a baseball, bobbed up and down as if sewn to elastic tissue. A thick wrinkled wattle, swollen crimson with blood, hung loosely under the bird's beak, down its fleshy neck. In slow motion, Albert raised his hand to his shirt pocket and slipped out his wing bone he had fashioned himself years before. It resembled a tiny trumpet, rubbed smooth and the color of butter. He put it to his lips and sucked gently on it, the way a man sucks on a newly lit pipe. The sound was a squealing yelp, crisp but not harsh—a turkey's love song, a note of primitive passion. Then more silence, each of us trying to be still as death.

Albert's finger moved again, certain as a compass needle. Equally suspicious the turkey moved to the west of the oak. It now stood enclosed in a thicket of vines and shrubs, an obscure vision of bronze and tarnished copper, soft browns, dappled grays and whites, an ancient dancer. It strutted magnificently, kicking up a cloud of leaves as its wings swept the ground. It was a performance that the bird evidently gave with some frequency, because the ends of its long wing feathers were worn and frayed. Like some fantastic spectacle in a cheap sideshow it paraded seductively behind its lacy green curtain, alternately swelling and deflating like a bagpipe. I looked at Albert. A smile had spread over his face. He yelped again on the wing bone and again the turkey moved, this time taking twenty minutes to perambulate twenty paces west and north.

To me the bird's movements were confusing, incomprehensible, exasperatingly senseless, the selfsame characteristics that I soon learned made these unnerving creatures so endlessly admirable. By midmorning the turkey had nearly circled us, and done so without coming any closer than eighty paces. Above the hills now, the sun warmed us. Albert worked the twin barrels of the shotgun; they flashed with sunlight. Instantly, the turkey disappeared, soundlessly, completely. Nature appeared double-edged: one side predictable and sure, the other mysterious and uncertain, all but invisible.

Albert put the shotgun against the oak, dug into his pocket, handed me a cold sausage biscuit. He took another for himself and poured a cup of hot coffee. "Nice bird," he said at last. "Young, though. And we don't need the meat. A good morning. The sun feels good. Warm."

We sat against the oak till noon. Albert napped. I watched the woods intently. Listened. My spine still tingled. The shotgun shells jingled in my pocket. It suddenly struck me that we had spent the entire morning unarmed. Albert had intended this turkey for the imagination, not the dinner plate. And I closed my eyes and saw again in every detail that wonderfully curious and beautiful bird with its dark haunting eyes. And its sound. The thought of it chilled my flesh. I felt that sound still filling me and the sensation of it thrilled me.

Later that day, Albert sat on the front porch, leaning back against the house in the big cane chair. He had propped the chair up with two thick books, *War and Peace* and a volume of Gibbons. The books kept the chair from catapulting him into the front yard should he fall into a pleasant dream and lurch forward.

Just before suppertime Emerson got back, the Ford truck rattling noisily into the front yard. Elias Wonder would live, he informed us, despite all that many had done to turn the tide in death's favor. Elias Wonder was forever threatening to die. It was his life's ambition. That and trout fishing. Someday he'd make good the threat, but this wasn't the time. This time it had only been a vague pain in his liver, eased by two pints of strawberries and a half-gallon of vintage whiskey. Last month it had been viral pneumonia. Six months before that it had been gout and a fever. Elias Wonder courted affliction and death the way other men courted passion. Because of a dose of mustard gas he had gulped somewhere during the First World War, he always had a temperature of 102 and was given to holding impromptu conversations with God, Marilou Pemberton, and Charles Darwin. Marilou Pemberton wrote Elias Wonder a Dear John letter in 1917 and had been dead since 1935. Died of polio, which Elias came down with in 1946 and recovered from miraculously in 1947.

"So he's okay?" asked Albert.

"Fine. Sleeping like the innocent lunatic he is."

Albert was up now, leaning casually on the porch rail watching the changing light in the sky as the sun set. There were broken, flat-bottomed clouds suffused with a ruby light, and Albert said how odd the earth was, really. Truth of it was, he said, that nature was cold, indifferent. Men thrust beauty on it and passion and all the qualities of life we yearned for, grasped for. We clothed it in our love and pain. Don't you think there's so much more to it than that, he asked absentmindedly, forgetting briefly that my father, for one, did not particularly want to fall under nature's spell. I nodded. "There's something just under its skin, something..." He stopped for a long moment. "Perhaps it is that something men call divine. Give it any name you please. It is a mystery, fascinating, soothing, damning, ruthless."

He talked on, said how the Reverend Biddle talked of Creation as though it had been a mere seven-day investment, like putting up a barn, a task with a beginning, middle, and a definite end. Not so. "Look out there," he said in a voice that suddenly demanded attention. "Creation is forever. Not made, boy, but being made, always. Does that sound silly, an old man's madness? I told you this morning that turkeys lead a man down curious paths." We went on looking at the sunset. Emerson was at the screen door now, watching too. Great streams of colored light poured through scattered clouds. Albert spoke again, almost in a whisper, a distracted thought, something about the sun coming and going in such faithful cycles and yet it never brought again what had passed. Never. And we sat there on the porch, each of us searching the fading daylight for omens.

In late March, just at first light on a windy Tuesday morning, it came up on the thready wind like the cry of some hopeless lunatic frightened by a waning moon. An old turkey gobbling down in the shadowy oak sloughs, heaping insults and warnings at a barred owl. The owl would hoot and the turkey would take up the challenge. "Sounds like something being tortured, don't it?" Albert said. "Something in terrible pain, like the sound a poor soul would make if he were being slowly flayed. It's no wonder so few sane and normal creatures have anything to do with turkeys. The beasts are moonstruck, loony as they come." And then the owl cut loose again, hooting a quick defiant run, seeming to enjoy the irritation its presence caused the caustic old turkey. And the tom's belligerent reply, the sound like something from a band composed of a zither, ukulele, union pipes, mellophone, hydraulic organ, glockenspiel, and carillon.

"You'd think something making that much racket would be

as easy to find as a wolf among sheep," mused Albert. "But not the wild turkey. For all his wailing, he's still a doppelgänger, all voice and no substance, ephemeral as air. Ask Wonder. He's seen them disappear into thin air." He was laughing now, his bony chest shaking so that you could almost hear his rib cage rubbing against his skin.

"You old son of a bitch," Emerson said, a wide grin working its way across his lips. "You know as well as I do that everything Elias Wonder sees disappears into thin air."

Emerson caught the laughter, then me. How I loved the sound of their laughter, how good it was just to laugh and laugh until you hurt, how the laughter took some of the pain out of the hard moments, the ones that hacked away at you day in and day out, impervious to resolution, to any remedy except that rising sound of the three of us laughing, laughing until we cried.

All that spring, I practiced on the wing bone until my lips blistered and cracked, and spent long hours in the oak bottoms studying turkeys. Always watching, observing, sure that if I studied hard enough and long enough, turkeys too, like trout and waterfowl and quail, would give me some sign, leave me a telling message. And they did. The message was always the same: survive. Carry on. It was like Elias Wonder's conversation with the crow he found in the middle of the Mount Hebron highway. That crow had been a messenger as well. What had it said to him? "There is common ground... there is common ground."

We took one good turkey that spring, a fine three-year-old tom that weighed maybe nineteen pounds. He showed up unannounced at the east end of the oakwood bottom on the last weekend of April. Pranced out of the blue shadows, all grace and ego, tiptoeing through the greening woods, full not of love, but of lust.

Albert had put his shotgun down to peel a hard-boiled egg. I touched his arm gently, caught his attention, moved my eyes toward the turkey, now fully in the open, perhaps 150 paces from where we sat back in the foggy shadows beneath a big oak tree. Albert licked his dry lips, yelped once, purred, a sweet, seductive call. The turkey's blue head bobbed once, twice. Albert had gotten its attention, piqued its interest. I leaned against the tree, concentrated on pure motionlessness. Coming closer, the old turkey became more suspicious with each step. And yet the distance steadily narrowed: 100 paces . . . 80 . . . 60. Albert laid a finger on my thigh, a signal to shoulder the big Winchester, ease off the safety. Albert yelped again, softly, his lips hardly moving. I had the big shotgun at my shoulder. The seconds passed like hours. My arms ached. I fought my muscles' urge to shake, tremble, give out. The turkey continued to move, passing from my right until he stood perhaps forty paces to Albert's left. Only the bird's head and long, fleshy neck were visible. Moving not by inches but by millimeters, I covered the turkey's head and neck with the shotgun's barrel, squeezed the trigger.

"This one's led a good, full life, son," Albert said as we stood over the dead turkey. "It's blood, all of its cunning and woodsmanship, is here, in the turkeys that are left. The earth provides. Perhaps some of this old birds' noble traits will mingle in our blood, improve our character."

I tied the turkey's legs together, slung it over my shoulder. Its flesh was still warm. I could feel the turkey's heat seeping through my jacket and shirt.

That was Albert's last day in the woods. I wish we had known then about the tumor that was killing him, emptying his brain. He might have wanted to stay a little longer, just resting, leaning back against the trunk of that big oak and feeling the warm April sun on his face.

Two nights later Albert fell down the stairs. I heard him out in the dark hallway, hours before dawn, shuffling about, talking in a hushed voice, calling out: "Karen," he said softly. "Karen, come to bed, dear, it's late."

I jumped out of bed, hurried into the hallway. "Albert!" I

yelled. "Albert!" He stood at the top of the stairs and appeared to reach out for something in the darkness and fell, tumbling down the stairs stiffly like a dropped mannequin. Down the ten steps he bounced, never uttering a sound.

Emerson and I carried him to the couch in the big room. A tender bruise on his thigh the size of a ripe melon. A small cut over his left eyebrow. Albert opened his eyes and smiled. "You guys wouldn't believe the dream I just had," he boasted. The next morning we drove him into Jonesboro to see a doctor. X-rays were ordered. When the doctor held the smoky image of Albert's brain up to the light, he saw the tumor, showed it to us, holding back the pride of his discovery of yet another patient's complaint. It was the size of a golf ball and white, an innocent white. I wondered how something of such a harmless color could be so lethal.

"You're dying," the doctor told Albert with cool professional detachment.

Albert rubbed the painful bruise on his thigh. "Who isn't, doc," he said calmly. "Who isn't."

Caring for Albert kept Emerson out of the woods for the rest of the year. Indeed, it was six months after Albert's death before Emerson went into the woods again.

We had gone into town with a truckload of fresh vegetables for Bates's store and decided to have the chicken-fried steak lunch at the café. While there, Emerson got involved in a conversation with Luther Higgins and Rowland Pugh about turkey hunting. The idea of a turkey hunter needing to be heavily camouflaged to outsmart a turkey was just then being touted.

Higgins had a perfectly bald head and heavy, sagging flesh. He claimed to be the best turkey hunter in the state and to prove it he wore a necklace of turkey spurs and a hat festooned with more than a hundred turkey beards.

Almost everyone thought Higgins to be a hardworking, God-fearing, and decent man. Emerson couldn't stand him.

"Murderer," Emerson said as Higgins kept telling everyone in the café that camouflage was the up-and-coming thing. "Once it's perfected, boys," Higgins said loudly, fingering the spurs around his neck with thick, meaty fingers, "I'll be invisible in the woods and there won't be a turkey that'll have a chance of slipping by me. I'll put an end to all them sly, feathered bastards."

Pugh and the others nodded in weak agreement, their eyes glazed with superficial enthusiasm.

"Murderer," Emerson repeated, taking a long pull of iced tea. "Hey, Higgins," he shouted across the room. "What's all this talk about colors got to do with turkeys, anyway? I been around a few turkeys in my time in various forms of dress and not a single turkey has ever registered a complaint against my attire. Turkeys don't much care what you wear, as long as it's not too ridiculous or completely out of fashion." Pugh got to giggling and from the kitchen we could hear Big Joe Dunklin let out a loud guffaw.

Higgins' eyes went wide with anger. "Who in the hell asked you, old man?" he said angrily. He was not used to having his pronouncements questioned. "This here's modern times and modern methods of guar-an-teed wild turkey success. This has got to do with stuff you know nothin' about—progressive high-tech killin'. Iffen the outdoor press says a man's got to be invisible to get a good turkey these days, then that's it. Chapter and verse. Get with the times, old man, or butt out!" Higgins spun violently around in his chair, turning his back on Emerson, who was laughing uncontrollably.

That weekend Emerson climbed up into the attic, holding a lantern to light his way in the pre-dawn darkness, and came down with a tattered box tied together with cobwebs and unraveling twine. As he cut the string, a great cynical smile edged across his face, and he pulled from the box a musty, faded Santa Claus suit, complete with white beard, mustache, and wig, a wide black belt, with large cracks meandering through the leather like open wounds, even a pair of knee-high black boots. He stripped down to his underwear and put the costume on, laughing all the while. I watched, bug-eyed, nervous, thinking it had finally happened. The loss of Elias Wonder and Albert had finally eaten beyond his firm heart, filled his mind with maddening grief. He had gone nutty too. Laughing even louder, he trotted to the mirror, adjusted the beard and wig, put the red cap on, and tossed me the key to the gun cabinet.

"Ho-ho-ho," he chanted, holding a gut he didn't have. "Be a good lad now and fetch Santa's shotgun and two twelve-gauge turkey loads."

He was still checking himself out in the mirror when I got back upstairs. "Are you okay?" I said. The words stumbled out awkwardly. My attempt at disguising my concern had failed.

"I'm not sure, son," he said, still facing the mirror, fluffing the white beard. "Am I invisible?"

"Hardly," I said, my voice cracking.

"Then all is well," he said. He held his hand out. "The shotgun and shells, please."

He put the shells in a small red velvet sack, which he flung over his shoulder as he bounced merrily down the stairs and out the back door and down toward the oak slough. "Ho-ho-ho, Luther!" I heard him exclaim as he walked out of sight.

A single shot shook the creek's solitude at a little after nine that morning. An hour later, Emerson, alias St. Nick, appeared at the edge of the woods, holding a huge old gobbler high overhead. "Ho-ho-ho!" he yelled at the top of his lungs. "Ho-ho-ho!"

Later that afternoon at the café the story was told, and he explained his antics as only an attempt to demonstrate that turkeys were spooked more by motion than fashion. "As long as you're still and quiet, you could wear kilts, for chrissakes," Emerson said with great conviction. It wasn't that he was against the wedding of turkey hunting and technology or even the notion, however curious to him, of hunters wanting to be invisible, if that's what they wanted to be; rather, it was just his belief that some of the old knowledge about woodsmanship was as good and reliable as the new. Emerson also made it clear that he felt no man should go into the woods holding more aces than whatever creature he might be after. In Emerson's own ethic, each time a man went into the woods he had the chance to return with some grain of solace as well as food.

Pugh and Big Joe Dunklin and Miss Donna all ogled the big turkey and Dunklin dressed it, stuffed it, and cooked it. By the next day Pugh had told everyone who gathered regularly at the café of what he'd seen and heard and that he'd seen Luther Higgins over at Bates's store and overheard him asking Bates about how a "cousin of his might go about orderin' a Santy Claus costume 'cause he had to play the old boy at his relations' this season." According to Pugh, Bates had looked Higgins hard in the eyes and asked him if he'd like a box of turkey loads for his "Santy's sack."

The next spring there were sightings, I later heard, of an obese man in a red suit loping in and out of every piece of turkey woods in the country and everyone knew it was Luther Higgins. And he must have been truly invisible, for there wasn't a single turkey killed in the hills that spring, fourteen months after Albert's death and six months after Emerson had died and been laid beside him up at Mount Hebron Cemetery. And across from them, over by the iron fence, lay Elias Wonder, his grave unmarked, already grown over with tall green grasses.

6. READINGS AT DUSK

Hell never welcomed two more kindly souls.

— The Reverend Conrad Biddle,
  Mount Hebron First Primitive Methodist
  Church, 1968

Everyone here 'bouts knows about them old men up the creek. Not even tryin' to make the land pay. Just fishin' and huntin'. Lord knows what-all. There hasn't been a day of my sixty years that I haven't cursed them and envied them.

— Big Joe Dunklin, chef, the Mount Hebron café, 1967

It had rained that night but when I woke up sunlight filled the room and it was cool. Sometime during the night, one of the old men had put a blanket over me. My duffel bag sat on the floor where I had dropped it. I stood at the open window for a long time. Birds fluttered excitedly in the woods beyond the barn. They too were on the move, heading south, following not so much the sun's light as its warmth. Whether or not they would survive depended, to a great degree, on its heat.

One of the old men had left a note on the kitchen table,

simple, to the point. "Eat, rest, and be merry, because at noon we go to work."

I poured a glass of milk, walked anxiously about the creaking house, not knowing what oddity might wait at every turn, lurk in every shadow. I found little because there was little to find. No television. No telephone. No washing machine or dryer. Not even a toaster. It seemed they didn't take to modern conveniences. "If I had a telephone," Albert told me later in a moment of deep thought, "then I'd be listed, wouldn't I? My whereabouts would be common knowledge. I cannot imagine a more desolate fate. Anyway, I'm not even sure I would know how to use the damn thing. Doesn't it involve a lot of bells, numbers, and cackling static?"

There was, however, a radio, housed in a huge walnut cabinet that sat in one corner of the big room. Albert turned it on each Sunday night so he could listen to a blues station in Memphis. He would sit on the couch with his Hohner harmonica and play along, often departing from whatever song the radio blared out, going off on his own into some deep, intricate blues melody and riffs of his own invention. He played with his eyes closed tight and his right foot counting the beat. The gritty chords and bent notes flooded the room. It almost seemed to sway, feel the pain in the bottomless notes, the agonizing tension of the bent notes suddenly exhausting themselves in gasping moments of only temporary resolution. That was Albert's brand of blues, touching the foul currents of tension and brief reconciliation. On warm nights, with every window in the house open, Albert's music drifted on the wind, dissipating finally in the stentorious rush of Starlight Creek.

On that first full day, I walked cautiously from the kitchen to the big room. That's when it first struck me, startled me. Books. Hundreds of them, everywhere. Stacked in teetering columns rising from the hardwood floors. Neatly shelved in pine bookcases that rose from floor to ceiling. Like towering sentinels, two bookcases stood shoulder to shoulder against every wall. Upstairs, more books. Each room not only a place to rest the body but work the mind. Each room a small library of smoldering words. Books scattered on the beds, their pages dog-eared. Books lying on the floors like a chain of exotic islands in a dark sea. Books tossed by the bedsides, passages marked in pencil, comments scribbled in the yellowing margins. Books piled in the bathroom, crammed in the closets along with large boxes of *The New Yorker,* issues dating back to 1927.

Everywhere I looked, books struggled for space, dominance, attention, the life readers alone can give them. On every surface a grand tour of history, science, rattled imaginations, prickly ideas, poetry, and fiction. They gave off an atmosphere you could feel, breathe, an air heavy with mankind's triumphs and foibles. Emotions leapt out of drawers, fell from bookshelves, hid beneath the sunken sofa, chuckled beside every chair.

All that morning, again and again, I walked through the house and the air was thick with the smell of old books. The house, like a library, had been divided into sections. The classics and a great deal of natural history were holed up in Albert's bedroom, battled there over matters of logic and reason, the real and the illusive, the question of fact and dream, carried on the rivalry between man's mind and his heart. "I get a kick out of the Greeks and Romans," said Albert over a dinner of squirrel and beans. "What a curious lot of old farts, but how they could write. Few things can get a man's mind off the hoe quicker than sparring with Plato or Aristotle." Albert had an abiding passion for clear thinking.

Novels swarmed about the big room, endless comment on the human condition rising and falling like a tide. The old men preferred the modern novel, which for them began the instant Cervantes pushed Don Quixote out into the world's madness. Humor stood equal with fiction, as it should. "What good is tragedy," Emerson said one evening, ruminating out loud. "To beat, the heart requires two chambers." Emerson loved a good laugh and would spend evening after evening in his rocking chair in the big room, a dune of books at his feet—Thurber, Waugh, De Vries, Benchley, E. B. White. Once he hurled a volume of Waugh across the room, a blur in the firelight. "Enough!" he shouted. "Enough! I can't take it. It's all too true, too painful." Indian history and biography in Emerson's room, dozens of books on the Plains Indians, the Sioux, the Cheyenne, the Blackfoot, and the Crow.

In size, their collection of books equaled the holdings of a modest library. And the old men had spent many winter nights reading them all, once, twice, who knows how many times. Yet with each reading came fresh details, new surprises, a chilled nerve, a stirred emotion, an unmasked thought or idea. For a long time, I would just touch the books, feel in their faded covers the longings of the two old farmers for whom they were a vibrant connection to life, to man and his world, a taste of lives lived beyond their own tenuous survival along Starlight Creek. If they hoped that trout would pull them back into the natural world, so too did they trust that their addiction to reading might somehow fill in the dark holes of their lives as human beings.

I would move around the big room, sidle like a crab across dangerous stones, shift from bookcase to bookcase, reading the spines of every book. Montesquieu, Freud, Emerson, H. L. Mencken, G. K. Chesterton, Blake, Hemingway, Flaubert, Keats, Diderot, Thoreau, Kafka, Schopenhauer, Ambrose Bierce, Goethe, Santayana, Jane Austen, Balzac, Cervantes, Baudelaire, Swift, T. S. Eliot, Yeats, Stendhal, Montaigne. Where to start? I would close my eyes, pull down a volume at random, begin to read, and could not stop. I began to take books from every shelf, lift them off the piles, stacks, drifts, read them slowly, deliberately, happily, wondering why fortune had dealt me not only the beauty and intrigue of the world beyond the back door, but these books as well, a storehouse of twitching humanity moaning in rich echoes deep in the Boston Mountains, along the banks of Starlight Creek. As a game, sometimes I would ponder how the writers would take their captivity there: Thoreau, naturally, would have loved it; Mencken would have puked, probably died; Keats would have breathed deeply of the land's raw beauty and endless solitude; De Vries would have lampooned it; Thurber would have bolted, thoroughly bewildered; E. B. White would have put in a garden, raised chickens, relaxed, been at ease.

Whether curled up at night in the big room with an armload of books, or out on the creek or up in the hills, I moved freely, like air through a cell's membrane, between two worlds, one natural, the other the chronicle of man, one a region of infinite possibility, the other a region of tension, torment, ephemeral joy and lament, regret, remorse, and ascension. More than anything else, the books seemed to reinforce what the world of the creek whispered—that life, more often than not, is unpredictable risk, a grasping from the old to the new, a dangerous and often fatal leap of faith, one that can never be fully known or completely explained.

This steady diet of books sustained the old men, both made them angry and gave them great pleasure. Like the creek and the hills, books tended to raise their temperatures. "The mind is a muscle too, of sorts," Albert said, fishing for some explanation of his passion for reading. He closed a volume of Gibbon he had been grappling with for days. "To get the best out of it, you've got to use it, put it to work." The books were not an escape, a barrier they had thrown up around themselves. They sought salvation not in fact, but in feeling, in experience. Man is matter. That is fact. He is a collection of minerals. That is fact. Reduced to his elements, though, the life went out of him. His calcium did not cry; his zinc did not love; his iron did not appreciate a good joke. Apart, something was missing, that spark of life, the electricity of the actual world, foreboding, nonsensical, haunting. Before and after the body, only ripeness, what some call spirit, the great mystery, remains alive in the grass, moving with the wind, swimming in all moving water. Albert's theory was that man needed the natural world, even though he denied the need, fought it. "Why do you think Hemingway's old man fought so hard for the great fish? Not so much because he wanted to, but because he had to. Such good books are not answers but guideposts, a vacillating compass needle, a vague message of where we've been and where we might be headed."

Emerson would spend weeks on natural history, glad to see that evolution was sweeping ahead with icy indifference. He liked the idea that no individual life was worth more than the survival of life itself. Only time would answer the nagging question of whether man is an evolutionary anomaly, a temporary error, or a creature of enduring worth, like the cockroach or the trout. So the old men firmly believed.

On a stormy night in February, Albert leapt up from his favorite reading position, stretched on the couch, flinging a copy of Plato's works on the floor with a thunderous whack. "Beareth all thing, believeth all things, hopeth all things, endureth all things." Albert offered the quote as though it were a timely invocation.

Emerson glanced over at me, rolling his eyes, knitting his bushy eyebrows up and down. "Groucho Marx?" he ventured.

Albert held back a laugh. "Close, you soulless backslider. St. Paul via the good Reverend Biddle. You never pay attention. Don't you remember the Sunday he made us write it down. A penance of some kind, I suppose. I can't get it out of my noodle. It pesters me day and night."

"Nature is often hidden, sometimes overcome, never extinguished," retorted Emerson, leaning back in his rocker.

Albert scratched his head. "Muddy Waters . . . No, no. Give me another chance now. Uh, Sonny Boy Williamson. Yeah, Sonny Boy Williamson."

"Francis Bacon," said Emerson.

Albert let out a long thoughtful sigh. "Well, maybe Mr.

Bacon, or some part of him, ended up as Leadbelly. Who knows?"

"Lie down, Albert," Emerson said in a consoling voice. "All the blood has gone to your feet."

"Amen, brother Emerson," said Albert, stretching back on the lumpy sofa, stuffing a big pillow under his head. "Do pass me the D. H. Lawrence, please. It's late and I need to spice up my dreams."

And the big room, dancing with eerie shadows in the dim yellow light, filled with the sounds of laughter.

On long winter nights, books lets us travel farther, deeper, than the big black atlas. They got us beyond fixed geography, known boundaries. The days' exhausting labor was soothed not only by the hills but by those rooms choked with books, so many enticing corridors into the heart of man, into the natural world. I read the same way I worked the fly rod, hungrily, wildly, indefatigably, and with great joy. Whether uplifting or shattering, I embraced each new book with innocent gratitude and wide-eyed expectation.

On blustery nights when the wind was shaking the windows, seeping in under the workshop's lopsided door, floating above the floor like pellicles of frost, Emerson would put on his overcoat and push the rocker closer to the fire, sit there with volumes of Muir and Burroughs and Thoreau. His teeth would clack and chatter, until finally Albert would insist that he take them out. "You sound like a cheap marimba band, for chrissakes," Albert scolded.

"That's right, chide a man while he's on the trail of eternal truth, cosmic enlightenment. This stuff is all the rage of the day, you know. Don't you listen to the gossip at the café. Why, these days even love's free."

"Crap," cried Albert. "Go to Memphis with that free-love stuff and see what you get. It's still two bucks a throw." He took his earmuffs off, warmed his hands, said almost regrettably, "Well, anyway, it was in 1920."

"Times change."

"Maybe," Albert conceded. "Or maybe it's just that everything changes and time just goes on, pressing us to either adopt its arbitrary devotions or toss in the chips."

"Speaking of devotions," said Emerson, slipping his gleaming false teeth back in, "it's about tea time." He turned to me. "Now, son," he said, like a sage passing down sacred knowledge, "remember that's one part tea to ten parts Mr. Wonder's warming tonic."

Emerson tossed back the tea in one great gulp, then leaned toward the fireplace to warm his hands. In a voice that was part sigh, part murmur, he began to speak, neither to me nor to Albert, who had his head buried in Darwin's *Voyage of the Beagle*, but, it seemed, to the fire itself, to every warming fire that had comforted him. "We are part of the great passion. I am of this place, this ground. Nature is the offspring of life. The earth and I share that much: we are both pieces of life's debris."

Suddenly, out of the corner of his eye, full of the fire's yellow light, he saw me listening and turned quickly to Albert, hoping, it seemed to me, to hide the emotion that had somehow escaped him. "Correct, brother Albert?" he said, breaking the room's cavernous quiet, his voice tinged with regret at having let the thought escape, breathe the air, the flames.

"Eh?" Albert replied. He had been at Darwin's side all evening, peering over the great man's shoulder. He did not welcome the interruption. "Eh?" he repeated, louder, irritated at having been so rudely hauled back to Trail's End before bedtime.

Although he had not heard Emerson, Albert, as always, had an answer anyway. "Eh, try a No. 16 Dun or a good Cahill at dawn. Soon as they see them, the trout rise waving a tiny white flag. A pitiful sight, really. By the way, old man, have you seen my edition of Plato?" Albert always suspected that Emerson was secretly dumping his collection of classics to make room for the ever-demanding modern novel. "It's not that I'm all that devoted to Plato, you undersand. I mean, Christ, I uttered the word 'utopia' last week in the café and cleared the place as sure as if I'd yelled FIRE! Even so, the classics are the classics and have a place, and I'm just not sure about the modern novel. All that endless wheedling and whining, all that hollow self-pity. Hasn't anyone in this house but me noticed the knee-deep pall of abstract thought flooding this room?" Then he fired off a Latin phrase or two, the words circling the room like rising smoke.

Emerson jerked his head toward the kitchen. My sign to make up another batch of tea. "For chrissakes, Albert, I haven't seen Plato for years. One thing, though. Quit bringing me messages from the past. I don't want to get bogged down in yesterday. If I stop and look back for too long, who knows, maybe I'll end up a frozen pillar of cement."

"Cement?" Albert wondered what cement had to do with securing Plato's recovery. "Cement," he chortled. "More like a pillar of crap, if you ask me."

Snickering like a fighter with his opponent on the ropes, helpless, Emerson threw his strength into a winning blow. "Look," he said, "Reverend Biddle says it happened in the Bible to the wife of some guy named Lot and she wasn't even looking for Plato or for the scribblings of any other dead dreamers."

Albert looked dumbfounded. "Lot's wife?" he said to himself, obviously searching his mind for someone named Lot. "Who the hell is Lot's wife and how did she finagle her way into this? Aren't you thinking about old lady Potts, the woman that died on the Mount Hebron highway in '59? Remember? Got run over by a bread truck. She'd gone out on the road to pick up a stranded dime and her back locked up on her. Loaves of bread were scattered over a mile of highway. We didn't have to buy bread for six months."

"No, no," insisted Emerson. "I tell you, this Lot is in the Bible. But that's not the issue. Lot or Potts, or anybody else's wife for that matter, or Plato, just leave me out of it. Want to bring me news, dear Albert? Tell me about now, this moment, or the next, how they mix, how the soup that is the past and present becomes the inevitable future. Tell me how the present feels and why it never lasts."

Albert had been heading to the kitchen for another glass of tea. He stood quietly in the doorway for several somber moments before he replied. "Because the earth is a gambler. She has a real lust for rolling the evolutionary dice. Too, whatever gods there are have a keen and rather slapstick sense of humor."

In the big room, night after night, each of them read, drifted in dreams, jousted with ideas, fiddled with thought, looked for reassurance and only rarely found it. Somewhere in that room ran an invisible boundary between their two worlds, a world within a world, a boundary as thin as a cell wall, one they passed through easily and gratefully, a boundary that did not separate them from life, but rather intensified the reality of their day-to-day struggles, their life of the heart and mind, a mixed salad of hope and hopelessness. The old men had lived for more then eighty years and from those worlds they had come to appreciate if not understand fragments of their own lives, the feeble nature of man, a creature that assumes itself to be the logical conclusion of creation instead of only a crude and rough beginning, a transitory life form, a brief evolutionary sideroad. Books were glimpses into man's fears, longings, passions. Too, books provided further evidence of their intimate connection to the earth, to the natural world, to every living thing. In that room overflowing with books, they read and in so doing traveled to exotic lands, listened to symphonies, attended operas, lost themselves in the melodies of time. Nightly, they were pilgrims and the good news was that all their roads eventually joined, brought them back home, back to the banks of Starlight Creek.

It seemed to me that the fate of the world rested as much with the old men of these mountains as it did with an auto worker in Detroit, the emperor of Japan, a herder in Nepal, the governor of Iowa, or a fisherman in Greece. "You know," Albert said to Reilly Larson at the Billups station as Reilly popped the hood on the Ford pickup, "we're all connected in some kind of way. I mean all the living things, and the inanimate too. Strange, isn't it? You, me, the Indian, the Chinese, the Russian, all of us thinking we're special and superior, yet all of us are fueled by the same mixture of blood and bone and minerals. Life is life when you get right down to it."

Reilly Larson came out from under the hood, frowning and wiping grease off his face with his shirtsleeve. "Is that so, Albert!" he snapped angrily, his patriotic American blood boiling. "Well, let me tell ya right here and now. I ain't a part of nothin' that includes niggers, rice eaters, redbones, or commies. Count me out of your happy world, you old lunatic." Larson tapped his plastic leg proudly. "I gave, bub. I gave because I am an American and America is worth any number of low-life godless pinks and soulless Japs. I ain't got nothin' left to give. Nothin'."

The old men kept reading, I think, because they hoped that one evening it would happen—they would stumble upon that sentence, that paragraph, that would at last take them beyond the material world, the technocratic world, and immerse them in the earth itself, stripped of pretense, the earth that was beyond the grasp of science and technology.

Winter gave us our most fitful nights of reading, like the February night Albert paced the floor turning the pages of a book on the natural history of the American Southwest. Emerson was outside gathering another load of wood. Five pieces each two and a half feet long. Albert stopped suddenly and stared blankly out the window. A cloudy night, with the wind out of the west shaking violently among the gray, leafless trees. A hard wind, one that felt of snow.

"Aspens," said Albert with a touch of deep longing in his voice. "Aspens in the early fall, leaves the yellow of young squash. Fresh snow in the high mountains shining in the morning light. Wide valleys, tall grasses bending in the wind. Cold mountain streams winding down the hillsides and onto the flat mesas. Cottonwood stands along the banks. Smoke rising from a small adobe house."

I sat by the fireplace and listened and the words built images in my mind that I thought surely I could reach out and touch. Emerson had come in and stood nearby, loaded down with wood.

"Moonlight on the creek," Albert said, continuing to stare out into the night. "A liquid light, soft and yellow. Trout rising from below. Goldenrod bending in an easy rain. Water flowing down from the Peaceable Kingdom over smooth rocks. A hawk on the wing. The call of a kingfisher nearby. Wild violets in spring." Then he paused, reflected on the book in his hand, the one proclaiming the beauty of the Southwest. A long pause as he considered his last words, his paean to the land beyond the back door. "Beauty is beauty," he said finally. "Rich, diverse. It's like Emerson's atlas, isn't it? The points of my compass bring me here . . . right here. Home."

Books enriched them without changing them. The old men were what they were, farmers, men of these mountains, not alien to the land, dispossessed. Many books reaffirmed this belief, no book ever altered it. Reading was not a quest for answers, assurances. Rather it was, like every aspect of their isolated and pinched lives, an effort to grasp whatever hold they could on the earth and mankind and their relationship to both. For me, the books had an even more compelling allure. Arriving at Trail's End, I had at first felt like an amputee, cut off, beyond reach. Norwell's secret, it seemed, had left me cold, insensitive, beyond feeling. Reading, like the Orvis fly rod, served as some new and amazing prosthesis, one that, in time, lost the feel of artificiality and took hold like a graft of living skin. I cannot remember the day or month, but it happened, and I recall waking up flushed and trembling with energy, soaked with sweat. The chill of life swept through me and I smiled.

As the tumor in Albert's brain grew, the one we never knew

he had until it killed him, he got David Woollum's disease. He started carrying on conversations with ghosts. In his case, dead writers. These exchanges were lively, heated, often controversial, and always one-sided. Since he was still alive, Albert always got the last word. Of course there were exceptions. He could not talk down Cervantes and found it impossible to get the drop on Twain, whom he loved immensely because Twain placed as much importance on old bastards like him and Emerson and Elias Wonder as he did on kings, presidents, and preachers.

"There, there," said Emerson when Albert kept turning to the chair next to him at the kitchen table, saying, "Eat up, Joyce. Okra is heap big magic! Might put a bolt of lightning in your prose, as if it needed any more juicing up—right, James, old boy?"

"There, there," cooed Emerson.

Thinking of them now, all these years later, the old men never struck me as crazy. Eccentric, yes. Odd, certainly. But no more than that. A couple of innocent old-timers who took from the land only what it cost to love it. No more, and often a good deal less. A week after I got off the bus at Mount Hebron, I traveled back to the town with the old men. Twice a month they went in for groceries. On this Saturday, they also needed a honing stone and five gallons of kerosene. As they talked with Mr. Bates, I walked up and down the aisles of the old store. I stared at the fishing rods and tackle, ogled the outdoor magazines in the rack near the double front doors, looked longingly at the polished and oiled shotguns that Bates kept locked in a glass cabinet behind the counter. On the third aisle I came across a stack of black notebooks, ledgers actually, one hundred blank pages per volume. Three for a dollar, the tag said. I picked up one, felt its weight, stared at the lined pages. A hundred of them. Such a vast white geography, a formless land between dark covers. Gathering up three of the ledgers, I tucked them under my arm, put a dollar bill by the cash register.

Bates took the bill with a cheerful grin. "Goin' to keep accounts, eh?" he said, with the firm authority of a man who had a clinched grip on the arcane world of economics and finance.

I shook my head. "No, sir. I thought I might keep a journal. You know, write things down."

Bates's grin collapsed into a worried frown. "A journal? You mean like 'Dear Diary'? Ain't you kinda old for that nonsense, boy?"

I shrugged my shoulders and watched Albert out of the corner of my eye.

"Got something to say, have you, son?" said Albert, patting me gently on the back. I felt his warm, sweet breath against my face.

Again I shrugged my shoulders. Why I had bought the ledgers puzzled even me. There was just something haunting about those pages, all that untouched whiteness. They were an invitation to a journey that was too tempting to resist. I thought of writing just a single word on one of the pages and imagined its dark shape, a smudge upon that perfect white world, a delicious flaw, an intriguing imperfection.

At home, I put the black notebooks on the bureau in my room. For days, each time I entered the room I looked at them, touched their covers. One night a week later, with only a slice of moon in the sky and a cold wind blowing down from the mountains, I sat on the edge of the bed, unable to sleep. Norwell crouched in the corner, a bloody sack of flesh and shattered bone, just waiting for me to drift into dream, waiting to whisper his secret to me again and again. I flipped on the bedside lamp, got one of the notebooks and a pencil, and stretched out on the bed. I opened the notebook to the first page and searched my mind for a word, a phrase, that would drive Norwell back into the shadows. This is what I wrote: "A good day. Clear and cold. We rebuilt the chicken coop. Albert calls our labor Ozark socialism, the most good for the most people, excluding, of course, the chickens. Albert thinks our chickens are hard-core revolutionaries out to change what he calls a 'fowl world.'"

After I had kept up my journal entries for a month, the old men, seeing I had no plans to give it up any more than I had plans to abandon the fly rod, built me a desk out of oak. They put it by the window in my room. "I suppose if he goes on with this," said Albert whimsically, "we'll have to make him a chair as well." And so they did, six months later, a fine chair, sturdy and straight-backed, and uncomfortable as hell.

"No writer writes, I hear tell," said Emerson, smiling broadly, "unless he's uncomfortable with something, even if it's just a chair."

I liked to think that, despite my age, I had known evil many times; but at Trail's End it was kindness I found, and two old men whose curiosity was as boundless as my own. For the most part, though, the residents of Mount Hebron thought Albert and Emerson were nuts, cracked enough to be locked away. And good riddance. Mount Hebron held a long list of faults and grievances against them. They were pikers. They were lazy. They gave the community a black eye, gave it a reputation as being backward. Every time good fortune or prosperity knocked at the door, the old fools refused to answer. They were different and enjoyed it. They didn't want what the community wanted, which was progress, a great big chunk of the American Dream, a long ride on any gravy train that could haul them out of their despair and poverty.

Everyone said you just couldn't trust a couple of old farts that went around town provoking folks, making trouble, telling them lies like technology wouldn't solve all their problems, bring them unblemished happiness, when every God-fearing and truly intelligent person knew damned well that technology would deliver them from their mindless labor and carry them into a new world of convenience, luxury, and instant gratification. All the really modern citizens of Mount Hebron knew that the old men up the creek were yesterday's news, outcasts, Oglala County's greatest embarrassment. Everyone just wished they would stay out of sight, go away, die and leave the world to those who could make a profit off it.

"Jesus Christ, they got no television, even," Miss Donna blurted out at the café on a Wednesday afternoon, while wiping tables. Bates was at the back table with Ethan Duffy, who had a place way down the valley, and Randy Chewes, who had his own backhoe and spent most of his time digging graves at the small cemeteries around the county. They were going through the list of reasons why people like Emerson and Albert gave farsighted, hardworking, modern-minded men like themselves a bad name. Miss Donna had hair that wasn't quite blond and wasn't quite red, thin lips, and angry eyes.

"What's that, Donna?" said Bates.

Donna had a reputation for contributing to every conversation the café spawned. She quit wiping tables, brushed her hair from her eyes. "I said they ain't even got a television. That right there oughta tell ya they ain't all the way right in the head, all the way modern and civilized."

Randy Chewes nodded in agreement. "That's a fact. Neither have they got themselves a telephone."

Bates sipped his tea, being careful not to slurp. "Christ, no television. No telephone. Worst of all, no aspirations. They're a black mark on us all, all of us decent and proper people trying to earn an honest profit from these worthless hills."

Donna took hold of her rag again, leaned over a table, rubbed it hard with soap and scalding hot water. "I'd almost forgive 'em," she said in a new tone of mercy, "if they'd just get born again, get right with God, believe what we the saved believe."

Mount Hebron prided itself on its closeness to God, the American God—tall, slim, and muscular, blond, blue-eyed, who loved them and all God-fearing Americans more than he loved Albanians, Kurds, Frenchmen, or anybody else who didn't fervently believe in the American way of life, a life that promised the faithful everything they wanted, from superiority over all the godless, sleazy little second-rate nations of the world to electric ovens, flush toilets, salvation, and a heaven free from mortgages, taxes, church, from having to mingle with the downtrodden, the vile, the unimportant, reprehensible, woeful, shabby, obnoxious, fetid, from the nut cases, perverts, criminals, or any other failed Christians.

Among their many crimes of taste and manner of living, Albert and Emerson had taken in the lunatic Elias Wonder, and while nearly every man in the county bought Wonder's whiskey by the gallon, that didn't mean they had to like him, associate with him, or stomach having him so near them that they could sometimes hear him laughing hysterically in the night like some wild, rabid beast stalking the woods, peeking into every window, just waiting for the opportunity to chop them up in little pieces.

Like many small towns, especially those that used to be so common in the southern mountains, Mount Hebron was a cell with a double nucleus. It revolved about two centers: one was Bates's store, where all matters secular were argued out, attended to. The other was the church, the Mount Hebron First Primitive Methodist Church. Here all matters spiritual received attention, were settled, provided for, and everything discussed at Bates's store was either ratified or damned.

Although there was much to worry about, the worthy people of Mount Hebron never worried about their place with God. God had not abandoned them. They had always been assured that all those who attended church three times a week, twice on Sunday and again on Wednesday, went to Sunday school, closed their eyes while praying, and gave at least $5 a month to the church were bound for heaven, in the express lane, whether they were with sin or without. All those who did not attend church and did not give at least $5 a month to the church, whether they could afford it or not and no matter their piety or faith, went to hell. Again, in the express lane. Indeed, those who didn't fork over the $5 went to what was known locally as "beyond hell." Deacon Jasper Wyatt told me with visible fear and appropriate trepidation that "beyond hell" was sort of like a Memphis dancehall on a Saturday night, a place that smelled of alcohol, throbbed with heathen music, and where every man was named Bubba and every harlot was named Wanda Sue.

It mattered little that Albert and Emerson were old men who kept to themselves, led simple lives that intruded on no one, and asked so little of the town. Yet when they did venture into town for groceries or gas or shotgun shells or a bowl of Big Joe's chili, they tended—unintentionally, I was always sure—to upset just about everyone they met.

"We are finite," Albert said philosophically to Mr. Bates, staring at him firmly across the cash register.

Bates backed way from the counter slowly, like a man backing away from the edge of a cliff. There was the look in his eyes of real terror, as if he feared any sudden move might set Albert off like a wild dog.

"S-s-sure," Bates stammered. "S-sure, Albert. It was a fine night. Stars. Moon. All that stuff."

"Ethiopia's hungry," Emerson told Miss Donna at the café, saying the words in a hushed tone.

Donna gave him an understanding look and thought he was whispering so as not to embarrass this Ethiopia, whoever he was. She knew Emerson was a soft touch for every bum that came through town.

"Fine, Emerson," she said, "but this ain't no welfare kitchen. If your pal's got the money or if you're paying, bring this Et-a-hope-ia fella in and I'll order up two bowls of chili for the loony-tune table."

She screamed the order to Big Joe, the one-handed cook who never told anyone exactly what he put in his chili. He made it late at night. You could see the café light on and hear Big Joe screaming like a bobcat and you knew the next's day's chili was perfect. "Hotter than hell's own fire," he had snorted after my first spoonful, a taste that was quickly followed by five glasses of iced tea. "Stuff's put away six truckers I know of and the law can't touch me, neither." Howling with pride and delight, Big Joe had sauntered back to the kitchen, where he ruled over the pots and pans with a cold ruthlessness.

"Every time I breathe, I inhale the world's horrors and its joys." Albert was talking out the truck window to Jacob Hupple. Hupple had giant green eyes, a blunt chin, and a sour disposition.

"Piss on you, Albert," said Hupple as he shoved another black spongy plug of chewing tobacco into his cheek, exposing a row of brown teeth as worn and rounded as the mountains. "Every time I breathe and smell crap I know you're around," he added, laughing peevishly.

"The spider and the horseshoe crab are both arachnids," chimed Albert knowingly.

The truck motors were idling noisily. Hupple, who hadn't heard clearly since he stopped wearing his hearing aid, only managed to grasp the word "arachnid." "That's their goddamn problem," he growled. "Ain't never been no arachnids in my valley and there ain't never going to be. And if there was, I'd run their foreign asses out. That's Hupple land. Five thousand an acre, Albert. Pure gold. I'm loaded."

A huge globule of cinnamon-colored tobacco juice edged slowly down his chin.

Hupple jostled the big Chevy into gear, started to pull away. "See ya in church, Albert," he said in the cheerful voice of a man who has just got the goods on another man. Hupple shook with laughter, spewing tobacco juice all over the dashboard. Suddenly he jammed on the brakes, shoved the truck into reverse, and backed up beside the Ford again.

Now tobacco juice was meandering out both corners of his mouth. As he spoke I could see his black tongue moving the sticky lump of tobacco from one cheek to the other.

"Albert," he said, his high-pitched voice serious now. "Tell that madman Wonder I need a quarter of his brew by Saturday.

I'll give him two bucks, which is a generous buck more than the lethal swill is worth. Oh, and tell him to leave out the kerosene, will ya. I'm trying to woo these Little Rock developers, not kill 'em. Two glasses of that stuff and I think I'm Patsy Cline."

"That's nothing," boasted Albert, his big head halfway out the window so he could yell out enough for Hupple to hear. "One sip and the boy here turned into a fly fisherman."

"Hey, kid," Hupple shouted, then spit the wad of tobacco into the street, where it looked like a mashed mouse. "When you want to do so real fishin', come on down to my place. I inject them red worms with air. Not only do they float, but they squirm something wonderful. They're in such agony, it drives the trout crazy."

Albert's face went completely white. He swallowed hard, leaned closer to Hupple, yelled at the top of his lungs, "Why don't you inject them with nitrous oxide, turn the whole ugly episode into a tragicomedy!"

Hupple shot Albert a suspicious look. "Yeah, but will they float like a balloon?"

Albert sighed deeply. Hupple steered the conversation to his favorite subject, his proposed Ozark Mountain Hillbilly Theme Park. "Think of it," he said wistfully. "Restaurants, motels, crafts shops pushing native crafts made in Taiwan, miniature golf, water rides, maybe a Hillbilly Space Needle, thousands of people emptying their blessed wallets in our town. And you can have a share, boys. A big share. I could make that rundown, no-good, worked-out wasteland of yours into a giant jackpot, one that keeps on giving. Think about it, boys."

Emerson thought about it and got a sickly, pained look on his face as Albert sped off down the highway toward the farm. I turned to look back. Albert grabbed me. "Watch it, son," he said sternly. "You might turn into a pillar of cement, or a partner in Hupple's hillbilly heaven." A moment passed. Albert's face bloomed with a fresh smile. "When we get back," he said, a hint of sedition in his voice, "walk down to Wonder's and place Hupple's order. Be sure to tell Elias that this here is a real special order, so he'd better up the normal dose of kerosene. If Hupple is Patsy Cline after two snorts, perhaps three will transform him into Howdy Doody." Laughter filled the cab of the truck. Even Emerson emerged from his deep funk and began to laugh long and hard.

Each visit to town was a time of high drama. But for all the kidding and needling the old men gave and took, it was never their intention to provoke or upset anyone. As for the townspeople and the other families in the valley, for all their harsh words about the old men, all of them seemed to care for them, respect them, even if personally they could not stand them. They pitied the old men and wanted earnestly to help them regain their senses, get with the times, join the rest of them in a rich and rewarding standard of living, a way of life that included in its future Hupple's Ozark Mountain Hillbilly Theme Park, a way for them to make a financial killing.

The old men honestly worried the good people of Mount Hebron, especially after they took in Elias Wonder. More than one resident of the valley believed that Wonder was probably on the lam from the FBI for some heinous crime, and each week a handful of people would stop by Bates's store to look at the new wanted posters that Bates tacked up on the back wall. Wonder spawned gossip and rumor the way a wildfire consumed oxygen. My favorite was that he kept his wife's skull in a tin box under his bed.

With the gentle prodding of the Reverend Biddle, the congregation of the Mount Hebron First Primitive Methodist Church voted to aid spreading the gospel not to the heathens of Africa, Russia, or New York, but to the two druids on Starlight Creek, shepherding them into the fold of the forever blessed. "Amen," screamed Miss Donna at a Wednesday night prayer meeting. She stood up, clapping her hands, rolling her prominent eyes. "There are troubled, tormented, misguided souls among us, at risk. Let us tend to our own." Brother Hupple was mighty glad to hear the good news and he seconded the motion because, while he didn't need their land for his theme park, he wanted it. A bigger park meant bigger profits and everybody got a share, he kept reminding everyone.

For years and years the congregants had voted a good portion of their humble missionary fund to bring Albert and Emerson back among them, among the truly saved. As for Elias Wonder, no one was that fond of his soul to begin with. Not a penny for Elias Wonder. Him they gave, and willingly, to Satan, feeling a sense of accomplishment at having rubbed out so great a sinner from their midst.

"Screw Hupple and his park," murmured the Reverend Biddle as he hopped into his two-tone green Pontiac with the shiny orange swooped-back Indian-head hood ornament on the last Sunday of every month to visit Albert, Emerson, and Elias Wonder and then, for a time, me.

The Mount Hebron First Primitive Methodist Church stood on the brow of Little Blue Ridge, just above the lower reaches of Starlight Creek. Where it passed below the church, the creek was wide and deep, its waters a darker green, like that of raw, unpolished emeralds.

A gravel road led up to the church from the Mount Hebron highway. On the highway stood a large white sign suspended from oak posts by links of noisy chains that creaked and clanked in every press of wind. On the sign was a four-foot black cross with a flaming, righteous red arrow pointing up the hill and white letters proclaiming "Mount Hebron First Primitive Methodist Church, Conrad Biddle, Reverend." The church itself was a long, narrow building, made almost entirely of wood, with a tin roof that flashed like sparks under a summer sun. The front of the church faced down the valley, overlooking, monitoring, soothing the handful of souls in its tenuous keeping. A large, simple wooden cross, painted white, was bolted to the roof above the double doors. The cross dominated the valley, a talisman visible from every point of the compass, from Bates's store out nearly to the county line. Only the hills to the north and west dwarfed it.

On the opposite end of the roof there stood what was left of a lightning rod. According to Albert, it had once been an angel teetering precariously on an iron arrow, but it had been struck so many times that it resembled a strange iron-black bird with enormous wings, a creature forever threatening to take wing, launch itself off the tin roof, lift weightless into the cool, uplifting wind. It never did. It just sat there on that high tin roof looking beyond the creek to the high country and, like the flock of souls it protected, stared yearningly at the horizon.

Jacob Hupple liked to stand behind the church on the bluff overlooking the creek, with the congregation around him, and describe to them the wonders of his theme park, how it would end their troubles, erase their despair, make them rich. "And everybody gets a share," he'd say. "The congregation would repeat YES! YES!, as though obeying Biddle's call to prayer on Sunday morning.

Inside the twin wooden doors, on either side of a narrow aisle, were stern ranks of polished hardwood pews. The pulpit was a hand-rubbed cherrywood lectern. Behind it, arranged in a semicircle, were twelve cane-backed chairs. Here the choir sang hymns of enduring faith, ultimate spiritual victory, life everlasting. The church had only two electric lights. Most of its light poured into the sanctuary through six stained-glass windows, each depicting a biblical tale of hope, tenacity, rebirth, firm belief, all told in streams of vivid, almost dizzying colors.

A few yards west of the church was Mount Hebron Cemetery. The graves were spread haphazardly beneath a stand of oaks and elms and the remnants of an old fruit orchard—death presented at random rather than orderly and precise. In the last hours of daylight, the weathered tombstones and humble white crosses had the soft glow of soapstone.

Actually, I heard the Mount Hebron First Primitive Methodist Church long before I saw it. Some weeks after moving in with the old men, a neighbor knocked frantically at the door. It was a miserably cold December day. Heavy gray clouds filled the valley, cast the mountains into abstract images in black and gray. Somber light fell across the spent fields, edged timidly into the woods. Norton Winton stood anxiously at the door, coatless, shivering from the cold. His pale blue eyes bulged with bad news. Albert brought him in, pushed him toward the fireplace, listened as he talked, his words rapid and sharp. A hunter from Jonesboro had shot a deer up near Miller's Ford, across the creek from the church. The man had risked a poor shot and wounded the deer. The deer had run; the hunter, angry at the waste of a cartridge, let it go, jumped into his truck and headed back to town.

As Winton spoke, Albert stared into the fire. He said nothing, only shook his head slowly. He walked to the hallway and put on his heavy coat. "Get Emerson," he told me, a bite to his voice. He went back to where Winton stood by the fire. I could still hear them, hear Albert saying that we couldn't leave the wounded deer in the hills, not in this cold, the wind heavy and strong and smelling of snow. The creature deserved better, a quick death, if nothing else.

Emerson came out of the kitchen, where he had been fixing supper. Albert unlocked the gun cabinet and took out his huge army .45-caliber pistol and three shells. He put the pistol in his coat pocket and headed out the door. "The deer will be on the ground by now, if it's still alive," said Emerson as he followed, putting on his coat, pulling a blue wool cap down snugly over his ears. "We've got to get it down quickly. Christ, don't you think a civilized man from town with a big truck and a bigger rifle could get it done neatly. At least show a little mercy, kill the beast cleanly. We've got to get it done fast," he said again, a swelling urgency in his voice.

Using the small wooden bridge over Blue Light Branch, we crossed the creek, parked the truck, walked hurriedly up the hill along a worn cattle path, and crossed into the dense woods of Bower's Hollow. Emerson found a fresh wallow in the damp brown grasses. Fallen leaves the color of beaver fur were smeared with dark red blood, still warm to the touch. The blood trail led to the creek, then back up the hill. In ever larger pools, the blood reflected the sky, becoming darker and darker, almost black against the muted colors of the winter ground. Fifty yards farther up, Albert found it, a young buck, perhaps a year old, lying on its side. The bullet had shattered its right front leg high up, near the shoulder. The deer tossed its head violently, gasped for air. You could hear the icy air rattling in its lungs. One brown eye stared at the graying sky, the dim light filtering through the leafless trees. Months later, on the creek, staring at that first trout, I would remember the deer's eyes as well. An indomitable light flashed in the trout's eye. I had seen that same light in the eye of the dying deer, even after the eye itself had glazed over, become opaque.

As we knelt by the deer, night was coming on fast and it had started to snow. Flakes of wet snow stuck to the deer's hide. We knelt there, all of us, a loose circle of humanity around one dying deer, and no one said anything or exchanged a look. Then I heard it—music. Deep, stirring music, reverent, inspiring. It came from across the creek, the notes clear and powerful, carried on the wind, mingling with the stream's hissing and the falling snow. Through the trees I could see the church atop the ridge. The whole building was bathed in light, decorated grandly for the Christmas season. Behind the stained-glass windows I could see dark shapes flickering in lantern light, shadows parading in the windows' liquid colors. Women and children carried candles. And the choir sang, loud and strong, like the pounding thunder of a sudden storm, a song that filled the entire valley. Sometimes, still, I hear that song, those strange lyrics:

> Brethren, see poor sinners round you,
> Trembling on the brink of woe;

Death is coming, hell is moving,
Can you bear to see them go?
See your fathers, see your mothers,
And your children sinking down;
Brethren, pray, and holy manna
Will be showered all around.

Albert reached into his coat pocket and took out the big pistol. The sound of the shot rose on the wind, joined the loud singing, became one more melded note in the old gospel song. Blood mixed with snow and we went about the work of cleaning the deer there on the hillside, leaving what could not be used behind us, food for the creatures already gathering nearby, their nostrils full of death's pungent smell. The rest we carried down the hill. Nothing could be left as waste. Nothing.

I never really knew how long it had been going on. Perhaps thirty years. Maybe more. By the time of my arrival among the old men, the meetings between them and the good Reverend Biddle had long since settled into an uncomplicated ritual. Biddle knew that Albert and Emerson and Elias Wonder were well anchored beyond whatever he might tell them, say to them, either as friend or reverend. That didn't matter, however, because he liked them, perhaps even admired them a little. Likewise, the old men liked the Reverend Biddle and often felt bad that they couldn't bring themselves to believe in the God that he believed in so totally and unconditionally. Sometimes, I thought that perhaps they envied him, as well.

The Reverend Biddle came to the house the last Sunday of every month. These Sundays were always looked forward to, for they involved a good meal, wine, hours of heady conversation. Biddle took it as his personal mission to save the old men from hell. He had determined years before that they should be led, willingly or not, into the magnanimous arms of righteousness.

Biddle had tired, mouselike eyes, a rounded, fleshy chin,

sunken cheeks, and a few tufts of silky gray hair on his melon-shaped head. He was given to moping about a great deal, and from his perpetually slumped shoulders one got the impression that he hauled the sins of the world, or at least his part of it, the congregation of the Mount Hebron First Primitive Methodist Church, 106 threatened souls, on his aching back. His followers worshipped him. They worshipped him because they not only suspected that he was in direct contact with God, they knew it. They knew it because Biddle had performed a miracle. The old ones never forgot the night it happened; the young ones grew up on their haunting stories of God's intervention through the Reverend Biddle's holy hands.

It happened on a Sunday morning in September 1945. While on his way to the church to prepare for the day's services, the Reverend Biddle saw an enormous dark hump in the road, curled up in the morning's fog and lacy shadows. He pulled his car off the road, got out to find Lloyd Haysberry's two-year-old milk cow laid out stiff as a frozen cat across the highway, just across from Haysberry's place. As for what followed, Haysberry saw the whole thing and it left him mute for two days until he finally blurted out the incredible story at the café, yelling at the top of his weak, hacking voice that quivered like a plucked guitar string every time he spoke.

The first time through, no one in the café could make out a syllable of what Haysberry was trying to say. It all came out as coughs or hiccups, incoherent rambling. It wasn't until Big Joe came out of the kitchen and poured a pitcher of iced tea over him that Haysberry settled down, sat on a nearby chair, and while crushing his brown fedora in his nervous hands told how the Reverend Biddle had raised his milk cow from the dead.

"She'd been there on the road nearly all night," whispered Haysberry, looking cautiously around the room, as if he half expected Satan to be among the gathering crowd. "I thought I'd heard a truck out on the road after midnight, and later thought maybe it had hit her good and kilt her dead. Guess she got

through the hole I never fixed along the roadside fence. Anyways, I walked out to the highway and put my hand on her.
Stone dead, I tell ya. Colder than January ice. No warmth in
her at all. I bent down and put my head to her chest. Nothing.
Quieter than a potato cellar. There was frost on her eyes and
mouth. I started cursing up a storm, I did, and finally went to
get the truck and a length of rope to drag her off the highway.
Thought maybe I could still salvage the meat.

"When I came back out the house with the rope, the Reverend Biddle was standing over her. I saw him touch her frozen
head, kinda kick her gentle like. He said some words over her I
couldn't make out and, I tell ya, that cow began to move. As
cold as it was, I broke out in a bad sweat. That cow moved its
legs and I dropped to my knees right there on the porch. My
cow got to her feet slow like, like maybe some other force was
helping her, some other hand was on her. Then the Reverend
Biddle—and this here's the eerie part—he don't think nothin'
if it. Just shrugs his shoulders, gets back into his car and drives
off. I spent nearly the whole of that day on my knees, tears
filling my eyes, and I couldn't speak. There must be some kinda
law that goes with divine miracles involving raising the dead
that whoever witnesses the miracle loses his speech for two
days. But, friends, I tell ya this: it was the hand of our Lord
workin' through the reverend."

And everybody gasped with reverence. This was something,
something indeed, that God would show up in Mount Hebron,
work a miracle in their midst. No one doubted Haysberry's story.
He was a good man, a good Christian, and no one had ever
caught him in a lie before. Why not, said the townspeople.
Stranger things had happened. God seemed to have a special
gift for manifesting himself in the most peculiar ways. Wasn't
there the Shroud of Turin, and the healing waters of Lourdes. It
seemed like every time you picked up the newspaper, God had
shown up in someone's Christmas lights, carved his image in a
beanfield, cast his shadow across some adobe hut in Wolfe's

Hole, Arizona, or been sighted mowing a lawn in France. So why not Mount Hebron's Holy Cow.

The faster Haysberry's story spread throughout the county, the more credible it became. News of the miracle on Mount Hebron highway swept over the countryside like some unstoppable virus. It touched everyone, refueled their broken faith, offered hope to the hopeless, promised salvation to the damned, health to the sickly, healing to the incurable. If the Reverend Biddle had the divine power to restore life to a lousy milk cow, said everyone, just think what he could do with their ravaged bodies and souls. And all with a painless touch of his hand.

"Touch me," pleaded Reilly Larson, as he stopped the Reverend Biddle in the street and lifted up his artificial leg to receive Biddle's magic touch. Biddle screamed and ran to his car. The more the good reverend denied his divine powers, the more his congregation flocked about him, yearning for his healing touch, the miracles in his fingertips.

As Biddle's reputation as a humble saint grew, so did the fame of Haysberry's milk cow. For as long as she lived, people traveled to her stall on the Haysberry farm to ogle her, pray to her, touch her, wonder why God had chosen to raise her from the dead. After all, she wasn't even a decent milk cow. Falling into fits of divine epilepsy, some worshippers cut off pieces of her hide for luck. Others flopped about Haysberry's barnyard speaking to her in tongues and were surprised to find that she responded. Her stall became a shrine, a place where people left flowers, simple gifts, photographs of dead relatives. The old cow took the adulation for as long as she could, then died. Haysberry toyed with the idea of having her stuffed, keeping her on as a paid attraction, twenty-five cents a look. But winter was coming on and so he ate her instead.

Biddle's resurrection of Haysberry's milk cow hounded him for the rest of his life. No one believed for one minute that he had nothing whatsoever to do with either the cow's life or death, and in the end he gave in and touched anyone who asked, just so they would go away and leave him alone. For years, no matter where he went he seemed to stumble on people who would throw themselves in his path, crying hysterically to be touched by his ineffable hand, the hand that had put the life back into Haysberry's milk cow. And Biddle would touch them quickly, wincing all the while. The whole matter reached its apex the Sunday Mrs. Priddy, from across Blackberry Run, showed up in the first pew loosely disguised in a freshly tanned cowhide. "Moo," she cried mournfully. Biddle stepped down from behind the lectern and touched her gently between her floppy ears, one brown and one white, because Mrs. Priddy had liver cancer and her luck had run out.

It never seemed to matter that no one the Reverend Biddle touched ever got better, recovered, reported a cure. No one really cared. No one seemed the worse for it—no one, that is, except Biddle, who boiled his hands in lye water three times a day and who had stopped sleeping at night. He dreamed of dead cows littering the highway.

One of Biddle's few escapes from his great burden of divine power was getting into his two-tone green Pontiac once a month and driving as fast as hell out to Trail's End, because Emerson and Albert thought the good reverend was kind and thoughtful rather than aloof and divine. While they thought he was a good man, they didn't believe he had the power to raise dead cows, especially Haysberry's old cow, which they knew for a fact had a habit of napping out on the highway. The asphalt held the heat and she liked that.

Still, walking about with the perceived power of immortality in his fingertips was a grave responsibility, one that the Reverend Biddle learned to shoulder with dignity and humility, even when the religious pilgrims who sought him out were less than satisfied.

"Ouch!" bellowed Garland Nobben. Nobben had sunk to his knees in front of the Reverend Biddle as he ate at the café. Nobben rubbed his forehead and climbed to his feet. "I asked you to save me, Pastor, not kill me, for God's sake!"

"Have you faith, brother Nobben?" mumbled Biddle, biting deeply into a bacon, lettuce, and tomato sandwich.

"Naturally," said Nobben reverently.

Biddle wiped a dab of mayonnaise from his lips. "Then go forth, read your Bible, lead a good, clean, and righteous life, and you will be saved, dear sir. I assure you."

After one such encounter, Biddle hopped in the Pontiac and drove like a madman out to the farm, showed up like a peddler wracked and bent from his load of pots and pans, a man of God seeking temporary refuge from his cargo of redemption, his flock of unquestioning believers. As the door opened, he almost fell into Emerson's arms. Slowly, he made his way to the big room, shed his stern black coat and collar, sank into the rocking chair and leaned his head back, his moist, tender eyes red with exhaustion, salvation's endless turmoil. He sat like this, like a reptile on a warm stone, for perhaps half an hour, letting all the tension in him dissipate, siphon out of his muscles like poison. Suddenly, he straightened up in the rocking chair, moistened his lips, began to speak.

"Wait!" Albert yelled, throwing his arms up in irritation. "For chrissakes, Biddle. All these years and you still can't keep the routine straight, can you? First the wine, then the sermon and so on."

Biddle laid his head back against the chair and whispered, "Yes, Albert. First the wine."

Albert made fruit and wild berry wines in the old copper still in the barn. There was always a big clay jug cooling in the waters of Starlight Creek. The jug sat on the bottom of the creek, secured by a rope tied around its neck at one end and a nearby gum tree at the other.

I fetched the jug, pulled it up out of the cool creek water, and we all gathered in the big room and the men drank the wine from large water glasses while eating a good meal. The old men always tried to have something special for the reverend.

Perhaps some fried quail and lima beans and cornbread, or a stuffed wild turkey with rice and gravy and fresh biscuits, or maybe just a good plate of beans and bacon, with fresh bread, butter, and plenty of cool wine.

And at last, Biddle took off his hat, revealing the perfectly round bald spot on the crown of his flushed head, a spot that gleamed, everybody said, just like a halo. Just another sign, boasted the proud members of the Mount Hebron First Primitive Methodist Church, that Conrad Biddle was no ordinary man. He had truly been touched by the hand of God.

The Reverend Biddle was neat, efficient, a man of telling ecclesiastical aplomb, who was against evil and for good, though he often, said Emerson, got the two confused. The old men felt sorry for him and worried about his fragile health. After all, should he die, who would be around to touch him and bring him back to life?

Biddle, in turn, worried about the old men. He even worried about Elias Wonder, even though he believed Wonder was moonstruck, crack-brained as he had ever seen, and therefore beyond whatever good his prayers might do for him. Biddle was greatly troubled about the old men because if he failed to save their tortured, misguided souls, they would spend eternity in the bowels of hell. It bothered him even more deeply that Albert and Emerson were so calmly resigned to doing just that—dying.

Biddle cleared his throat, couched his words in a cloak of deadly gravity. "But don't you know what waits beyond the grave for the unforgiven," he implored them, a drop of wine on his bottom lip.

"Rot," answered Albert cheerfully, as though he were the only child in a classroom who knew the answer to a difficult question. "Followed by ripeness."

Biddle adjusted himself in the rocker, pursed his lips in thought, tried again. "Death for those not reborn in Christ is death," he explained, lamplight collecting in the soft dark folds of skin under his eyes.

Emerson then came to life. "Death! Why, brother Biddle, you say the word as though it were something altogether deplorable. Why not death? An end to things. A beginning for other things. What better solution to a man's life than his death?"

Biddle took out the red bandana he kept in his pants pocket, wiped his face, and asked for another glass of wine. And the hours went by and the wine flowed, as did the debate, which was always friendly and often comical. Unable to stay seated once his theological blood had been warmed, the Reverend Biddle, his dinner eaten and his resolve renewed, leapt up out of the rocking chair and paced the room, his hands jammed in his pockets. He laid a frayed Bible in the seat of the rocker. To me the book looked twice the size of Albert's big black atlas.

The more Biddle paced, the more impassioned he became. Meanwhile, Albert and Emerson, a congregation of unflappable infidels, relaxed on the truncated couch. It wasn't their refusal to believe in a supreme life force that saddened and aggravated Biddle; rather it was their refusal to believe in God, an omniscient, omnipotent God who spoke English, was certain of Anglo-Saxon heritage and preferences, a God who loved America and Americans more than he loved, say, the Japanese, a fact that Biddle defied anyone to disprove.

"Poverty," said Albert, raising his hand.

"Where?" shouted Biddle suspiciously.

"Right here," Albert replied good-naturedly. "You just had supper with it."

At moments like these, Biddle always had some wise theological saying, something to parry whatever thrust the old men poked him with. "Every spiritual investment yields eternal returns," he shouted, waving his hands jubilantly in the air.

"Yeah," mused Emerson. "but at what cost and what rate of interest?"

As the evening wore on, debate gave way to a dueling chorus of anxious questions and uncertain answers.

"There is no single right faith," lamented Emerson. He and

Albert, it seemed, had dabbled in them all over their long lives. Buddhism, Confucianism, Lamaisam, Taoism, Hinduism, Zen. They had bowed to the East, prayed to the West. They had tried to be upstanding Lutherans, Baptists, Mormons, Shakers, Catholics, Mennonites, Dunkers, and Moravians. They had sampled the wisdom of Martin Luther, Muhammed, Joseph Smith, John Wesley, John Calvin, Christ, Buddha, even Nazareth D. Whipple, who had a place down by Elk Fork. Whipple believed he had found the place where God had holed up after man got out of control. It was out in New Mexico, down in the wild, mean country of the Rio Grande Gorge. Whipple was a persuasive man and had up to thirty-nine believers and every year they would all pack up and go out to New Mexico. They never found anything except some pretty rocks and a lot of good Indian blankets. Whipple made his last expedition in 1940, alone. Again, he came back empty-handed. That was the summer he predicted the world would end on December 31, 1943. Nazareth Whipple died in the summer of '42; the world, for better or worse, kept going.

Nothing they tried had calmed the old men, had answered their questions, eased their doubts.

"What questions?" asked Biddle

"Adam and Eve had sons?" said Albert cautiously. "Who had the daughters?"

Having caught the rhythm, Emerson piped up, without missing a beat. "How did God spend his time before the Creation? Did he have another line of work?"

"Heaven," speculated Albert. "I don't get heaven. Where is it, exactly? Up? Down? East? West? Another planet? Another universe? Or is it just out the back door, down by the creek? If it's not in my neighborhood, do I have to go? You know how homesick I get, brother Biddle."

Emerson was up now, collecting the supper plates. He turned to Biddle with a quizzical look. "If God is our father, who is our mother?"

"Is God against disease, ignorance, litter, bad plumbing, malnutrition?" needled Albert. "And if so, how can we tell?"

"Why not just happiness?" Emerson shouted from the kitchen. "Why not serenity? Why homelessness? Why war and dead young soldiers, and tooth decay? And tell me, dear Conrad, why are there so few happy endings? You tell me of sinners. Show me the saints."

Biddle jumped to the floor, Bible in hand, and like the happy evangelist he was, pummeled them with the good word, the good news. He was like a modern-day oracle, his quiver loaded with sacred arrows.

"Surely the day is coming; it will burn like a furnace. All the arrogant and every evildoer will be stubble, and that day that is coming will set them on fire, says the Lord Almighty. Not a root or a branch will be left to them. But for you who revere my name, the sun of righteousness will rise with healing in its wings. And you will go out and leap like calves released from the stall. Then you will trample down the wicked; they will be ashes under the soles of your feet on the day when I do these things, says the Lord Almighty." Biddle threw the Bible down on the chair for effect, for the sound was like rolling thunder. "Heed the word of Malachi," he said with exhaustion. Tears welled in the corners of his eyes. Gathering his composure, he again raised his arms toward the ceiling and brought the words up deep from his round, lumpy belly. "Repent, sinners, and assure your place in God's heaven before it's too late."

"It's too late," sighed Emerson almost every Sunday that Biddle came for his visit until the old men died.

One Sunday, Biddle arrived to find the madman Elias Wonder stretched out on the floor in front of the fireplace, a pillow propped under his enormous head of thick shiny black hair.

"Qué pasa, Padre?" Wonder said as cheerfully as he ever said anything.

Elias Wonder's black eyes were always sizing up Biddle. Whenever the Indian was at hand, Biddle doubled up on his wine.

"How's the soul business, Father?" Wonder said, knowing that the words were like splinters under Biddle's skin.

"It's Reverend, not Father," Biddle corrected calmly. "And you should count your blessings." He said the words carefully, as though he were fondling the beads of a rosary.

"My blessings!" howled Wonder, his eyes rolling back in his head, his head falling off the pillow with an audible thud. Then those black Indian eyes became narrow, reptilian slits staring at Biddle. "What blessings?"

"Why, everything," chimed Biddle, knocking back half a glass of wine. "Remember Psalm 86:5: 'Thou, Lord, art good, and ready to forgive; and plenteous in mercy.'"

A growl came from deep in Wonder's throat. Refusing the wine, he instead reached for the flask of whiskey and cold creek water he kept in his coat pocket. "Blessings," he repeated, rubbing his chin. "Oh, you mean my opulent dwelling down the creek? My six fingers? My seven toes? Perhaps my one lung or my skipping heart, or that cloud of mustard gas that keeps following me around? How many blessings is that? Shall I go on, mention my throbbing head, my chronic cough, the pain in my eyes when I'm sober?"

Biddle raised his right index finger, held it high, as if pointing the way to salvation. "I am the door: by me if any man enter in, he shall be saved, and shall go in and out, and find pasture."

"Get this, Albert," sneered Elias Wonder. "I'm dying a thousand deaths and the Reverend Biddle's offering me hay."

"You are alive, brother Elias," counseled Biddle, "and that's something." He tried to sound uplifting, hopeful.

Wonder rearranged the pillow, flipped over on his stomach. "Yeah, I'm alive and tomorrow I could catch Morley's disease and be dead, no thanks to you or God."

"What's wrong with Mr. Morley?" asked Biddle, genuinely concerned, for Morley was one of his congregation, a man of abiding faith.

"Beats me, Priest. But whatever nails him, I'll get as well. Good ol' E. W., the human guinea pig. You know, your Holiness, frankly I think God's got it in for me and will get me in the end. I'm only sixty-six years old and death has been nibbling away at me ever since I can remember."

"'I will not leave you comfortless'... John 14:18," quoted Biddle, looking sadly down at Wonder, hoping the words would connect. "Life could be worse, Elias."

"Life could be a damn lot better, Rabbi," said Wonder, nursing his flask.

As a sign of solidarity, a unity of feelings, if not ideas, Cody coiled up at Elias Wonder's feet and went to sleep. He had no doubts. God and heaven came with the sunrise and he wanted to be well rested to greet them.

"Chaplain," Albert began, picking up the loose, unraveling thread of the conversation.

"My God, Albert, I'm 'Reverend,'" interrupted Biddle.

"Right, kind confessor, but my question is this: should we follow so blindly, so willingly, so indiscreetly a God whose master plan includes baldness, warts, senility, diarrhea, lumbago, dermatitis, pinkeye, St. Anthony's fire, and bunions?"

"Yeah!" interjected Wonder with fierce approval. And why not. He had suffered from every ailment Albert had listed, except for baldness. Indeed, Albert could have gone on and on. Elias Wonder prided himself on surviving every malady the world had flung so maliciously at him.

Chewing on a quail bone, Albert continued. "Is such a God a just God? A merciful God? The God of goodness and joy?"

A smile edged triumphantly across Biddle's face, even tracking into the sad pockets of his cheeks. "One and the same," he beamed. "The Lord shall give thee rest from thy sorrow'... Isaiah 14:3."

"Why pain?" inquired Emerson sincerely, the two words spoken in a low voice, more a thought than a question. "You know, Conrad, even death can be accomplished without it. Out there in the natural world, it happens all the time. You would think that God, whatever or whoever he is, with all that power at his command, could have at least eased pain."

"Yes," moaned Elias Wonder, who was suffering from a stomach ulcer at the time. "Just ease the pain."

"With all that power," Emerson reflected, "imagine not what he came up with, which seems an awkward blunder, especially in putting together man, but what he could have done. All that possibility wasted."

"'The Lord my God will enlighten my darkness.'" Biddle prayed. "Psalm 18:28." Opening his eyes, he turned to Emerson. "How can you cling to what passes, what is without hope?" Biddle wondered aloud. He loosened his collar, sipped the sweet wine.

"Don't good Christians believe that they are made in God's image?" Emerson said. "Well, I had a dream once, Conrad. A long time ago, but I remember it clearly. It was that God was more like us than we were like him, and we were all on the same road, always changing, evolving not in a void but in the belly of life's chaos. Even the earth was not still, but on the move, the very ground I stood on drifting like a boat upon a dark sea. All was rock and geography, the animate and inanimate joined. Life to earth and stone and back somehow to life again. Variety and richness, like the earth itself, like the rocks and air and water, the things that are the same on both sides of the grave. And though we were all one, neither were we one and the same. There were always differences, a wonderful arpeggio sung by the universe itself and shaped by the earth. It was some dream, Friar. Only such dreams have brought me a dose of comfort and understanding."

Biddle worked the pages of the big Bible. "'All things work together for good to them that love God' . . . Romans 8:28."

Elias Wonder, like a great beached sea lion, had again flipped over on his belly, resting his head in his wrinkled, rough hands. His breath, smelling of kerosene and hickory, spiced the room's atmosphere.

Whiskey brought out the orator in Wonder, made him a regular jawsmith, silver-tongued and irresistible. His voice dropped to a mellow, searching tone. "Cardinal, I had me a dream once, too. Just once, right after I walked into that daisy-yellow cloud of mustard gas. Everything went black and then a sun like no other sun I had seen, a sun of boiling reds and rusty oranges, rose over a land I did not recognize. Suddenly there was a naked creature with long black hair and somber eyes standing at the edge of a great green forest that stretched without a break to the horizon. The creature had an eagle feather in its hair.

"Preacher, I knew instantly that that creature was man. It was us. Nature had spit us out as if we were something sour, unnatural, tainted, grotesque. And the creature took the eagle feather from its hair and flung it to the ground, stomped on it, took an oath of revenge on the earth, the earth that would not let him back in. The man had a troubled heart and sought to soothe it by conquering the earth, subduing it. He would be the highest creature of them all. He would be king, the earth's master. But you know, your Eminence, even his own kind would turn on him, bring him bad news. Soon, that dolt Copernicus would tell him that this world wasn't the center of the universe, that everything did not revolve about him in contrite submission. And that dumpy, scruffy-looking limey Darwin would spring the surprise of evolution on him, kick him out of the lap of the gods and into the trees with the apes. And that nut case Freud hurt man most of all, shattering his moral heart and mind, letting him know that he was instead a creature of considerable perversion. A troubled creature indeed.

"You want to know the rest of the dream, Vicar? It's just

black teeth, sharp-pointed teeth and pitted molars, grinders, thousands of feet high and everywhere gobbling, gobbling, consuming, consuming, without thought or reason. And then I woke up in a hospital bed and discovered I was Robert E. Lee, which was a great disapointment because I had always wanted to be Crazy Horse, or Gall, or Sitting Bull."

Biddle slammed the Bible down hard into his open fist and in a great apocalyptical voice, a voice that boomed and proclaimed, shuddered, "'The Lord is my shepherd; I shall not want.'"

"I want," Albert groaned.

"Want what?"

"To know why!" Albert shrieked.

"Why?"

"Why lockjaw? Why cold sores? Why toxic goiter? Why shingles? Why Cleveland? Where are the trout of yesteryear?" yowled Albert.

Biddle stood tall, unshaken. "All answers come to him that believeth in the Lord thy God," he said in his best revival-tent voice. "Without accepting Christ, you risk the hereafter, heaven itself."

"Oh, no, your Holiness. Not at all," chortled Wonder, who was flushed now from the whiskey and the warmth of the fireplace. "No, we'll be back. Life's immortality is more important than our own. My father told me that. His name was He That Follows the Sun. He was a true Sioux. He was wise. His brains had not been scrambled by the white man or by mustard gas or by any of civilization's contrivances. We'll be back, not as ourselves, of course, but as life, the life we have led. We will rise like trout in a dark mountain stream, rise bravely to the surface."

"Amen," said Albert, lifting his glass high.

"You're doomed," cried the Reverend Biddle, drowning a sly smile with a glass of sweet apple wine.

Wiping his mouth on his shirt, Albert turned to Biddle with a new look of intense seriousness. "Is it true, Conrad, that Satan hails from New Jersey?"

Biddle stopped pacing the floor, came to a dead stop, rubbed his bald pate. "Could be," he mused. "I mean, why not. Hell is hell."

At the end of each of these Sunday meetings, as the day's light faded like a mist beyond the hills and shadows crept out of the woods, spread over the fields, the Reverend Biddle would offer a prayer for the old men's souls. He always asked God to look after them, even though they were not "official Christians." And the happy, contented old atheists would see him off, then gather up their fly rods and hurry on down to the creek to feel it cold against their thighs and watch the last of the light flicker like candlelight off its surface and feel the cold evening air against their faces. Once, I remember Albert saying, as his line performed a perfect series of arabesques behind him, "Tell me, Emerson. Do you think that if God had to live as we do, he would?"

And a month later, Biddle would return, take up his assault, hurl the gospel at them, pray to God to forgive them, implore them to follow Christ to heaven.

"I like this world," answered Albert after one such drubbing. Silky sunlight flooded the big room. "It's home. Why would I want to spend eternity somewhere else, skipping about in a white dress and strumming a harp? What kind of a Paradise is that, anyway? Perhaps the only thing that is eternal is eternity. This harp business really bothers me, brother Biddle. You know I'm a harmonica man. Is there a place in heaven for a man that plays the blues? What's Satan's side of all this? What's he offering? Does hell have a blues band?"

Biddle muttered a long prayer and the old men would go on about life, how they loved it because it was like a rising fog, refusing to take definite shape, become fixed. It was fickle, erratic, amorphous, a great unpredictable energy, as easily changed as clouds in storm-tossed winds. This was its charm, its unending allure. And the God the old men didn't believe in was a part of it all, immersed in it, there and not there. Elias Wonder's Great Mystery.

Albert and Emerson seemed to fit no modern niche. They were certainly not Economic Man or Military Man. Neither did they have much in common with the emerging Psychological Man or Technological Man. They were Transitory Man. Farmers. Subsistence farmers. Men of the earth. And that was enough for them, as long as they had the creek, the smell of the sweet earth, the sun's heat on their skin, the bobcats screaming in the hills, trout rising in the creek, a daily rite of resurrection, ongoing redemption. Blessed were the transitory: the past and present vouchsafing the future. The equation seemed simple enough: decay to fertility, fertility to decay. On and on.

"Watch your step," Albert warned the Reverend Biddle. "The earth is always on the move, even as we stand, inching beneath us like an ancient worm."

The last Sunday I saw the Reverend Biddle while the old men were still alive was much like the others, a heady mixture of wine and fascinating conversation, the usual prayers and scriptures; the familiar doubts and endless questions from the aging nonbelievers. Biddle had a little more wine than was his custom and near twilight Albert took him by the arm and lead him to the back porch. The door was open and I could hear the waters of Starlight Creek splashing over, wearing down ancient stone. The two men walked down the steps and out toward the path that led down to the creek. A film of yellow moonlight shimmered on the water. A coyote howled in the distance. Albert stopped, put his big hand on Biddle's bent shoulders, and said softly, "Welcome, brother Conrad, to the Kingdom of God. You stand at heaven's gate. Won't you enter?"

Even in the muted, hazy moonlight, I could see Biddle regard Albert with a crooked but generous smile. "Blasphemer," he whispered as though he might indeed have been in his pulpit at the Mount Hebron First Primitive Methodist Church. He took a great gulp of the brisk night air.

"Amen," said Albert, and he pulled Biddle closer to him and both men began to laugh, until Albert stopped short. "Look here, brother Biddle," he said, "perhaps you could do an old heretic a Christian favor. Lately, I can get to the creek; I can cast my line and dry fly; indeed, I can do everything but get these satanic trout to gobble up my humble offering. There wouldn't by chance be a Psalm or catchy prayer to take care of a malady like this, would there? You know, maybe something that begins 'Almighty Lord, why is it my rod and my reel have turned on me? Bring back their comfort, their grace, their luck.' . . . You know, something like that."

And Biddle just went on laughing, laughing so hard he finally had to drop his wine glass and tumble to the ground in helpless sobs.

After a time, the old men came in. Biddle gathered up his coat, his hat, his Bible. He buttoned up his collar, took a drink of cold water to wash out his mouth. The instant he walked out the door he took on that bent posture of his, the wrinkled look of an accordian. He swayed gently as he walked across the grass toward his car, so heavy was his load of goodness and piety and saving grace.

"It is fitting that such a good and kind man is among the chosen," commented Albert. "Bless him."

"Yes, bless him," echoed Albert.

"Chili vinegar," said Elias Wonder faintly, but proudly.

"Eh?"

"Chili vinegar. It's the whiskey's secret ingredient. I stole it from Big Joe's chili recipe."

Albert touched Elias' arm gently, knowing he had, again, slipped back into the invisible cloud of mustard gas that followed him about like his shadow.

Down the drive, they could hear the good Reverend Biddle

singing loudly, singly over the drone of the Pontiac's big engine, a hymn called "The Old Gospel Ship."

I have good news to bring
And that is why I sing.
All my joys with you I'll share.
I'm going to take a trip
In the old Gos-pel ship
And go sailing through the air.

Chorus
O I'm gon-na take a trip
In the old Gos-pel ship,
I'm going far beyond the sky;
O I'm gon-na shout and sing
Until the heavens ring,
When I'm bidding this world good-bye.

7. DAYS OF WONDER

He was like trout. You never knew when he might rise out of the darkness. And even when he did, like trout he kept his mystery intact.

— *Emerson Newell on Elias Wonder, 1966*

As we walked toward the mailbox alongside the Mount Hebron highway where I was to catch the school bus, I started counting in my head. Counting schools, all the schools I had attended. The old men had gone into the fields early, right after breakfast, and Elias Wonder kept me company, walked beside me. I had counted up to seven schools when I noticed that Wonder was barefoot again. An old Indian custom, he told me. Shoes were an artificial barrier between a man and the ground, kept a man too far removed from the good earth. He liked the feel of cool, damp grass under his feet, between his toes. He never wanted to stop feeling the earth. To hell with shoes.

Elias Wonder said pure Sioux blood ran in his veins. He was half Sans Arc and half Brulé. I never doubted him—not with that ruddy complexion, high cheekbones, wide, defiant mouth, broad, powerful chin, and dark eyes that held the light like the surface of polished stones. Eyes heavy with untold stories of despair, anguish, grief, heartache. Elias Wonder rarely smiled. He was short and squat, with thick lampblack hair combed straight back, massive hands, and bowed legs.

I slumped against the mailbox, feeling sluggish, bogged down in an ooze of sticky depression. School! I certainly had not mentioned the subject, and for a full two weeks the matter had never come up, so I assumed—okay, hoped—that my education was to be left in the capable hands of Albert and Emerson. Then Emerson showed up at my bedroom door, and said it—"School tomorrow."

"What?" I mumbled as I looked up from the pages of De-Voto's *Across the Wide Missouri*, hoping I had somehow misunderstood him.

"School."

No, he had said it, all right. The word seemed to fall out of the air like a stone: something final, inescapable. I was angry to learn that modern education had succeeded in setting up shop in such a beautiful place as this narrow, isolated mountain valley. It just didn't make sense. From what I had seen, there seemed even fewer souls to educate than to save.

I would be attending the Oglala County Junior and Senior High School, grades seven through twelve. The bus, county school bus No. 2 (out of five), would pick me up daily between 7:00 and 7:15 in the morning.

"It's not Harvard, son, but there's something there worth knowing, I'm sure," Emerson said with appropriate empathy. Albert, sporting a scholarly smile, stood just behind him. Neither of the old men had made it through high school.

And now here I was waiting for the bus. Another bus. I leaned my rucksack up against the stump onto which the mailbox was nailed.

Elias Wonder's eyes searched the fog-shrouded highway. "There," he said with a start. "There, by that old hickory. That's where I decided to finally do it."

"Do what?" I asked fearlessly. I had already learned that

since Elias Wonder was completely loco he was probably the sanest man in Oglala County. He was harmless.

He said, "Die, just die."

I looked at him, the high forehead, those raven-black, haunting eyes, the muscles twitching just below his cheekbones. The color of his skin reminded me of damp red clay.

"Just die," he said again, his voice tinged with regret that he hadn't died all those years ago by the hickory tree just down the highway.

He turned and faced me, his eyes almost liquid in the early morning light. I always found it impossible to accept that behind such kind eyes sat an unhinged mind.

"And I would have, too, if those two old white men hadn't spotted my body, chipped me out of the snow and ice, thawed me out. I remember opening my eyes and thinking surely I had gone to the bad place, the land of no rest. Goddamnit, I thought, even dead I'm surrounded by white men. But I wasn't dead yet and finding that out was a great disappointment to me."

And it was, because for as long as anyone in the valley could recall, Elias Wonder had been threatening to die.

The old men had found Elias Wonder alongside the Mount Hebron highway in the winter of 1927. It had been snowing for two days. They wrapped the Indian's body in wool blankets and rushed him to the farmhouse. His skin had turned the dull gray color of zinc. They pulled him out of a threadbare army coat, a blue wool shirt, and a pair of jeans. Socks but no shoes. He had been dragging a baby-blue steamer trunk along the highway, up and down the hills until he got to the hickory tree and decided to go to sleep and let the cold sing him death's lullaby.

They fed the Indian hot tea and honey, gave him warm, dry clothes. They made a bed of quilts and blankets for him by the fireplace. The first time Elias Wonder came to, he introduced himself as General Robert E. Lee. Emerson was thrilled to finally meet the man his father had served under.

"I surrender," moaned Elias Wonder, his cold body shaking horribly. "I give up."

"No harm in that," Albert said with soothing reassurance. "We all do sooner or later."

It was the next time he floated up to the surface of consciousness, opened his eyes, that Elias Wonder thought he had gone to hell because he was eyeball to eyeball with two old, ugly white men. And when they came into sharper focus he fainted, fled back into the dark, warm, insular safety of his coma.

Papers in the pocket identified the owner of the coat as one Elias Wonder, former corporal in the United States Marine Corps, 1916–1918. Race: American Indian. Place of birth: Unknown. Year: Unknown. Age: Approximately 33. Comments: Non compos mentis resulting from inhaling mustard gas (dichlorodiethyl sulfide, C4H8CL2S), France, 1917. Prognosis: Poor. Treatment: Permanent institutional care. (Signed) Major E. H. Cranby, USMC.

Where had the Indian been between the war's end and 1927? No one knew, including Elias Wonder. When asked, this is what he said: "Looking for someone kind enough to accept my surrender so I could hurry up and die."

Albert's theory was that Elias Wonder had probably just walked out of some bureaucratic bughouse, packed the pretty blue steamer trunk, and hit the road. Who would care, after all? Just one less delirious, crack-brained, slaphappy, pixilated Indian to worry about.

Albert and Emerson had a long and bedeviling tradition of extending help to drifters, bums, free-roaming nut cases, the homeless, the luckless. Their compassion drove the good citizens of Mount Hebron into fits of zealous outrage because they were certain that someday one of these grateful derelicts, one of these revived vagrants, one of these thankful pikers, would skulk into town and want to stay put.

But none ever had. None, that is, except Elias Wonder. And Elias Wonder really scared them because he almost never came to town, where they could keep an eye on him. And when he did show up, he liked to mope about, talking under his breath.

"Land stealers. Rapists. Killers of the old, the young, the innocent. Murderers," Elias Wonder muttered to everyone he bumped into.

"What's he sulking about?" asked Bates nervously, backing away from the Indian. Every time Wonder came in the store, Bates would stand behind the counter fondling the 12-gauge shotgun loaded with buckshot he kept there.

"Beats me," Albert chirped. "Seems he's an Indian with a gripe. Some silly notion that white folks did his people harm, injustice, or some such nonsense. Probably that mustard gas talking. Follows the poor bastard like a cloud. You're safe as long as he's not Robert E. Lee."

Bates stood behind the counter, runnels of sweat coming down his forehead. "Unless he's *who?*" he shouted in a voice shrill with panic and disbelief. When his nerves were about to go, Bates's voice always had a high squeal to it. He began toying with the shotgun trigger. "Just what happens when this lunatic turns into Lee?" he asked, his eyes squinting, following Wonder's every movement about the store.

Albert leaned over the wooden counter, put his mouth close to Bates's ear. "He wants to surrender."

Bates regarded Albert with wide-eyed incredulity, a look equal to that of any madman. "Surrender what?"

Albert shrugged his shoulders. "Beats me, Bates. Beats me." And he put a pound of sugar on the counter along with coffee and flour. "But if I were you and Elias wanted to surrender, I'd graciously accept."

Every time Elias Wonder showed up in town, tried to talk with someone on the street or in the café or in Bates's store, they would smile stiffly, nodding their heads while backpedaling like crazy to get away from him. "I do, General Lee," Mrs. Hinson would holler every time she laid eyes on Elias Wonder.

"I do accept your surrender... And by the way, General, Mr. Hinson would like a pint of whiskey by week's end."

Wonder always stood there shaking his head, whispering to Emerson. "White man, everybody in this one-horse town is nuts. Who the hell is this Lee guy, for chrissakes, and why is he surrendering?"

The news that he sometimes walked back into that cloud of mustard gas and exited as General Lee surprised Wonder, disappointed him. "When I was a kid," he said sadly, "I used to dream that I would wake up as Crazy Horse."

So, unlike all the other nameless, down-and-out men that Emerson and Albert had taken in, clothed, and fed, Elias Wonder, once he thawed out, seemed in no hurry to grab his blue steamer trunk and move on. And the longer he stayed, the more fearful the good people of the valley became. Strangers were one thing. Strangers who were daffy Indians with a habit of walking in and out of reality were intolerable. When it became clear that Wonder planned to stay, for weeks hardly a day went by that someone didn't call Little Bo Hopkins, the county sheriff, screaming that Elias Wonder was at the door preparing to do them in, his body doused in war paint, his maniacal eyes bugging out of his head, but these reports always turned out to be bogus, one hoax after another. The closest thing to an intruder Sheriff Hopkins ever found was a runaway goat draped in a checkered tablecloth eating beer cans piled on Lester Wooten's front porch.

Even after years had passed, no one was entirely sure why Elias Wonder had decided to stay. I asked him once as we waited by the mailbox. This is what he told me: "I know many red men whose insides are white, but those old men back there are the only white men I know whose insides are red."

Both Emerson and Albert took an immediate liking to the eccentric Indian. They all shared common miseries and common joys. "Besides," Albert said, remembering Elias months later, "how often does a crazed Indian walk into a man's life, an

Indian who is not only an expert fly fisherman and a mystic, but a mixologist of the first order, capable of converting corn into a grog with more grace than altar wine, more punch than methane, an Indian of such depth that he could, at a moment's notice, turn into Robert E. Lee? . . . I loved him."

Elias Wonder was more suspicious than grateful when the old men offered him the rundown cabin on Starlight Creek. After all, the history of his tribe was one of seeing white men taking land, not giving it up, especially for free.

"I don't have to sign a rigged treaty?" Elias Wonder prodded, the words oozing with spleen.

Albert said he didn't.

Wonder fidgeted with the bear's tooth he wore on a piece of leather tied around his haggard neck. "You won't take it back next year, make me move to Arizona to live like a reptile in the hot sands? You won't discover oil or gold or uranium there and burn me out or buy me out with cheap jewelry or force me to take up hog farming in Iowa? You won't sneak up on me, infect me with some deadly white man's virus, some lousy bacteria my innocent Indian blood can't take?"

The old men shook their heads and Elias Wonder dragged the big blue steamer trunk downstream to where Susan's Branch joined the creek, to the ramshackle cabin on the far side of Karen's Pool, and set up housekeeping. He built a still and began making the best whiskey anyone in the valley had tasted in years, and the good Reverend Biddle, although upset that the Indian hadn't moved on, accepted his presence, this new burden, this new test of his faith, and decided to save not only Emerson and Albert's tormented souls, but Elias Wonder's too.

Wonder did little to the old cabin. There was a pot-bellied Franklin stove, the three-legged lawn chair, a bed with no springs. Instead, the mattress rested on a tapestry of ropes that Wonder had tied snugly across the sideboards in a crisscross pattern. At the foot of the bed sat the steamer trunk that everyone worried about. The trunk fueled rumors that lived on decade after decade. A great many of the valley's residents believed that Wonder kept something especially hideous in the trunk. Perhaps a white man's skull. Others, believing themselves more modern and practical, believed the trunk to be as empty as the old Indian's brains. Still others feared it might contain enough canisters of mustard gas to turn every brain in the valley into jelly.

Failure was hard work and getting harder. One slip, the old men knew, and something drastic might happen and make the farm a profit-making enterprise. Consequently, Albert and Emerson made Elias Wonder a full partner in the farm. For his effort at helping them keep the place as backward as it had always been, they paid him a good portion of the corn corp, the free cabin, meals, and friendship. In turn he heaped on them excellent liquor, heated opinions, his short temper, and his always delightful, alluring, and mysterious company.

Emerson remembered the first time he fished with the Indian, how much at ease he was in the creek, at home. The natural world seemed to embrace Elias Wonder as one of its own rather than as some temporary intruder. To the old men, Wonder belonged to the natural world, was inseparable from its noisy silences, its great unknowns. In my mind they all were alike: they heard a music few men cared to hear, music played without end by the natural world, which I too desperately wanted to hear, be part of. I never thought of Elias Wonder as a madman. He was, rather, a happy eccentric, a trait he shared with Albert and Emerson.

None of them ever gave in, let go. Hard luck never succeeded in driving them from the land. Ironically, it only increased their bond to it. They marveled at the earth with a child's wonder and never tried to explain life, interpret it, dissect it. They had no use for the notion that human beings were evolution's great triumph, its epitome, its darling rather than its spoiled child. Living was enough; the land was enough; the creek was enough. Their ties to the earth eased time's burden, history's lingering memory, their loneliness as men.

By the time I arrived in Mount Hebron, Elias Wonder was as much a fixture in the valley as the old men themselves. Most of the farmers and their families ignored him with the same bottomless compassion that fueled their pious contempt for Albert and Emerson. Despite the passage of so many years, whenever Elias Wonder made one of his infrequent trips to town, people tended to stay indoors, off the streets. The years had answered so few questions about the Indian, where he had come from, why he had stayed to terrify them. A private man, Elias Wonder never said. He made his whiskey, worked the old farm, spent hour after hour on the creek casting dry flies over the noses of belligerent trout. He did not take ducks to eat, or quail. He left wild turkeys alone, thereby proving his inviolate sanity. Trout alone obsessed him, possessed him.

As we fished the rock-strewn waters of the Peaceable Kingdom above Karen's Pool on a cool evening in March, Elias Wonder startled me by speaking. Normally, conversation bored him; silence was his tongue, his speech. "When I was a boy," he said, "it was the custom among my people that the young men take a wild creature as their cipher, a mark of their approaching manhood, a badge of character. On a raw spring day the young men assembled by the big river that snaked across the prairie. The sun was just rising and the dawn spread across the vast plains, a land that seemed to reach beyond time itself. And we young men then chose. Fox. Panther. Eagle. Deer. Bear. Horse. When my turn arrived I said loudly, clearly, proudly, 'Trout.' My father smiled and was not ashamed. From that moment on, the trout and I have been inseparable."

That's what thrilled me most about Elias Wonder, why I admired him, loved him. He had a great, warming mystery about him. I never knew what a moment with him might yield, except that whatever came would surely be laced with the unusual. The old Indian was a glorious enigma, one I never desired to unravel, figure out.

On that first morning when he walked with me to the mail-box where I was to catch the school bus, he did not stay. Important matters called him back to his cabin. No, not the whiskey still, but a spider that had strung its web in his door-way. Its eggs had hatched, the spiderlings had gone. Now the old female spider was dying. "She never complains," said Wonder, smiling. "Each day she gets weaker and weaker and now she no longer mends her web. The wind, or the intensity of the light, tells her it is time to rest, that her work is over. She has kicked the future out and now waits in her comfortable web to die."

Elias Wonder had been waiting too, and for a long time. He never really forgave the old men for saving his life. An Indian, he said vehemently, had the right to die when and where he liked. And Elias Wonder wanted to check out as quickly as possible. For years the old men worked feverishly yanking him from death's nimble and inexhaustible grasp. Wonder played with death the way a kitten plays with yarn, hoping to become wrapped up in it. The man never spent a day that didn't spawn some horrendous new crop of symptoms that he was certain would be the ones to finally do him in. Fever blisters, recurrent malaria, minor strokes, diurnal epilepsy, chronic cramps, colic, lumbago, arthritis, rheumatism, benign tumors that cost him great chunks of flesh from his stomach, thighs, and right cheek. And every time disease struck him down, Elias Wonder would just chuckle approvingly, telling the old men that sooner or later he'd come down with something they couldn't cure him of. "You can't keep me here forever," he told them. And Albert would baste him with a balm of witch hazel and blue ointment, take his temperature, paint his sores with peroxide and tincture of iodine.

Elias Wonder kept on smiling slyly while coming down with devil's grip, pinkeye, angina pectoris, hemorrhoids, and perni-cious anemia. Albert and Emerson would get up in the middle of the night, slip their coats over their pajamas, light a lantern, walk downstream to Wonder's cabin and wash the floors and walls with lye soap and force-feed the happy victim laxatives, Bromo-Seltzer cut with whiskey, milk of bismuth, and sassafras tea. Everything worked for a while and nothing worked for long. After every remedy, Elias Wonder gleefully fell victim to some other malady. Hard as he tried, however, no matter how sick he became, he always fell just inches short of dying. "Maybe I'm trying too hard," he told Emerson, managing a fey grin while recovering from a bout of bacillary dysentery.

"Not a chance," quipped Emerson, wiping the deep reddish folds of Wonder's face with a cool rag. "Not a chance."

When Elias Wonder limped in his bare feet from Bates's store to the café, children often would point at him and stare in bewilderment, a kind of distant awe. The old Indian had high blood pressure. His arteries were clogged with gooey clumps of cholesterol. He suffered from foggy vision. He had one kidney, one lung, no gallbladder or spleen. He was missing fingers and toes and the children couldn't take their eyes off the old man who seemed to be disappearing before their eyes an organ and an appendage at the time. Their parents would make the children turn away, as if Elias Wonder were the Angel of Death set loose to cast its shadow among them.

Elias Wonder was, despite his fascination with death, in love with life. In was just that since he was well acquainted with life on one side of the soil, he was eager to sample conditions on the other side, down where the roots of grasses and trees mingled.

"But why?" pleaded the Reverend Biddle, his face contorted with disbelief. "The bread of life is not of this world," he yelled, thoroughly flummoxed by Elias Wonder's determination to feel a warm, dark blanket of earth over his bones at last.

"Why not?" Elias Wonder answered, fluid rattling in his one good lung. "Why not?"

· · ·

For months, Elias Wonder walked with me each weekday morning to the mailbox by the highway. Sometimes we talked. More often we didn't, and would just sit there on the ground until we heard the low grumble of the school bus crawling up the hill and he would slip away, moving barefoot through the grass as quietly as a small wind over the surface of the creek. One morning, just before disappearing, he tapped me on the shoulder and said, "During the war, every minute of every day four human beings died. Imagine that."

I thought of Norwell, multiplied him by four, then by hours, days, weeks, months, years, and turned red-faced and shocked. I stared into those dark Indian eyes and said, "I can't. I can't." And Elias Wonder smiled and stepped back into his cloud of mustard gas and vanished as if he too was unable to imagine the carnage, the mountains of bone and gristle and vacant eyes.

It took Oglala County school bus No. 2 exactly thirty-six minutes to creep down the valley past Old Siles, the town that wasn't a town anymore, to the broad meadow where the old school sat. The Oglala County Junior and Senior High School, known as Mountain High, would be the twelfth school of my long but as yet undistinguished educational career. An even dozen from Kaiserslautern, Germany, and Fort Leavenworth, Kansas, to Hampton Roads, Virginia, Okinawa, and Orléans, France. Not a single one stood out in my mind. My first day at Mountain High, as I looked out the window of the bus, I remember thinking that at the least the buildings weren't renovated Quonset huts. Attending a wide variety of schools tends to mold the wandering student into a well-rounded and experienced veteran of higher learning. A dozen in fourteen years. I felt rightfully smug, as though I understood schools the way Cody knew ducks.

The school that sat beguilingly in the open meadow looked like a minimum-security prison. Chain-link fence around three small two-story red brick buildings, the newest of which had been built in 1953. A modest gym, decorated in the school's colors, lobster red and mulberry purple. A huge mural of the school's mascot had been hand-painted on the gym's dull green brick walls behind the single set of bleachers. On studying the mural, my first tentative guesses were wildebeest or feral hog. Recognizing my honest confusion as I looked at the immense, puzzling mural, a fellow student rescued me, whispered, "We're the Panthers." The Oglala County Panthers, 283 all-American students who spent every school day planning their imminent escape from the valley to Memphis, Little Rock, St. Louis, Anywhere.

I reported to the office, where a chubby blond woman with intricately teased hair and apathetic eyes handed me my schedule. "You're the new kid, huh?" she said while lazily adjusting a bright orange miniskirt. I nodded. "We had a dickens of a time getting transcripts on you. You an orphan, a runaway, or what?"

I folded the schedule and tucked it into my shirt pocket. "A refugee, ma'am," I said politely, coating the words with just the right mix of sentimental lacquer.

She looked up at me finally, managed a thin sympathetic smile of almost honest welcome. "Poor dear. And you've been put with those goofballs up the valley. Keep an eye on 'em, young man. My mother knows about those old men. Both nutty. Keep a wild Indian on the place, a mad killer wanted for hideous crimes in who knows how many states." She extended her hand—small, alabaster, white, a ring on every finger. "Always glad to welcome a new Panther," she purred weakly. "Your first class is science, Mrs. Hobhouse."

I shuddered.

Outside the office in the long, gray-green hallway flanked on either side by a row of lockers, I pulled out my schedule card. After Hobhouse came social studies with someone named F. Nozzel, then math with one C. L. Riggles, followed by lunch, followed by English with T. J. Elliot, a sad-eyed man who, I would learn, was extremely sensitive about his name, as though he were only too painfully aware that a couple of misplaced consonants had cost him a life of literary genius. After English came Spanish with Señorita Wanda Tripling and then, last period, physical education overseen by Coach Orel "Dash" Fowler, who, I guessed, stood a little over five feet tall, weighing in at well over three-hundred pounds, and smelling, even across the locker room, like a 100-pound vat of rotten herring.

For weeks I tried in earnest to fit in, become one of the gang at Mountain High, a loyal Panther. Go Red and Purple! Mountain High was the first public school I had ever attended and, as I had always suspected, public school was only moderately more interesting than army-post schools. But all my efforts at acclimatizaton ended in exasperation. During Spirit Week, I had no spirit; weekly pep rallies found me listless, anxious, pepless, my mind constantly preoccupied with the old men, the hills, the creek, the wonder of rising trout. The world beyond the schoolyard fence seemed indomitable, held me under its alluring spell. As an ameliorant to my youthful despair, Mountain High failed to ease my mind, comfort me. At lunch I would pace nervously along the fence, for I knew even then, in those first weeks in the mountains, that my time there, my time with the old men along the creek, was limited, a temporary reprieve, and I was determined not to waste a moment. Soon enough, I was spending more time not attending school than attending it. Mr. Fortnip, the principal, didn't seem to mind. Indeed, it came as a great surprise to him that any relative of the old fools on Starlight Creek had any interest in proper education at all.

Sometimes, though, I did hunger for school, not because I loved the work or had any great educational aspirations, but because the other kids were a great source of information, a link to the world beyond the hills. Through them I learned how the world I had disappeared from so suddenly was faring. It was at Mountain High that I learned that the little Asian war in Vietnam had grown up, become bogged down, bloody, controversial. The young Marine on Okinawa had evidently been wrong.

One well-armed U.S. Marine could not clean the communists out of Vietnam in a week. It was now going on two years. Still, spirits were high, at least at Mountain High. The President, I was told, had said it was time to nail the coonskin to the barn door. Victory was at hand; the enemy was on the run. Raymond Solomon, a junior who had been held back twice, grabbed me one day on the basketball court. He saw my dog tags, which I had bound together with a piece of duck tape. "What's this shit, butthead," he growled, holding the tags in his sweaty hands. "You ain't been in Nam, you little shit." And he pulled the chain tight about my neck, cutting into the flesh.

I pulled his hand loose. "Refugee," I said, coughing.

His voice took on a new tone, one of sympathy and genuine interest. "You're right. I'm much too young to go to war. I have to wait until I'm eighteen. I have a note from my mother." Laughing, he let go of my dog tags, told me how he had already signed up. That in another month he'd be an indestructible U.S. Marine.

I thought of Norwell. Of Elias Wonder. Raymond Solomon couldn't wait. When he talked, his pale blue eyes lit up with youthful ferocity. "Man, I want to get my hands on one of them M-16s. What a groove, man. I'm gonna keep that sonofabitch on full auto, man. Full rock 'n' roll. Kill me a shitload of them dinks and see the wonders of Asia."

He seemed to know a lot about the war. "Are we winning?" I asked him one day between classes. My interest was genuine. I didn't know. I'd had no news.

"Goddamn it, kid," Solomon groaned, "don't you listen to the news on television? It's right there every friggin' night. Hell's bells, boy. Goddamn right we're winning. Ain't a country on this earth that can take the U.S., especially some backward, ignorant, Stone Age gang of rice-eatin' commies. We kick ass."

I wondered if we'd crossed the DMZ, taken Hanoi, were heading for China. "How do you know we're winning?" I asked.

A giant grin galloped across Solomon's bright face. "Easy,

kid. Every week someone tallies up the dead. Since we're killing more of them than they are of us, we're winning. Simple mathematics." The gallantry of attrition. Victory by numbers. The glory of mathematics. What Elias Wonder had whispered to me about his war, World War I, flashed through my mind. Four lives every minute. How many now, I wondered, and had Norwell been number one?

Solomon was hardly alone. All the older boys at Mountain High had the itch to go, get in on the excitement. After all, it wasn't every generation that had a war, a chance to join up, fight for their country, travel, be shipped off to far-off seductive lands and legally kill the local inhabitants. Such a prospect— the allure, the thrill—crackled through the boys of Mountain High like waves of high-voltage electricity.

Will Igam was leaving in a month. First to Fort Bragg, then to Nam. "I can't stand the waiting," he crooned. Igam, like Solomon, was eighteen, immortal, and had the world by the ass. "I hear them Viet-a-mese women are all nymphos," he told us every chance he got. "After I get me some medals, I'm sure as hell gonna spend some time in Saigon. Watch out, you sweet little slant-eyed darlings, old Will is coming to free ya and love ya all night long. Old Will Igam and his Great American Magic Flute are coming to town!"

"Ain't ya gonna say good-bye, wish me luck, you little bastard," Raymond Solomon said to me on his last day at school. I shook his hand, wished him luck, great luck. "What can I write on my helmet cover?" he asked. "You know stuff. Give me something that'll shock the pants off everybody." My mind went blank. Here I was, part of the generation with a message, and I had no good words. So I wrote down what I had written in black Magic Marker across my own helmet cover the day Norwell picked up that grenade, pulled the pin, evaporated: Beati Pacifici. Blessed Are the Peacemakers.

Solomon grabbed the slip of paper from my hand, looked at it. "Shit, man," he said, "what does it mean?"

I let a moment pass and lied to him. "Loosely translated, it could mean 'Kill 'em all and let God sort 'em out.'"

"Hot damn," said a grinning Raymond Solomon who was on his way to war. "Hot damn."

He gave me a hearty slap on the shoulder and I whispered under my breath, *"Dulce et decorum est pro patria mori."*

"Huh?" Solomon was staring at me and I saw that he hardly looked eighteen. Not a mark on his soft white skin. He poked me in the gut. "Hey, Einstein, what's it mean?"

"Oh, nothing," I said. "It's a line from a war poem. Just a line." And I did not recite the rest of the poem I had read in my room just days before, on a night that Norwell kept slipping bloodily in and out of my dreams. "Means something like 'How sweet and good it is to die for one's country.'"

"Damn straight," said Solomon, and turned and walked out of the school and off to war. No bands played and no crowds cheered and no one came to see him months later after he'd been torn apart by a booby-trapped 105mm shell that took his right arm and left leg and all of his mind and left him in a wheelchair, speechless, heavy straps around his waist and chest, a brace around his rubbery neck. His blue eyes had gone dark and gray. A small glass was taped to his chin to catch the drool that spilled from the corner of his mouth, out the end of a plastic tube. Each morning his mother would wheel him out onto the porch and each evening at sunset she would wheel him back into the house. I went by and saw him, helped his mother empty the glass of drool, then refit it under his slack lips. All I could think of to say to him was "There, there, Ray. There, there." He had been riding in a truck sent to the rear on a beer-finding mission when it found the waiting 105mm shell. Two men were killed; Solomon became a vegetable. All were doused with beer and glory.

It was at Mountain High, in the summer of 1966, that I discovered that I had the honor of bringing up the rear of the 60's generation, a generation, I was told, like no other in history, one determined to change the very nature of the world and mankind. "Make Love Not War" went the motto.

"Can that be done?" I wondered aloud.

"You bet your sweet ass it can," said the beautiful girl who was three years my senior and who had already been accepted at Columbia University, "no matter who or what we have to bring down, crush, destroy along the way." She had long red hair, a gorgeous array of freckles, and deep green eyes, and was wearing a pink T-shirt with yet another message coming out of a giant multicolored flower. This was the message. "We Are All One." It was some message and I bucked up my courage and asked her if by being all one, it would mean the end of natural diversity, the excitement of change, chance, possibility.

"Huh?" the beautiful senior said, squinting at me as if I were not quite in focus.

I repeated the question, adding, "Do we have to all be one? Can we be something else, travel another road?"

She leaned into me, so close that I could feel her breasts moving beneath the pink T-shirt, rising and falling with the psychedelic flower. I wondered if there was the slightest chance of her and I becoming one for a half-hour or so. "Give Peace and Love a chance, you slimy little establishment geek," she said tenderly, brushing my cheeks with the wisp of a kiss. "We Shall Overcome."

"We who?" I asked as she walked triumphantly out of the lunchroom.

Free Love. Revolution. We Shall Overcome. Peace. Raised Consciousness. Save the Whales. Kill the Pigs, a slogan I found curious at first. I mean, how many more hogs could we do in each year? Then I was rescued again and told that "Pig" was our generation's moniker for policemen. I saw my first peace symbol at Mountain High. New Realities. Better Living Through Chemistry. Bob Dylan sang and the words seemed true—there was indeed a lot happening beyond the hills and to me, not yet fifteen, most of it seemed like a load of bullshit. It was at

Mountain High that I heard the Beatles again and was shocked to learn that not only had they learned to carry a tune but were considered the most important band in the brief history of rock 'n' roll. If all else failed—if Peace failed, if Flower Power failed, if Universal Oneness failed, if chemicals failed—our souls could still be saved by music, by rock 'n' roll.

During my short tenure at Mountain High, I fell in love three times. The last one was Martha Wrye. I was convinced she was the most beautiful girl in the world. Certainly, she was the most gorgeous female I had laid eyes on in months and I yearned for her tragically. I could pause now and tell you about her milk-white skin, her heartbreaking smile, the seductive way sunlight fell on her silky blond hair, her kind eyes, her soft voice. But I won't. The inventory is hardly new. All men, I suppose, fall under its spell sooner or later. Beautiful Martha Wrye. Her mother had been Miss Alabama in 1947. She was a knockout, too.

"I can make you happy in ways you've never imagined," said the note Martha Wrye passed to me from her seat behind me in Spanish class. Señorita Wanda Tripling brought her hand down violently on her desk and demanded to know what the note said and I replied, *"Eigner Herd ist Goldes Wert,"* a phrase I remembered from Germany and which I prayed still meant "There's no place like home."

At lunch, I took my fresh, cool apple, and stood by the fence, looking out at the mountains. The wind felt good against my face, the way, I fantasized, that Martha Wrye's caress would feel. A hard flat blue light came off the high ridges and there were no clouds over the entire valley. The wind picked up and I delighted in its energy. Everything beyond that schoolyard fence seemed in motion, even the hills. Out beyond the fence, I thought, all things were not one, no matter how many slogans were pinned and tacked upon the earth. Rather, everything stood poised for change. All that was alive was mutable, eternally chaotic. And I was again overcome with the desire to escape the schoolyard, jump the fence, run to the creek, cast a line, give in to the infinite possibilities of swift water and trout.

The bell rang. Martha Wrye stood beside me, traces of sunlight on her smooth hair. The wind blew harder still and across the road I saw a single sumac leaf, oxblood red, spiraling in the wind. The first leaf of autumn. Another sign, I thought. Surely, a sign.

And so it was, for when I got home that afternoon I learned that Elias Wonder was dead. After so many years of trying, he'd finally made good his threat.

Albert and Emerson had come in at noon and after lunch Albert carried a box of tomatoes, cucumbers, squash, corn, some empty Ball jars to be refilled with whiskey orders, and half a dozen dry trout flies downstream to Wonder's cabin. It had been a grand week for Elias Wonder. Nothing more serious than a head cold—a cough and a runny nose.

Albert stood in the doorway of the cabin, saw the old Indian lying on the bed, dressed, shoeless, dead.

"How?" asked Emerson, who turned toward the kitchen window after Albert told him, raised it to let in the cool, fresh air pushed by the building wind.

"A cold."

"Figures," sighed Emerson. "The old bastard. Like him to lull us all these years with cancers and heart attacks and whatall and then give in to the common cold."

Emerson went into town to speak with the Reverend Biddle, who in a hurried meeting with the church leaders won their grudging permission to bury the old pagan in the cemetery beside the First Primitive Methodist Church on Mount Hebron. There was, however, a condition: that the grave be dug along the north fence, "well away from those who had earned heaven."

A message was left with Miss Donna at the café to ask Randy Chewes about digging the grave. But it was a busy week for him, and though he paid his respects, he told us he just couldn't ignore the paying dead to dig a free hole for Elias Wonder. If we could come up with $40, though, he could have the backhoe over at the cemetery in twenty-four hours.

That evening we drove the Ford down through the woods to Wonder's cabin. In the truck bed were six thick wool blankets and ten yards of strong rope. Emerson lit the lantern by the doorway and the cabin's deep purple shadows retreated before the smoky orange light. I stood at the foot of the bed looking at Wonder and felt a sourness in my stomach, a chill at the base of my spine. A breeze brushed my skin and I was sure it was the old Indian's voice. I held to that feeling and it helped ease the loneliness, temper the sadness. The three of us stood there in the shimmering lantern light and let Elias Wonder go. We knew that what had been Elias Wonder was already becoming something else, something new.

Death is awkward, stiff, heavy as anchor chain. The body, looking so at rest, turned to stone once in my grip. Albert tore a bed sheet into strips and tied Wonder's hands together, then his feet. Emerson and I struggled with the corpse, sliding pieces of rope around the shoulders, waist, and calves. Emerson spread the blankets on the gritty cabin floor, then we laid the rigid corpse on them, folded the blankets over, and again bound the sack of dead flesh with rope. We hauled it outside and somehow managed to lift it onto the truck bed. "While he lived, Elias was never a burden. But in death he's quickly wearing my ancient ass out," gasped Emerson, leaning heavily against the Ford.

"Amen, Brother Emerson," Albert wheezed. "Amen."

One of Elias Wonder's feet had come loose, poked out of the blankets, toes stiff as plaster, the sole no longer pink but white as Italian marble in the moonlight. Albert pushed it back under the blankets, then put his arm around my shoulder, drew me near him. "Don't take it too hard, son," he said. "Elias is not there. He, like his body, is becoming something else. Who knows what. That's the beauty of it all. Who knows what's next. Elias is home. I bet he's already some wild wind blowing out toward the Great Plains, headed home."

We drove back to Trail's End, the body that had been Elias Wonder sliding back and forth in the truck bed like a loose tire. I covered my ears, tried thinking of Martha Wrye and instead thought of what the old Indian had often said when he hooked into a good trout. "Goddamn it, boy! There it is. Life, the feel of it, the sound of it. Full and mature and good."

That night Elias Wonder's body stayed in the back of the truck and was finally impervious to the weather, pain, loss, sorrow, to man's every legacy, to everything but the earth.

Early the next morning we put three shovels and a pickax in the truck and drove up to Mount Hebron Cemetery. The morning's thin light seemed to gather about the white cross on the church's rooftop, giving it a high platinum shine. A mockingbird perched on the roof chided us noisily, as if the clatter of our shovels had spoiled its morning.

Albert set to work marking the gravesite. He used his compass to point the head of the grave slightly north of west. What seemed cold precision was in fact an act of passion. "It's only right that Elias' head should lie toward Dakota's Black Hills," he explained. My sadness produced in me a frightening strength, a brooding power. Grief did not bring paralysis but a deep shock that demanded action, pulled relentlessly at me, a fierce emotion that had not boiled in me since Norwell pulled the pin on that grenade and became in an instant a bloody cloud of flesh and shards of bone.

Taking one of the shovels, Albert outlined the grave's boundary, a seam of gently disturbed dirt, dead-leaf brown, three feet wide by six and a half feet long.

My heart beat wildly, threatened to lose its rhythm. It pounded in great bursts against the muscles of my chest. I thought surely at any moment it would tear through the inadequate hold of my skin. "Let me," I suddenly hollered, taking up the pickax and lashing at the ground between the marked lines. "Let me, please."

Sorrow is a fuel greater than pure oxygen, greater than a surge of adrenaline. I swung the pick again and again. Sunlight poured over the hills and across the creek and surged up the hillside and over the church and cemetery and still I hacked and slashed violently at the ground. In great chunks the hard earth gave way, as though it knew what was at hand and had been waiting patiently. The pick's heavy iron head felt almost weightless as I wielded it high overhead and then straight into the ground, and with each stroke ragged pieces of ground filled the plot. I stripped off my coat and shirt, took up the broad, flat-faced shovel, cleared away the loose dirt. As I worked, a livid-brown dune rose beside the widening hole. Sweat covered my face and hands, dripped from my chin and fingertips, clung to my flesh and the sunlight came off it as though it were dew on the grass. My arms did not ache, nor my hands blister. The hoe had prepared me well, calloused my hands, strengthened my back.

All through the morning I assaulted that gaping brown hole, roughing its sides with the pick, then scraping it clean with the shovel, and thinking all the while that I was digging not one grave, but many. A grave for Elias Wonder. A grave for Albert, who was dying. A grave for Norwell. For Raymond Solomon. And the dune beside the grave rose higher and higher, throwing a shadow across my handiwork, making the hole look gray and bottomless.

Albert and Emerson stood far back from me, said nothing, left me to my work. When my shoulders had dropped from sight, fell below the top of the hole, they brought Elias Wonder's body from the truck and laid it on the side of the grave across from the high mound of moist, sweet-smelling earth. I used the shovel to tidy up the hole and never looked up, never looked at the hard, stiff bundle. Elias Wonder was gone. Albert was leaving. Time was running out. That was the way of things. I could not stop it, any of it. I could only strike out with the pick, dig a good grave, say good-bye. What message had the November geese brought? Carry on. Carry on.

When I climbed out of the hole, my body was soaked in dirt and sweat, giving it the color of rust. The good Reverend Biddle had joined us, his black coat off, his collar loosened. He asked me to dig a small hole at the head of the grave. When I had finished, he took a mallet and sank a wooden cross painted white. On it he had burned one word: WONDER. He stood behind the cross, hands folded, hat off, his figure throwing a long indigo shadow over the grave. "Just in case the Lord should forget where we laid him, the old heretic," he said, the words soft and forgiving.

Albert and Emerson took hold of the rope tied around the blanket covering the body. I lifted the shoulders and head and carefully, loyally, sorrowfully, we let it down into the hole. Then the sound of the first shovelfuls of dirt hitting the body, a quick series of dull slaps, hollow thuds.

When it was done a dome of mountain earth covered the hole. I stood behind the little cross and a wind came up, fresh and strong. How cool it felt against my naked shoulders. How good it felt to be alive.

Clouds on the wind momentarily covered the sun and moved on, looking like sheets of dull copper as they caught the afternoon's flat, fading light.

Emerson took the shovels to the truck and came back with a book wrapped in leather, which he had found in Elias Wonder's blue steamer trunk, along with an old buffalo skull, its horns tightly wrapped in pieces of tanned animal hide, and two musty, decaying eagle feathers tied to a wooden peg drilled into the forehead. There were two circles painted in earth tones on the skull. The inner circle was the soft yellow of cottonwood leaves in the fall; the outer circle was a deep, ferruginous red, dark as blood. Radiating from the outer circle were seven arrow points, also painted red. None of us knew the skull's exact meaning. Albert was sure, though, that to Elias it had meant family, his ancestors, the union of the Sioux with the earth, the Great Mystery. "Perhaps it's a map home," said Emerson as he laid the cinerous old skull at the base of the white cross. Then his voice loud and firm, he read from the book he'd found in Elias Wonder's trunk.

'Every part of this soil is sacred in the estimation of my people. Every hillside, every valley, every plain and grove, has been hallowed by some sad or happy event in days long vanished. The very dust upon which you now stand responds more lovingly to their footsteps than to yours, because it is rich with the blood of our ancestors and our bare feet are conscious of the sympathetic touch. . . . And when the last Red Man shall have perished, and the memory of my tribe shall have become a myth among the White Men, these shores will swarm with the invisible dead of my tribe, and when your children's children think themselves alone in the field, the store, the shop, upon the highway, or in the silence of the pathless woods, they will not be alone. At night when the streets of your cities and villages are silent and you think them deserted, they will throng with the returning hosts that once filled and still love this beautiful land. The White Man will never be alone. Let him be just and deal kindly with my people, for the dead are not powerless. Dead, did I say? There is no death, only a change of worlds.'

"The words of Chief Seattle," said Emerson, "spoken in 1854." He closed the book and tucked it under his arm.

"Wonder? Wonder who?" said Albert in the truck as we drove home. He held his head in his big hands and rubbed the pasty-white skin of his forehead, and I knew the tumor in his brain had just erased another memory.

Emerson stopped the truck at the mailbox, reached in, got the day's meager mail—the weekly edition of the church bulletin. He sat there in the dissolving light, reading it. I had leaned my head back against the seat, hoping that exhaustion would finally overwhelm me.

Then suddenly a burst of cackling laughter from Emerson. "Lord, would you just listen to this," he yelped happily, and began reading an ad printed on the back of the bulletin. "'Are you tired of cleaning yourself. Let me do it for you. I'm a cheap Christian woman.'" A name and telephone number accompanied the ad. I still had my eyes closed but I could feel the laughter welling up in Albert. The trembling in his arms turned into an uncontrollable quaking of his shoulders. And then there was no stopping it, as we all howled at the top of our voices and the old truck rocked back and forth there by the mailbox off the Mount Hebron highway.

I felt Albert's bony elbow in my side. "Okay, son," he laughed, "now you can get me a tel-e-phone."

8. LEGACY

I was lucky. I had these mountains, trout, blues music, and family.
Without these things, I would have cashed in my chips long ago,
thrown my arms cheerfully around insanity.

— *Albert McClain, 1966*

A month after Elias Wonder's death, Albert gave me the
bear tooth the crazed old Sioux shaman had worn around his
neck. I put it on the chain with my dog tags. Now I carried
Norwell in the rippled strawberry-colored scars on my hands
and arms and Elias Wonder around my neck. Where would I
carry Albert and the old man, I thought late one night as Albert's tumor made him walk the dark upstairs hallway calling out
for dead wives, lost trout, vanishing memories. But I knew. I
knew. In my blood.

"How long?" Emerson asked the smiling doctor in town after
Albert had leapt up from the examining table and walked out
the door barefoot, his pants unzipped.

The doctor said, "Who knows," seeming surprised at the
directness of the question. He explained that malignant tumors
were such finicky things. So unpredictable. No two behaved

alike. All they had in common, really, was one thing: they were all killers. Otherwise, just so much perplexing deadliness. This one would kill Albert. It might take a week, a month, six months, but it would kill him.

The doctor wrote out a prescription and handed it to Emerson. "Toward the end there might be great pain," he said. His voice had changed, had taken on a more remorseful tone. "This will help. You know, keep him calm, comfortable." He sighed heavily, tapped his pen nervously on his fake-wood desk.

Emerson stood silent, knowing there was more, something the doctor hadn't said.

Another sigh. The doctor regretted having to say everything so precisely. He seemed annoyed that Emerson could not read his implied meanings. Finally, he spoke again. "Look, there's a better than even chance that the old man will lose what little memory he has left. His last days may well be completely incoherent. He won't know you or the boy or much of anything else. His mind will disintegrate, sort of." You could see the relief on the doctor's face. There, he had said it and was done with it. He all but jumped up, left the room.

A month after we buried Elias Wonder, Albert was much worse. His tumor went on and on, eating not only tissue and bits of bone, but memory and experience as well. His strength had gone, evaporating quickly like a thin mist over summer pasture. Each day found him capable of doing less. His body became a burden over which he had no control. The muscles in his legs and arms went soft, the nerves shut down. Day after day, I watched the light fade from his eyes. Finally the morning came when the pain in his head exploded and he could not move from his bed. He screamed for me to shut the curtains because the sunlight tortured his brain. I didn't tell him that a solid layer of smoke-gray clouds hung over the valley, blocking out the morning sunlight like an impenetrable door. There was not enough daylight coming through his window to chase away the night's lingering shadows.

Later that day, I saw him dipping his harmonica. As always, first dousing it in a glass of I.B.C. root beer, then in a glass of creek water, then working the holes, blowing all the water and root beer out until he got the tone he wanted. At first the notes were weak, thready, broken, but he played on and as he played the music gave him a new strength. He saw me watching. Our eyes met for the first time in days and I was scared. No, not of his dying, for by now death and I were fast companions, true friends. No, what terrified me was the thought of Albert not knowing me. I was not ready for the tumor to eat the part of his brain where I existed.

"McKinley Morganfield," he said, the words snapping like a whip, and my stomach jerked and cramped up, my legs trembled. McKinley Morganfield? Had it happened already? Was it a name from the past? Had Albert's tumor suddenly transformed me into McKinley Morganfield? My throat went tight, my mouth sour and dry. I could feel my lips straining to move. Nothing came out. No sound at all.

Then that wry smile. Albert's smile, a smile of remembrance.

"McKinley Morganfield," he said again. "A man from Clarksdale, Mississippi. A Delta man. A singing man. And when the people heard him sing the blues he became somebody else altogether. A man and a place and a way of living. He was like the old river, that voice deep and wide, restless and rolling. And so they called him Muddy Waters, blues man. Any man who leads an honest life, feels life, sings the blues." Albert, frail and white as flour, sat on the cool wood floor, put the Hohner harmonica to his lips, and played. I sat there with him and he played all afternoon, playing and singing Muddy Waters, Howlin' Wolf, John Lee Hooker, Memphis Slim, Big Walter Horton, and Mississippi John Hurt. I thought of nothing else but the words and the music, the wailing harmonica, as Albert blew tragedy in and drew compassion and understanding out. Exhaustion at last took him down and he crawled into his bed and slept. I covered him with a blanket and left the darkened room, leaving the hall light on in case he woke up, felt compelled to walk the house looking for those whose names he had forgotten, whose faces had become blank and lifeless.

"Who's there?" I had heard him call out on one of his nocturnal excursions. "Are you there? . . . Diane, is that you? Why have you cut your hair?"

At school, Martha Wrye tried cheering me up, suggested Primal Screaming, Zen, a talk with some Hindu guru whose ad she had clipped from a California street paper she subscribed to. He had a sale on: eternal bliss for only $9.95. No refunds. I thanked her kindly. Nothing worked. The problem was that while everyone at Mountain High was trying to get the hell out of the mountains, I was trying just as desperately to stay in them. This is what the kids at Mountain High said to the mountains: No way. No chance. No thanks. After I had taken a battery of state and national scholastic tests, Miss Adams, the school guidance counselor, called me to her office. I found her studying my scores with hopeless eyes. She greeted me with a vapid grin, asked if I had ever considered a career in the military. I ran for the door and kept on running all the way to Starlight Creek.

Emerson found me hiding out above Karen's Pool. "Come on," he said. I followed him to the Ford, put my fly rod in the truck bed.

Except for a darkening of the soft flesh beneath his eyes, the strain of Elias Wonder's death and Albert's dying had left no visible mark on the old man. His days in the garden and fields were now twice as long. Often, he did not come back to the house until well after sunset and I would cook him dinner, make him coffee mixed with what remained of Elias Wonder's whiskey. He had not fished or even walked in the woods for weeks. He only worked, caring for Albert and the land.

In the mornings Emerson would wake me and we would get Albert to the bathroom, clean him, get him dressed. We fed him, even though he always vomited the food back up, saying in a plaintive voice, "Death's a messy thing, isn't it?"

I made Emerson's breakfast, too, and he stayed with Albert until I got home from school, then he would go into the fields and work until the light was gone.

When Emerson found me at Karen's Pool, he did not drive me back to Mountain High. Instead, he turned the Ford toward town. I saw the doctor's white prescription slip lying on the dashboard. Emerson said nothing until we had passed beyond Mount Hebron.

"Pain's come." Emerson kept his eyes on the highway, downshifting for a steep curve. The muscles beneath his deeply tanned forearm pushed against his old skin as he jammed the gearshift forward. Making the curve, he shifted again, turned to me, his eyes capturing mine, told me that Albert had hollered out in awful pain early in the morning and the torment had not let up. Not fear's scream. Not the sound of anguish or mere discomfort. But pain's throbbing voice—a howling of nerves, paroxysms of rasping, gnawing agony, vocal lacerations, wracking misery. The old man nodded toward the rear of the Ford and there I saw the familiar shape of bundled wool blankets.

"The doctor said this medicine would make things easier on him. He's never had things easy. Maybe now's the time." The bundles? Shotguns—the Fox, the Winchester Model 12, and the Remington—and two bamboo fly rods. Emerson knew a man in town who would buy the lot. Cash money. Money to mollify Albert's pain, perhaps lead him into numbing unconsciousness. His only escape. Biddle was at the farmhouse. We had to hurry.

The man in town was polite, kind, sorry that death had to be his charm, the cause of his sudden good fortune, the bearer of such fine shotguns, such perfect fly rods. I took the old Orvis from the truck, offered it to him as well. Once, Albert had parted with it to ease my pain. I only wanted to do the same. A good trade. A rod for no pain. The man smiled, took the rod, pressed the folded bills into my hands. I did not look back.

The medicine made Albert's eyes heavy, took him far away. He no longer knew me and it did not matter. "I feel warm. No pain. No pain. It's not so bad at all," he said as the pills took hold. Now only Emerson stayed with him, only he was allowed in the room. Only he passed through that doorway between the living and the dying. I worked the fields, split wood, and in the evenings cleaned and recleaned Albert's one remaining fly rod. Before I walked down the stairs that last time, Albert had said to me, "Go fishing, son. The dying need to die."

And so he did, exactly one week later, early on a Tuesday morning, just at daylight. And this time everything was ready, taken care of. Randy Chewes had dug a fine hole for twenty percent off his normal grave-digging fee, and George Lightman, of Lightman's Funeral Home & Water Well Services over at Owl Creek, had sold Emerson a damaged pine coffin at a good price. Emerson dressed Albert in his blue wool shirt, Montana string tie, and green work pants, and kindly refused Lightman's gracious offer to drain Albert's body of blood and pump in some high-powered preservatives, and generally "make him look good and alive for no extra money."

Emerson, Lightman, the Reverend Biddle, and I carried the body to the coffin, which had been placed in the back of the Ford. We all met up at Mount Hebron Cemetery and lifted the coffin to the grave in the shade of the trees and lowered it down into the hole with the same ropes we had used to lay Elias Wonder's body to rest.

As I shoveled the dirt into the grave, a cool wind came up out of the northwest, a wind that smelled of rain. Lightman and Biddle stood with their hats in their hands and their heads bowed, but not Emerson. He kept his head up, straight, firm. Biddle had asked to read one brief Bible passage. Emerson saw no harm in it. Albert had always liked the Reverend Biddle, despite his vocation. Biddle stepped to the head of the grave. He looked relaxed, like a man who had given salvation all he had but knew that while the church might claim the old men's bodies, it could not claim their souls. He turned to Psalm 1:3 and read: "'And he shall be like a tree planted by the rivers of water, that bringeth forth its fruit in its season.'"

And I heard the men say "Amen" as I followed Emerson back to the Ford.

"Get the rods," said Emerson.

I brought them and we walked down to the creek and fished all day, even after the rain came, cold and hard. Late in the afternoon, I heard him yell from up at Karen's Pool. I laid Albert's Phillipson fly rod down carefully in the damp grass and ran frantically upstream, thinking of every possible calamity. The old man was standing on one of the huge gray stones which hung over the pool, runnels of rainwater pouring from his hat brim. The driving rain had pressed his shirt tight against his chest, stuck his pants to his legs like clumps of papier-mâché. Attached to his line, there in the shallow water around the stone, was an enormous brown trout, a leviathan, as beautiful a trout as I had ever seen. Ornery, taciturn, incorrigible, noble. The old man was beaming. He kept pointing almost hysterically to the trout's great jaws. "The fly, damn it! Look at the goddamn fly!"

I moved closer, looked down into the water, saw the big fish just below the surface. In the disturbance caused by the pelting rain, it looked abstract. The fly hooked in its massive jaw was unlike anything I had ever seen or heard of, anything with a known reputation, that is. It was a fabulous concoction that flashed traces of green, yellow, and red thread, a dazzle of chicken feathers.

Emerson kept hollering at the top of his lungs, his voice rising above the pounding of the rain against the rocks and the surface of the creek. "An anomaly!" he cried. "A one hundred percent Albert trout anomaly!"

Then I knew. The fly was one of the fantastic trout fly patterns the old men had never tired of tying during the long winter months. And now it had finally happened. One of their efforts had at last tempted and hooked an admirable trout. Calming his elation, Emerson came off the rock and into the water. He worked the hook out of the trout's jaw and held up the soggy, extraordinary-looking fly. A remarkable fly. Outlandish. A genuine absurdity.

"I suppose we ought to name it," Emerson shouted above the rain. "Christ, this is no fluke. This one works."

Both of us thought a moment, then I blurted out, "How about Albert's Delight?"

Emerson's eyes lit up. "Yeah," he said, his lips now purple from the chilly rain. "Sure. 'Albert's Delight.' The old son of a bitch would sure gloat over that, wouldn't he?"

That night over a supper of lima beans, venison steaks, boot-black coffee, and whiskey, Emerson said he wanted me to know Albert's last words. They were for us both. His good-bye. This was what he said before the tumor gobbled up the last morsels of his mind: "Hand me my rod. There are trout in the creek."

A week later the letter came. I saw the APO postmark and knew. My sister's handwriting. My father never wrote letters. Words just didn't have the power, the volume his expression demanded. He preferred corresponding by taped message. He especially liked recording the messages while in combat, under fire. Heavy fighting seemed to add impact to whatever he had to say. Don't be too hard on him, my mother told us time and again. He suffers from a rare form of combat stress, she said; he thinks he's Edward R. Murrow.

A second envelope was stuffed inside the big one. More bus tickets. Time to strike the tents again, get the caravan back on the road. Where to this time? Virginia. School number thirteen.

My sister's words were sweet, kind. She was a saint. She was

also something of a celebrity, being a member of a select society
—the graduates of Okinawa's Kubasaki High. True, she was the
one that broke a heavy dinner plate over my head in Germany.
But I was grateful. The whack dissolved the brown fog in my
left eye.

"I see everything clearly," I had squealed, getting up off the
kitchen floor.

"Goody," she had said with what I felt was less than appropriate enthusiasm. "Then how about grabbing the dish towel
and start drying before I bean you again."

Before my sister smashed the plate over my head I hadn't
seen anything clearly in months because I had vision only in my
right eye after I lost control of my sled on an icy hill and
slammed into the sled ahead of me. Its right blade pierced my
left eye. I couldn't see at all. All that snow, all that whiteness,
and all I saw was black, total blackness. Not even gauzy
shadows or pinpoints of distant light. Calmly my sister led me to
my mother, who took me to a bored army medic who put me in
a chair and asked me how many fingers he was holding in front
of my face.

"None," I said.

"Nope," he said in a disappointed tone. "Ten." Having
completed this thorough scientific exam, he turned to my
mother. "The boy seems to be blind."

Then he wiped away the frozen blood and snow from my
eyes and tried again. This time he held up three fingers. "How
many do you see?" he asked with cold medical professionalism.

"All of them," I said.

The medic giggled with delight. Evidently, I was the first
patient he had cured so effortlessly. "He can see, ma'am," he
told my mother as he swabbed the eye with creams and solu-
tions, dressed it in bandages, and put a dashing black patch over
it.

At school I lifted the patch and Captain Mark's daughter
Kimberly screamed "It's dead!" and fainted.

My prognosis was poor until my sister hit me over the head with the plate and saved my sight. She was the apple of my father's eye and carried on the family's military tradition by marrying a young, handsome armor officer. My father couldn't have been happier, though secretly he still didn't trust any soldier who rode to war. "That was Patton's whole problem. He never got any exercise!"

I packed my duffel bag. On a cool, cloudy Monday morning, Emerson drove me into Mount Hebron and parked across from Bates's store. He shook my hand firmly, drew me close, said, "You know, son, it wasn't supposed to turn out like this. Any of it." I nodded. He gave me a bag of sandwiches and I crossed the street, got on the bus. When I looked out the window, Emerson was gone, headed home.

Somewhere in eastern Tennessee the bus stopped and I bought a root beer, opened the bag, dug out a fried Spam sandwich and a hard-boiled egg. At the bottom of the bag, wrapped in a clean cloth, was Albert's harmonica.

Emerson died in the winter of 1967. Death was kinder to him, took him in his sleep. When I heard, I wondered if he had been dreaming, and if so, of what. I imagined that, like Albert, at the end he dreamed of the mountains, the creek, the trout, the good earth.

Over Christmas break, I left high school and drove back to the Arkansas mountains, drove down out of Virginia and across the cold countryside of Tennessee, then north and west into the Ozark hills and pulled into the narrow valley, onto the winding Mount Hebron road. I got there on a Sunday. Heavy gray clouds, a hard, cold rain falling. I did not go by the farm, which had been sold, nor did I stop in town. I drove up to the cemetery and walked to the iron fence and saw them there, the two graying stones, Albert's already threatening to topple. The white cross that had marked Elias Wonder's grave was gone, and so was the buffalo skull he had been carrying home in his blue steamer trunk. All three men were there, under the Reverend Biddle's eye at last, if not his authority. They were of the earth, totally, completely. I stood in the rain for a long time, just looking and trying hard not to think at all, for I had no wish to make judgments, nor seek answers, nor harvest messages. It was only important that I had come one last time to this place, a boy's sanctuary. His solace. His home.

How dull the stones looked in the rain against the black-browed hills, the dark sky. Only here in these mountains, here with these old men, amid the creek, the trout, the natural world, had I ever ceased to feel alone. I recalled those winter nights on the roof of the farmhouse when we waited for the geese to come overhead and I'd felt like a giant nautilus adrift in a boundless sea. Yet how contented had I felt, even in that reverie, for all I was, all I would be, was inexorably with me there in my chambered shell. Albert, Emerson, Norwell, Elias Wonder, the wildness of the mountains, all of it was with me, and the weight of it all, my time here, set my course, marked my way. So it was still; so it would always be.

I drove down the hill, turned toward town, saw the great scars of construction at the upper end of the valley. Signs cluttered the road, each one announcing the site of Hupple's Incredible, Magnificent, Fun-Filled, All-American Ozark Mountain Theme Park just ahead. Two Miles Ahead and the Fun Begins. Amazing Sights and Adventures Ahead.

I saw a sparkling Piggly Wiggly supermarket where Bates's store had been. Progress. Hupple had promised everyone a share. I wondered if anyone had stayed to collect it.

I pulled off the road for a moment. The radio was on. I dialed in Memphis, the blues station. There he was again: McKinley Morganfield, Muddy Waters, his voice raw as a plow busting through hardscrabble Delta ground. I turned it up, studied the topographical maps I had with me of Montana, took out my compass, plotted my course. There were mountains there, wild, humped-back, merciless. Trout, too, feral and arbitrary.

Evil-eyed and belligerent. As fickle as the swift waters that held them, as elusive as shadows, as uncompromising as life itself. West, then, north and west. I thought I saw Martha Wrye standing outside the Piggly Wiggly, her arms around a short man wearing a bright yellow Nehru jacket and a black turban. His skin was a lovely hazel brown that glistened in the rain. The California guru, the grand yogi, Martha's old friend Pujari Nesbit with a booth at Hupple's Ozark Mountain Theme Park peddling tickets to cosmic enlightenment right next to the hog-calling booth? Martha. And I fell in love again, yearned for her terribly as I drove out of the hills heading west.

On the radio, Muddy Waters gave way to Willie Dixon and Homesick James Williamson. In the back seat sat a choir of willowy, supple fly rods, rods with trout in them and stories to collect, gospels according to Orvis, Powell, R. L. Winston, and Phillipson.

There was news on the radio of a truce in Vietnam, a cease-fire honoring the observance of the Vietnamese New Year. Tet. 1968. Year of the Monkey.